LIBRARY OF CONGRESS CLASSIFICATION

FOURTH EDITION

Social Sciences:
Economics

LIBRARY OF CONGRESS CLASSIFICATION SCHEDULES

For sale by the Cataloging Distribution Service,
Library of Congress, Building 159, Navy
Yard Annex, Washington, D.C. 20541, to which inquiries
on current availability and price should be addressed.

A	General Works
B–BJ	Philosophy. Psychology
BL–BX	Religion
C	Auxiliary Sciences of History
D	History: General and Old World (Eastern Hemisphere)
E–F	History: America (Western Hemisphere)
G	Geography. Maps. Anthropology. Recreation
H–HJ	Social Sciences: Economics
HM–HX	Social Sciences: Sociology
J	Political Science
K	Law (General)
KD	Law of the United Kingdom and Ireland
KE	Law of Canada
KF	Law of the United States
L	Education
M	Music
N	Fine Arts
P–PA	General Philology and Linguistics. Classical Languages and Literatures.
PA Supplement	Byzantine and Modern Greek Literature. Medieval and Modern Latin Literature
PB–PH	Modern European Languages
PG	Russian Literature
PJ–PM	Languages and literatures of Asia, Africa, Oceania. American Indian Languages. Artificial Languages
P–PM Supplement	Index to Languages and Dialects
PN, PR, PS, PZ	General Literature. English and American Literature. Fiction in English. Juvenile Belles Lettres
PQ, Part 1	French Literature
PQ, Part 2	Italian, Spanish, and Portuguese Literatures
PT, Part 1	German Literature
Part 2	Dutch and Scandinavian Literatures
Q	Science
R	Medicine
S	Agriculture
T	Technology
U	Military Science
V	Naval Science
Z	Bibliography Library Science

SUBJECT CATALOGING DIVISION
PROCESSING SERVICES
LIBRARY OF CONGRESS

CLASSIFICATION
CLASS H
SUBCLASSES H–HJ

Social Sciences:
Economics

FOURTH EDITION

LIBRARY OF CONGRESS
WASHINGTON 1981

The additions and changes in Class H, Subclasses H–HJ adopted while this work was in press will be cumulated and printed in List 201 of **LC Classification—Additions and Changes**

Library of Congress Cataloging in Publication Data

United States.   Library of Congress.   Subject
   Cataloging Division.
   Classification, Class H, Subclasses H–HJ,
social sciences, economics.

   Includes index.
   Supt. of Docs.: LC 1.2.Sol
   1.   Classification—Books—Social sciences.
2.   Classification, Library of Congress.   I.   Title.
Z696.U5H–HJ   1981   025.4′63   80–607827
ISBN 0–8444–0353–9

For sale for $10 by the Cataloging Distribution Service, Library of Congress, Building 159, Navy Yard Annex, Washington, D.C. 20541. Subscribers to the card service can charge purchases to their accounts; others must pay in advance by check or money order payable to the **Chief, Cataloging Distribution Service, Library of Congress.** Payment from foreign countries may be made with UNESCO coupons. Price includes postage.

PREFACE

The first edition of Class H was published in 1910, with a second and fundamentally unchanged edition published in 1920. More than a quarter of a century was to pass before the appearance of the third edition in 1949, which incorporated developments during, between, and immediately after the two world wars. A reprint edition was published in 1967, which included supplementary pages of additions and changes made through 1964. Because of the size of the H schedule, the fourth edition of Class H has been issued in two parts, H–HJ and HM–HX. HM–HX was published in July 1980 as an unrevised cumulation.

This fourth edition not only cumulates all additions and changes made since the third edition through June 1980 but also contains many revisions of geographic listings in order to reflect the current political situation. Major geographic revisions have been made throughout the schedule, but changes are most noticeable in HA, HC, and HJ, where list of countries with Cutter numbers have been replaced by lists of countries with whole numbers or by numbers from the geographic tables. As a result, the classification of many countries, particularly those in Africa and Asia, has been substantially affected. Subclasses HD, HF, and HG contain many changes in topical captions resulting from the inclusion of new concepts and the restatement of existing captions. Throughout, many of the documents captions have been replaced by captions for periodicals. Many numbers that formerly provided for laws and legal topics have been eliminated because legal materials now are classed in the appropriate subclasses of Class K. Where complete revision was neither possible nor desirable, the schedule has been improved by arranging notes and references to conform with current practice and deleting parenthesized numbers.

The present revision is the product of the cooperative efforts of social sciences catalogers Regene Ross, Raoul leMat, Gabriel Horchler, James McGovern, and Donald Panzera, under the direction of Nicholas Hedlesky (now retired). The overall technical supervision was the responsibility of Eugene T. Frosio, principal subject cataloger. The editorial work for this edition was supervised by Lawrence Buzard, editor of classification, who also prepared the index.

Mary K. D. Pietris
Chief, Subject Cataloging Division

Joseph H. Howard
Assistant Librarian for Processing Services

SYNOPSIS

HD

ECONOMIC HISTORY AND CONDITIONS

ECONOMIC HISTORY AND CONDITIONS

HD

TRANSPORTATION AND COMMUNICATIONS

HE

PUBLIC FINANCE - Continued

	Periodicals. Serials
1.A1-2	Polyglot
.A3-Z	American and English
3	French
5	German
7	Italian
8	Other languages, A-Z
9	Yearbooks
	Societies
10	International
11	American and English
13	French
15	German
17	Italian
19	Other languages, A-Z
	Congresses
21	International
22	American and English
23	French
25	German
27	Italian
29	Other languages, A-Z
	Collected works (nonserial)
31	Several authors
33	Individual authors
35	Addresses, essays, lectures
	Dictionaries. Encyclopedias
40.A2	General works
.A3-Z	Polyglot
41	American and English
43	French
45	German
47	Italian
49	Other languages, A-Z
.5	Terminology. Abbreviations. Notation
50	Directories
	History
51	General works
53	By region or country, A-Z
	Biography
57	Collective
59	Individual, A-Z
	Theory. Method. Relation to other subjects
	Including social philosophy
61	General works
.2	Classification
.3	Electronic data processing
.4	Forecasting in the social sciences
	Cf. CB158+, History of civilization
	HB3730, Economic forecasting
	HD30.27, Management
	HN101+, Social prediction, by region or country
	T174, Technological forecasting
	Statistical methods, see HA29+
	Relation to history, see D16.166
	Relation to international law, see JX1249
	Communication of information
.8	General works
.9	Information services

1

	Study and teaching. Research
	Cf. LB1584+, Elementary school education
62.A1A-Z	Periodicals. Societies. Serials
.A3A-Z	Congresses
.A5-Z	General works
.3	Problems, exercises, examinations
.5	By region or country, A-Z
	For individual schools, see H65+
	Museums. Exhibitions
63	General works
64	By region or country, A-Z
	Under each country:
	.x General works
	.x2 Individual institutions, A-Z
	Schools. Institutes of social sciences
65	General works
67	Individual schools. By city, A-Z
69	Syllabi, outlines
	General works, treatises, and advanced textbooks
71	To 1789
81	1789-1870
83	1871-1975
85	1976-
86	Elementary school textbooks
87	Secondary school textbooks
91	General special (Special aspects of the subject as a whole)
92	Pictorial works
93	Popular works
95	Juvenile works
97	Public policy (General). Policy sciences
99	Charts, diagrams, etc.

Class here general works on
    social science statistics and
    censuses, including statistical
    data and methodology. For sta-
    tistical data alone, <u>see</u> HA154+
For works on the general theory and
    methodology of statistics, <u>see</u>
    QA276+
For special applications of statis-
    tics in the social sciences, <u>see</u>
    the special field, e. g. HD1421+,
    Agricultural statistics; HF1016+,
    Commercial statistics

1	Periodicals. Societies. Serials
12	Congresses
	Collected works (nonserial)
13	Several authors
15	Individual authors
17	Dictionaries. Encyclopedias
19	History
	Biography
22	Collective
23	Individual, A-Z

<u>Theory and method of social science statistics</u>

	General works
29	English
.5	Other languages, A-Z
.6	Juvenile works
30	Frequency distribution
.3	Time-series analysis
.4	Index numbers
	Cf. HB225, Prices
31	Tabular and graphic methods
.15	Forms
.2	Sampling
.3	Regression and correlation
.5	Hypothesis testing
.7	Estimation
.9	Decision theory

<u>Study and teaching. Research</u>

35	General works
.15	Problems, exercises, examinations
.3	By region or country, A-Z

<u>Organizations. Bureaus. Service</u>

36	International
37	By region or country, A-Z
	Under each country:
	.x1-19 Periodicals. Serials
	.x2A-Z General works
	.x3 By region, province, state, etc., A-Z
	.x4 By city, A-Z

              Registration of vital events. Registration (General)
                    Including registration of births, marriages,
                       deaths, etc.
                    Cf. HB848+, Demography
38.A1A-Z   General works
              By region or country
                 United States
  .A2-5   General works
  .A6-Z   By region or state
39   Other regions or countries, A-Z
                    Under each country:
                       .xA-Z General works
                       .x3   Local (States, etc.), A-Z
              Statistical data
                    For data of special fields, see the field
                 Universal statistics
154   Periodicals. Societies. Serials
155   General works
                 By region or country
                    Class here general statistics and cen-
                       suses, including population and vital
                       statistics if consisting of the broad-
                       est groups of data. For population and
                       vital statistics limited to a more
                       specific subject, see HB884+, e. g.
                       HB1321, Mortality
                    Under each country (unless otherwise
                       provided for):

20 nos.	10 nos.	5 nos.	1 no.	
				Official
(1)	(1)	(1)	.A1-3	Main serial
(2)				Statistical abstracts
(3)				Other serials
(4)	(1.5)	(1.5)	.A4-5	Censuses. By date
(5)	(2)	(2)		Other monographic works
				Administrative reports of
				the census and other
				statistical bureaus, see
				HA37+
(9)	(3)			Miscellaneous
		(3)		Nonofficial
(14)	(5)		.A6-Z	Serials
(15)	(6)			General works
(16)				Manuals
(17)				Miscellaneous
(18)	(7)	(4)	.Z9A-Z	By state, etc., A-Z
(19)	(8)	(5)		By city, A-Z

                 America
175   General works
195-730   United States
                       Official
                          Serials, see HA203
195   General works
                             Class here works summarizing the results
                                of more than one census period

Statistical data
  By region or country
    America
      United States
        Official — Continued
201   Censuses. By date
202   Statistical abstracts
203   Serials
205   Other monographic works
            Administrative reports of the Bureau
              of the Census and other statistical
              bureaus, see HA37.U1+
209   Miscellaneous
          Nonofficial
214   Serials
215   General works
216   Manuals
217   Miscellaneous
218   Regions (covering several states)
          Individual states
              Subarranged by assigning nos. (1) - (7)
                of 10 number table, p. 4
              For counties, see subdivision 7
221-227   Alabama
231-237   Alaska
241-247   Arizona
251-257   Arkansas
261-267   California
271-277   Colorado
281-287   Connecticut
              Dakota Territory, see HA631+
291-297   Delaware
301-307   District of Columbia
311-317   Florida
321-327   Georgia
  329.1-.7   Hawaii
331-337   Idaho
341-347   Illinois
351-357   Indian Territory
361-367   Indiana
371-377   Iowa
381-387   Kansas
391-397   Kentucky
401-407   Louisiana
411-417   Maine
421-427   Maryland
431-437   Massachusetts
441-447   Michigan
451-457   Minnesota
461-467   Mississippi
471-477   Missouri
481-487   Montana

Statistical data
  By region or country 1/
    America
      United States
        Individual states - Continued

491-497	Nebraska
501-507	Nevada
511-517	New Hampshire
521-527	New Jersey
531-537	New Mexico
541-547	New York
551-557	North Carolina
561-567	North Dakota
571-577	Ohio
581-587	Oklahoma
591-597	Oregon
601-607	Pennsylvania
611-617	Rhode Island
621-627	South Carolina
631-637	South Dakota
641-647	Tennessee
651-657	Texas
661-667	Utah
671-677	Vermont
681-687	Virginia
691-697	Washington
701-707	West Virginia
711-717	Wisconsin
721-727	Wyoming
	Counties (General)
	For the counties of a given state, see
	the state, subdivision (7)
729	Official
.5	Nonofficial
	Cities, A-Z
730.A1-5A-Z	Official
.A6-Z	Nonofficial
740	Greenland
741-750	Canada
750.5	Saint Pierre and Miquelon Islands
751-760	Latin America
761-770	Mexico
781-790	Central America
791-800	Belize
801-810	Costa Rica
811-820	Guatemala
821-830	Honduras
831-840	Nicaragua
841-850	Salvador
851-854	Panama
855	Panama Canal Zone

1/

   For subarrangement, unless otherwise provided, see tables, p. 4

Statistical data
By region or country 1/
America
Latin America - Continued
West Indies. Caribbean area

855.5	General works
861	Bahamas
865	Barbados
866	Leeward Islands 2/
867	Trinidad and Tobago
868	Windward Islands 2/
871-880	Cuba
881-885	Haiti
886-890	Dominican Republic. Santo Domingo
891-900	Jamaica
901-910	Puerto Rico
911-915	Virgin Islands of the United States
916	British West Indies
917	Netherlands Antilles
	French West Indies
918	General works
.7	Guadeloupe
.9	Martinique
921-930	Bermuda
931-940	South America
941-960	Argentina
961-970	Bolivia
971-990	Brazil
991-1010	Chile
1011-1020	Colombia
1021-1030	Ecuador
	Guianas
1031	General works
1033	Guyana
1035	Surinam
1037	French Guiana
1041-1050	Paraguay
1051-1070	Peru
1071-1090	Uruguay
1091-1100	Venezuela
	Europe
1107	General works
.5	European Economic Community countries
1110-1116	Commonwealth of Nations
1121-1140	Great Britain. England
1141-1150	Northern Ireland
1151-1160	Scotland
1161-1170	Wales

1/ For subarrangement, unless otherwise provided, see tables, p. 4

2/ Subarrange: .A1A-Z General works; .A3-Z By island, A-Z

Statistical data
By region or country 1/
Europe - Continued

1170.1-.5	Ireland. Irish Republic
1171-1190	Austria
1191-1200	Czechoslovakia
1201-1210	Hungary
1210.5	Liechtenstein
1211-1230	France
1230.5	Monaco
1231-1250	Germany
	Including West Germany
1341-1349	East Germany
1351-1359	Greece
1360-1379	Italy
1379.5	San Marino
1380	Malta
	Benelux countries. Low countries
1381-1390	Netherlands
1391-1410	Belgium
1411-1420	Luxemburg
1431-1450	Soviet Union
1450.5	Finland
1451-1460	Poland
1461-1470	Scandinavia
1471-1490	Denmark
1491-1500	Iceland
1501-1520	Norway
1521-1540	Sweden
1541-1560	Spain
1563	Andorra
1565	Gibralter
1571-1580	Portugal
1591-1610	Switzerland
1611-1620	Balkan States
1620.5	Albania
1621-1630	Bulgaria
1631-1635	Yugoslavia
1641-1650	Romania
	Asia, see HA4551+
	Africa, see HA4671+
	Atlantic Ocean Islands
	Iceland, see HA1491+
2280	Azores
	Bermuda, see HA921+
2285	Madeira Islands
2287	Canary Islands
2289	Cape Verde Islands
2291	St. Helena
2293	Tristan da Cunha
2295	Falkland Islands

1/
For subarrangement, unless otherwise provided, see tables, p. 4

Statistical data
By region or country 1/ - Continued

	Indian Ocean Islands
2300	Maldive Islands
2301	Seychelles
2303	Comoro Islands
2305	Mauritius
2307	Réunion
2309	Karguelen Islands
3001-3010	Australia
3171-3190	New Zealand
4001-4010	Pacific Ocean Islands
4010.5	Trust Territory of the Pacific
	Including Mariana, Caroline, and Marshall Islands
	Hawaii, see HA329.1+
	French Polynesia
4011	General works
.5	Tahiti
4012	Guam
4013	Papua New Guinea
4014	Solomon Islands
4015	New Caledonia
.5	New Hebrides
4016	Fiji Islands
.5	Wallis Islands
.7	Gilbert and Ellice Islands
4017	Tonga
	Samoan Islands
4018	General works
.5	American Samoa
.7	Western Samoa
4020	Arctic regions
	Greenland, see HA740
.5	Antarctic regions
4021-4026	Communistic countries
	Official
4021	Serials
4022	Monographs
	Nonofficial
4025	Serials
4026	General works
4551-4737	Asia and Africa. Table VIII
	For Table VIII, see pp. 341-340. Add country number in Table to 4000

1/
For subarrangement, unless otherwise provided, see tables, p. 4

ECONOMIC THEORY

	Periodicals. Societies. Serials
1.A1A-Z	International or polyglot
.A2-Z	American and English
3	French
5	German
7	Italian
9	Other languages
21	Congresses
	Collected works (nonserial)
30	Polyglot
	American and English
31	Several authors
33	Individual authors
34	Addresses, essays, lectures
36-39	French 1/
41-44	German 1/
46-49	Italian 1/
51-54	Other languages 1/
61	Dictionaries. Encyclopedias
62	Terminology. Abbreviations. Notation
63	Directories
	Economics as a science. Relation to other subjects
	Cf. HB131+, Methodology
71	General works
72	Relation to philosophy, religion, ethics
	For relation of economics to specific religions, see BL-BX
73	Relation to politics and law
74	Relation to other special topics, A-Z
	Anthropology, see GN448+
	Demography, see HB849.42
	International law, see JX1252
	.P8 Psychology
	Sociology, see HM35
	Study and teaching. Research
.5	General works
.6	Problems, exercises, examinations
	By region or country
.8	United States
.9	Other regions or countries, A-Z
	History of economics. History of economic theory
	For the economic history of individual countries, see HC
75	General works
	Biography
76	Collective
	Individual, see HB101+
	By period
77	Ancient
79	Medieval
81	Modern to 1700
83	18th century
85	19th century
87	20th century

1/

Subarranged like HB31-34

Economic theory
   History of economics. History of economic
      theory – Continued
      Special schools
         For biographies of individuals, <u>see</u> HB101+

90	Comparative economics
91	Mercantile system. Cameralism
93	Physiocrats
94	Classical school
	Cf. HB161+, Economic theory
95	Liberalism. Laissez faire
	Cf. HF1713, Tariff policy
	JC571+, Political theory
97	Historical school
.5	Marxian economics. Socialist economics
	Cf. HX39.5, Karl Marx
98	Austrian school of economics. Marginalists
	Cf. HB201+, Value
.2	Neoclassical school. Cambridge school. Marshallians
.3	Chicago school
99.3	Welfare economics
	Cf. HB846+, Welfare theory
.5	Institutional economics
.7	Keynesian economics

     By region or country
       Under each country:
         .A2A–Z History
         .A3A–Z Collective biography
         .A5–Z   Individual biography

101	Austria
.5	Czechoslovakia
102	Hungary
103	Great Britain
105	France
107	Germany
	Including West Germany
	For the biography of Karl Marx, <u>see</u> HX39.5
.5	East Germany
108	Greece
	Balkan States
.2	General works
.3	Bulgaria
.4	Yugoslavia
.5	Romania
109	Italy
	Low Countires
111	Netherlands
112	Belgium
113	Soviet Union
114	Poland
.3	Finland

Economic theory
  History of economics. History of economic
    theory
    By region or country - Continued

	Scandinavia
115	General works
116.2	Denmark
.3	Norway
.5	Sweden
117	Spain
.5	Portugal
118	Switzerland
119	United States
121	Canada
	Latin America
122	General works
123	By region or country, A-Z

                Under each country:
                    .x   History
                        Biography
                  .x2   Collective
                  .x3   Individual, A-Z

	Asia
125	General works
126	Individual regions or countries, A-Z
	Subarranged like HB123
.3	Arab countries
	Africa
127	General works
.5	Individual regions or countries, A-Z
	Subarranged like HB123
129	Australia
.5	New Zealand
130	Underdeveloped areas

  Methodology

131	General works
133	Information theory in economics. Economic cybernetics

    Mathematical economics. Quantitative methods
          For special applications, see the field
            of application

135	General works
137	Economic statistics

          Including data collection techniques; for
            statistical data, see HC or the field
            of application
          Cf. HC28, Survey techniques
      Econometrics

139	General works
141	Econometric models
.5	National income accounting

          Cf. HC79.I5, Economic history

142	Input-output analysis. Interindustry economics

          Cf. HC79.I57, Economic history

.5	Flow of funds accounting

          Cf. HC79.F55, Economic history

Economic theory
  Methodology
    Mathematical economics. Quantitative methods –
      Continued

143	Mathematical programming
	Cf. T57.7, Industrial engineering
.5	Electronic data processing
.7	Optimization techniques
144	Game theory
	Cf. HD30.26, Management games
	T57.92, Industrial engineering
145	General equilibrium. Comparative statics

  General works, treatises, and textbooks
   Medieval period, see HB79
   Before Adam Smith to 1776/1789

151	English and American
153	French
155	German
157	Italian
159	Other languages
161-169	Classical period, 1776/1789-1843/1876

     Cf. HB94, History of economic thought
     Subarranged like HB151+
   Recent, 1843/1876-
    English and American

171	General works
.5	Textbooks
	Including outlines, syllabi, etc.
172	Microeconomics
.5	Macroeconomics
173	French
175	German
177	Italian
178	Russian
.5	Spanish
179	Other European languages, A-Z
180	Oriental languages, A-Z
181	Other languages, A-Z
183	Juvenile works
195	Economics of war
	Cf. HC79.D4, Economic impact of defense and
	disarmament
199	General special (Special aspects of the subject
	as a whole)

  Industrial organization and market structure, see
  HD2321+
  Value. Utility
    Cf. HB98, Austrian school of economics

201	General works
	History of theory
203	General works
205	By region or country, A-Z

Economic theory
   Income. Factor shares
      Interest - Continued
         By region or country
           United States

545	General works
547	By region or state, A-Z
549	Other regions or countries, A-Z
551	Usury
601	Profit

             Cf. HC79.P7, Economic history
                 HF5681.P8, Accounting
                 HG4028.P7, Corporation finance

615	Entrepreneurship. Risk and uncertainty

             Cf. HD30.22, Managerial economics
                 HD61, Risk in industry (Management)
                 HG8053, Insurance

        Property
           Including ownership
             Cf. HX550.P7, Socialism and property

701	General works

          Private property

711	General works
715	Inheritance

             Cf. HJ5801+, Inheritance tax
         Public property, see HD3840+, JK1601+, etc.

      Consumption. Demand
         Cf. HC79.C6, Economic history

801	General works

        Household consumption. Consumer demand
           Cf. HC79.C63, Consumer protection
               HF5415.3, Consumer research

820	General works
822	Personal saving. Propensity to save

             Cf. HG7920+, Finance

831	Leisure classes

             Cf. GV1+, Recreation

835	Ethics of consumption and wealth
841	Luxury

             Cf. BJ1535.L9, Ethics
        Aggregate demand

842	General works
.5	Aggregate consumption
843	Aggregate saving and investment

             Cf. HC79.S3, Economic history
               HG4516, Finance

      Welfare theory
         Cf. HB99.3, History of economics
            HV1+, Social and public welfare

846	General works
.2	Cost benefit analysis

          Cf. HD47, Management

.3	Externalities

<u>Economic theory</u>
  <u>Welfare theory</u> - Continued

846.5	Public goods
.6	Theory of second best
.8	Social choice
	Business cycles. Economic fluctuations, <u>see</u> HB3711+

DEMOGRAPHY. VITAL EVENTS

Including statistical works on specific aspects
  of population and vital events, as, for
  example, HB1321+, Mortality. For works presenting
  the broadest groups of data relating to population
  and vital events, <u>see</u> HA155+
Cf. HQ750+, Eugenics
    RA407+, Medical statistics

848	Periodicals. Societies. Serials
849	Congresses
	Collected works (nonserial)
.1	Several authors
.15	Individual authors
.2	Dictionaries. Encyclopedias
.25	Terminology. Abbreviations. Notation
.3	Directories

<u>Theory. Method. Relation to other subjects</u>

.4	General works
	Relation to anthropology. Demographic anthropology, <u>see</u> GN335
	Relation to biology. Population biology, <u>see</u> QH752
.41	Relation to economics
	Relation to education, <u>see</u> LC68+
.42	Relation to philosophy, religion, ethics
	Cf. HQ766.2, Moral and religious aspects of birth control
	Relation to population genetics, <u>see</u> GN289, QH455
.43	Relation to psychology. Population psychology
.44	Relation to sociology
.47	Cohort analysis
.49	Demographic survey techniques
	Cf. HA38, Registration of vital events
.5	Electronic data processing
.51	Mathematical models
.53	Population forecasting
.55	Stable population model
	Communication of information
.6	General works
.65	Information services

Study and teaching. Research

850	General works
.3	Problems, exercises, examinations
.5	By region or country, A-Z
.8	Museums. Exhibitions

Demography. Vital events - Continued

    History of demography

851	General works
852	Special schools
853	By region or country, A-Z

    Biography

855	Collective

      Malthus

861	Writings of Malthus
863	Criticism and biography
865	Other individual, A-Z

    General works, treatises, and advanced textbooks

867	Through 1834

      Malthus, see HB861+

871	1835-
873	Elementary textbooks
883	Juvenile works
.5	Population policy

      Cf. HQ766.7, Population control

    By region or country, see HB3501+

884	Underdeveloped areas
.5	Population assistance

      Including aid by individual countries to
        several countries

      Class aid for a specific country with the
        recipient country in HB3501+

885	General special (Special aspects of the subject as a whole)

    Births. Fertility

      Cf. HQ766, Family planning

901	General works
902	Birth intervals

      Fecundity, see QP251+

      Sterility, see RC889

      Illegitimacy, see HQ998

911-1107	By region or country. Table II 1/

      Under each country:

2 nos.	1 no.	
(1)	.A3A-Z	General works
(2)	.A5-Z	Local, A-Z

Marriages. Nuptiality

    Cf. HQ503+, Marriage and family

1111	General works
1113	Age at marriage
1121-1317	By region or country. Table II 1/

      Subarrange each country like HB911-1107

Deaths. Mortality

1321	General works
1322	Life tables

      Cf. HG8783, Actuarial science

.3	Life expectancy
.5	Maternal mortality

      Cf. RG530, Obstetrics

1/
    For Table II, see pp. 331-340. Add country number in table to 910 or 1120
as the case requires

Demography. Vital events

Deaths. Mortality – Continued

1323   Other special subjects, A–Z

            .A2 Accidents

               Afro-Americans, see .B5

               Alcoholism, see RC565

            .B5 Blacks. Afro-Americnas

            .C5 Children

                Cf. RJ59+, Pediatrics

            .I4 Infants

               Occupational mortality, see .P8

            .P8 Professions. Occupational mortality

            .S5 Sex

            .S8 Suicide

1331–1527   By region or country. Table II 1/

               Subarrange each country like HB911–1107

Age. Age distribution

             For specific age groups, see HQ767.8+

1531   General works

1541–1737   By region or country. Table II 1/

               Subarrange each country like HB911–1107

Sex

1741   General works

1751–1947   By region or country. Table II 1/

               Subarrange each country like HB911–1107

Population geography. Migration

            Cf. GF1+, Anthropogeography

               GN370, Ethnology

1951   General works

1952   Internal migration

            International migration. Emigration and immigration,

            see JV6001+

            Migrant labor, see HD5855+

1953   Population density

1954   Residential mobility

               Cf. HD7285+, Housing

1955   Rural-urban migration

1961–2157   By region or country. Table II 1/

               Subarrange each country like HB911–1107

Urban population

            Cf. HT201, Urban sociology

2161   General works

2171–2367   By region or country. Table II 1/

               Subarrange each country like HB911–1107

Rural population

            Cf. HT421+, Rural sociology

2371   General works

2381–2577   By region or country. Table II 1/

               Subarrange each country like HB911–1107

1/

    For Table II, see pp. 331–340. Add country number in table to 1330, 1540, 1750, 1960, 2170 or 2380 as the case requires

Demography. Vital events – Continued
   Professions. Occupations
      Cf. HD5701+, Labor market
          HF5381+, Vocational guidance

2581	General works
2582	Classification
2583	Productive life span
2591–2787	By region or country. Table II 1/

         Subarrange each country like HB911–1107
      Classes, see HT601+
      Individual nationalities, ethnic groups, etc., see
        the particular group in D–F, e. g. Jews, DS133+

3501–3697	By region or country. Table II 1/

         Subarrange each country like HB911–1107

BUSINESS CYCLES. ECONOMIC FLUCTUATIONS
Cf. HD49, Management

3711	General works
3714	History of theories
	History of crises
3716	General works
3717	Particular crises. By date
	Relation to special topics
3718	Social and psychological aspects
3719	Costs, profits, and cycles
3720	Investments and cycles
.5	Inventories and cycles
3721	Consumption and cycles
	Finance and cycles. Financial crises
3722	General works
3723	Money and cycles
3725	Banking and cycles
3727	Speculation and cycles
3728	Agriculture and cycles
.5	Sunspots and cycles
	Astrology and cycles, see BF1729.B8
3730	Economic forecasting
	Cf. HD30.27, Management
3732	Economic stabilization
	Cf. HC79.W24, Wage price policy
	HD82+, Economic policy
3741–3840	By region or country. Table I 2/

         Class here general works only; for particular
           crises, see HB3717
         Cf. HC95+, Economic history

1/
   For Table II, see pp. 331–340. Add country number in table to 2590 or 3500,
as the case requires
2/
   For Table I, see pp. 331–340. Add country number in table to 3740

10	Periodicals. Societies. Serials
13	Congresses
	Collected works (nonserial)
.2	Several authors
.3	Individual authors
14	Yearbooks
15	Dictionaries. Encyclopedias
21	General works
26	Theory. Method. Relation to other subjects
	Communication of information
27	General works
.2	Information services
	Study and teaching. Research
28	General works
.5	By region or country, A-Z
	Biography
29	Collective
	Individual, see subject and country
	History
	By period
	Prehistoric, primitive, see GN448+
	Antiquity
31	General works
33	Egypt
	Cf. HC531+, Egypt (Modern)
35	Orient
37	Greece
39	Rome
	Middle Ages
41	General works
42	15th century
	Modern
51	General works
.5	16th century
52	17th century
.5	18th century
	19th century
53	General works
.2	General special
	20th century
54	General works
55	General special
56	World War I, 1914-1918
	Reconstruction, 1919-1939
57.A15A-Z	Periodicals. Societies. Serials
	Documents
.A2	League of Nations
.A3A-Z	Individual countries

	History
	By period
	Modern
	20th century
	Reconstruction, 1919–1939 – Continued
	Conferences
57.A5	International
	Cf. HC57.3, Genoa conference, 1922
	HC57.4, Hague conference on Russia, 1922
	HC57.6, Monetary and economic conference.
	London, 1933
.A6	Other
.A62–Z	General works
.3	Genoa conference, 1922
.4	Hague conference on Russia, 1922
.6	Monetary and economic conference. London, 1933
58	World War II, 1939–1945
59	1945–
.7	Underdeveloped areas
	Class here general works only
	Cf. HD82+, Economic development
	For special topics, see HD1417, HF1413, etc.
	Technical assistance. Economic assistance
	Including aid by individual countries to
	several countries
	For aid for a specific country, see the
	recipient country in HC95+
60	General works
.5	United States Peace Corps
79	Special topics, A–Z
	Class here general works only
	For these topics in specific geographic areas, see HC94+
.A4	Air pollution
	Anti-poverty programs, see .P63
.A8	Auditing and inspection of state enterprises
	Class here works limited to socialist
	countries only
.A9	Automation
	Cf. HD45, Automation in management
.C3	Capital. Capital productivity
	Cf. HB501+, Economic theory
	HD39, Industrial management
	HD57.5, Industrial productivity
	HG4028.C4, Corporate finance
	Conservation of natural resources, see S900+
.C6	Consumer demand
	Cf. HB801+, Economic theory
	HF5415.3, Marketing
.C63	Consumer protection
.C7	Cost (Industrial)
	Cf. HD47+, Costs (Industrial management)
	HF5686.C8, Accounting
.D4	Defense and disarmament, Economic impact of.
	Economics of war
	Cf. HB195, Economic theory
.D45	Disasters, Economic impact of
	Cf. HV553+, Disaster relief
.D5	Distribution of industry. Industrial location
	Cf. HD58, Industrial
	HD1393.5, Industrial property

79   Special topics, A-Z - Continued
      Diversification in industry, see HD
      Economic assistance, Domestic, see .P63
.E5   Environmental policy
      Cf. HC79.A4, Air pollution
          HC79.P55, Pollution
          HD69.P6, Industrial management
.F3   Famines
      Cf. HV630+, Famine relief
.F55   Flow of funds
      Cf. HB142.5, Economic theory
      Gross National product, see .I5
.I5   Income. Income distribution. Gross national
      product. National income
      Cf. HB141.5+, Economic theory
          HB522, Economic theory
      Industrial location, see .D5
.I52   Industrial productivity
      Cf. HD56+, Industrial management
.I53   Industrial promotion
.I57   Input-output tables. Interindustry economics
      Cf. HB142, Economic theory   *H53 High Tech.*
.I6   Inventories
      Cf. HD55, Industrial management
.L3   Labor productivity
      Cf. HD57, Industrial management
      Location of industry, see .D5
      National income, see .I5
.P55   Pollution
      Cf. HC79.A4, Air pollution
          HC79.E5, Environmental policy
          HD69.P6, Pollution control policy
            (Industrial management)
.P6   Poor. Poverty
      Cf. HV40+, Charity and public relief
.P63   Economic assistance, Domestic. Anti-poverty
      programs
      Prices, see HB231+
.P7   Profit
      Cf. HB601, Economic theory
.R4   Research, Economic inpact of
.S3   Saving and investment
      Cf. HB822, Economic theory
          HG4516, Finance
.S6   Socialist competition. Stakhanov movement
.S8   Strategic materials
.S9   Subsidies
      Cf. HD3641, State and industry
.T4   Technological innovations
      Cf. HD45, Industrial management
.W24   Wage-price policy
      Cf. HB236, Price regulation
          HB3732, Economic stabilization
      War, Economics, of, see .D4
.W3   Waste
      Cf. HD62, Industrial management

79   <u>Special topics, A-Z</u> - Continued
         .W4   Wealth
              Cf. HB251, Economic theory
         .Z6   Zoning economics
              Cf. HD260, Real estate
                  HT169.5+, City planning
                  HT390+, Regional planning

92   Economic geography of the oceans (General)
         Cf. GC1000+, Marine resources
     By region or country
         Class here general works only; for particular
           industries, <u>see</u> HD
         Under each country (local numbers used under
           countries only):

10 nos.	5 nos.	
		Collected works
		Documents
(1.A1-3)	(1.A1-3)	Serial documents
		Separate documents
(1.A4)	(1.A4)	Administrative documents. By date
		Other documents, <u>see</u> General works
(1.A5-Z)	(1.A5-Z)	Periodicals. Societies. Serials
(2)		Dictionaries. Encyclopedias
(2.2)		Directories
(2.5)	(1.5)	Biography
		For particular industries, <u>see</u> HD
		.A2 Collective
		.A3-Z Individual
(3)	(2)	General works
(3.5)	(2.5)	Natural resources
		By period
		Period divisions vary for different countries
(4)		Early
		Including Medieval
(5)		Later
	(3)	Local
(7)		By state, etc., A-Z
(8)		By city, A-Z
		For local annual reviews of "Commerce,"
		"Finance," "Trade," etc., <u>see</u> HF3163 and
		HF3221+, subdivision (10) under each
		country; general, HC14
(9)	(4)	Colonies
		Including exploitation and economic conditions
		For colonial administration and policy, <u>see</u> JV
(10)	(5)	Special topics (not otherwise provided for), A-Z
		For list of topics, <u>see</u> HC79

1 no.	
.A1A-Z	Periodicals. Societies. Serials
.A5-Z6	General works
.Z7A-Z	Local, A-Z
.Z9A-Z	Special topics (not otherwise provided for), A-Z
	For list of topics, <u>see</u> HC79

	By region or country 1/ - Continued
	America. Western Hemisphere
94	General works
	North America
95	General works
	United States
101	Periodicals. Societies. Serials
102	Dictionaries. Encyclopedias
.2	Directories
.5	Biography
	For specific industries, see the industry,
	e. g. HG2463, United States bankers
.A2	Collective
.A3-Z	Individual
103	General works
.5	Syllabi, outlines
.7	Natural resources
104-106	By period
104	Colonial
105	1776-1900
	1860-1869
.6	General works
.65	Confederate States
.7	1870-1879
	1901-1945
106	General works
.2	World War I, 1914-1918
.3	Reconstruction, 1919-1939
.4	World War II, 1939-1945
.5	Reconstruction, 1945-1961
.6	1961-1971
.7	1971-
107	By region or state
	Under each state:
	.x General works
	.x2 By region, county, parish, A-Z
	.x3 Special topics (not otherwise
	provided for), A-Z 2/
107.A1-195	Regions
.A11	New England
.A115	Northeastern States
.A118	Atlantic States
.A12	Middle Atlantic States
.A124	Potomac Valley
.A127	Appalachian region
.A13	South
.A135	Tennessee Valley
.A137	Ozark Mountain region
.A14	North Central States
	Including Great Lakes region
	and Old Northwest

1/

For subarrangement, unless otherwise provided, see tables, p. 23

2/

For list of topics, see HC79

By region or country 1/
America. Western Hemisphere
North America
United States
By region or state

107.A1-195	Regions - Continued
.A145	Northwestern States
.A15	Mississippi Valley
.A16	Ohio Valley
.A165	Southwestern States
.A17	Western States
.A172	Missouri Valley
.A175	Pacific Southwestern States
.A18	Pacific coast
.A19	Pacific Northwestern States
.A195	Columbia Valley
.A2-W	Individual states, A-W
	For table of states, <u>see</u> p. 344
108	By city, A-Z
109	Territories and possessions (General)
110	Special topics (not otherwise provided for), A-Z
.5	Greenland
111-120	Canada
121-130	Latin America
131-140	Mexico
	Central America
141	General works
142	Belize
143	Costa Rica
144	Guatemala
145	Honduras
146	Nicaragua
147	Panama
.5	Panama Canal Zone
148	El Salvador
151	West Indies. Caribbean area
152	Bahamas
.5	Cuba
153	Haiti
.5	Dominican Republic. Santo Domingo

1/

For subarrangement, unless otherwise provided, <u>see</u> tables, p. 23

By region or country 1/
America. Western Hemisphere
Latin America
West Indies. Carribbean area - Continued

154	Jamaica
.5	Puerto Rico
155	Virgin Islands of the United States
.5	British West Indies
156	Leeward Islands
.5	Windward Islands
157	Trinidad and Tobago
.5	Netherlands Antilles. Dutch West Indies
	French West Indies
158	General works
.5	Guadeloupe
.6	Martinique

161-170	South America
171-180	Argentina
181-185	Bolivia
186-190	Brazil
188	Regions, states, A-Z
189	Cities, A-Z
191-195	Chile
196-200	Colombia
201-204.5	Ecuador
204.5	Special topics (not otherwise provided for), A-Z 2/

	Guianas
205	General works
206-210	Guyana. British Guiana
211-215	Surinam. Dutch Guiana
216-220	French Guiana
221-225	Paraguay
226-230	Peru
231-235	Uruguay
236-239.5	Venezuela
239.5	Special topics (not otherwise provided for), A-Z 2/

	Europe
240	General works
.9	Special topics (not otherwise provided for), A-Z 2/
	European economic integration
241	General works
	European Economic Community
	For special topics, see HC240.9
.2	General works
.25	Relation to individual regions or countries, A-Z
.4	European Free Trade Association
	For special topics, see HC240.9

1/
  For subarrangement, unless otherwise provided, see tables, p. 23

2/
  For list of topics, see HC79

	By region or country 1/
	Europe - Continued
243	Northern Europe. Baltic States
	For individual Baltic states, see HC337,
	e. g. Estonia, HC337.E7+
.5	Sovet ékonomicheskoĭ vzaimopomoshchi. Council for
	Mutal Economic Aid. COMECON
	For special topics, see HC244.Z9
244	Central Europe. Eastern Europe
.5	Southern Europe. Mediterranean area
	Commonwealth of Nations
245	Collected works (nonserial)
246	General works
251-260	Great Britain
253	General works
	By period
	Middle ages
254	General works
.3	Manorial system
.4	1485-1600
.5	1600-1800
255	19th century
	Including Modern (General)
	20th century
256	General works
.2	World War I, 1914-1918
.3	Reconstruction, 1919-1939
.4	World War II, 1939-1945
.5	1945-1964
.6	1964-
	Local
257	By region, country, etc., A-Z
	e. g. Buckinghamshire, England, see HC251+
	.N58 Northern Ireland
	.S4 Scotland
	.W3 Wales
258	By city, A-Z
	e. g. .L6 London
260.5	Ireland. Irish Republic
261-270	Austria
	Czechoslovakia
270.2	Periodicals. Societies. Serials
.225	Dictionaries. Encyclopedias
.227	Directories
	Biography
.23	Collective
.232	Individual, A-Z

1/

For subarrangement, unless otherwise provided, see tables, p. 23

2/

For list of topics, see HC79

	By region or country 1/
	Europe
	Czechoslvoakia - Continued
270.24	General works
.25	Natural resources
	By period
.26	To 1918
.27	1918-1945
.28	1945-
.29	By region, county, etc., A-Z
.292	By city, A-Z
.295	Special topics (not otherwise provided for), A-Z 2/
271-280	France
274	To 1600
275	1600-1900
	20th century
276	General works
.2	1945-
280.5	Monaco
281-290.5	Germany
	Including West Germany
	20th century
286	General works
.2	World War I, 1914-1918
.3	Reconstruction, 1919-1945
.4	World War II, 1939-1945
.5	1945-1965
.6	1965-1974
.7	1974-
287	States, A-Z
288	Regions, A-Z
289	Cities, A-Z
290.5	Special topics (not otherwise provided for), A-Z 2/
.7-.795	East Germany
	Divided like HC270.2-.295
291-300	Greece
	By period
294	Byzantine Empire
295	Modern Greece
300.2-.295	Hungary
	Divided like HC270.2-.295
301-310	Italy
310.2	Malta
	Benelux countries. Low countries
.5	General works
311-320	Belgium
321-329.5	Netherlands
329.5	Special topics (not otherwise provided for), A-Z 2/
330	Luxemburg

	By region or country 1/
	Europe - Continued
331-340	Soviet Union
	By period
334	To 1861
	1861-1917
	1917-1950
335	General works
.2	1917-1927
	1928-1950
.3	General works
.4	1928-1932
.5	1933-1937
.6	1938-1945
.7	1946-1950
336	1951-1958
.2	1959-1965
.23	1966-1970
.24	1971-1975
.25	1976-
337	Local, A-Z
340.2	Finland
.3	Poland
341-350	Scandinavia
351-360	Denmark
360.5	Iceland
361-370	Norway
371-380	Sweden
381-390	Spain
	For Canary Islands, see HC593.5
390.5	Andorra
.6	Gibraltar
391-394.5	Portugal
	For Madeira, see HC593
	For the Azores, see HC592
394.5	Special topics (not otherwise provided for), A-Z 2/
395-400	Switzerland
395	Periodicals. Societies. Serials
396	Dictionaries. Encyclopedias
397	General works
	Local
398	Regions and cantons, A-Z
399	Cities, A-Z
400	Special topics (not otherwise provided for), A-Z 2/
	Balkan States
401	General works
402	Albania
403	Bulgaria
405	Romania

1/   For subarrangement, unless otherwise provided, see tables, p. 23

2/   For list of topics, see HC79

	By region or country 1/
	Europe
	Balkan States - Continued
	Turkey, see HC491+
407	Yugoslavia
411–415	Asia
415.15	Middle East. Near East
	Turkey, see HC491+
.2	Cyprus
.23	Syria
.24	Lebanon
.25	Israel. Palestine
.26	Jordan
	Arabian Peninsula. Arabia
.3	General works
.33	Saudi Arabia
.34	Yemen (Yemen Arab Republic)
.342	Yemen (People's Democratic Republic). Southern Yemen. Aden (Colony and Protectorate)
.35	Oman. Muscat and Oman
.36	United Arab Emirates. Trucial States
.37	Qatar
.38	Bahrein
.39	Kuwait
.4	Iraq
	Iran, see HC471+
416–420	Afghanistan
422	Burma
424	Sri Lanka. Ceylon
425	Nepal
426–430	China
	By period
427.6	Early to 1644
.7	1644–1912
.8	1912–1949
.9	1949–1976
.92	1976–
.94	Outer Mongolia. Mongolian People's Republic
.95	Macao
430.5	Taiwan. Formosa
	South Asia
431–440	India
435.1	1918–1947
.2	1947–
439	Famines
440.5	Pakistan
.8	Bangladesh. East Pakistan
	Sri Lanka, see HC424
441	Southeast Asia. Indochina
	Including French Indochina
	Burma, see HC422
442	Cambodia
443	Laos
444	Vietnam

1/

    For subarrangement, unless otherwise provided, see tables, p. 23

	By region or country 1/
	Asia
	Southeast Asia. Indochina - Continued
445	Thailand
.5	Malaysia. Malaya
.8	Singapore
.85	Brunei
446-450	Indonesia
451-460	Philippine Islands
460.5	East Asia. Far East
461-465	Japan
	By period
462.6	Early to 1867
.7	1867-1918
.8	1918-1945
.9	1945-
466-470	Korea
	Including South Korea
470.2	North Korea
.3	Hongkong
471-480	Iran. Persia
491-495	Turkey
	Arab countries
498	General works
.9	Special topics (not otherwise provided for), A-Z 2/
499	Islamic countries
	Africa, see HC800+
	Atlantic Ocean Islands
	Iceland, see HC360.5
592	Azores
.5	Bermuda
593	Madeira Islands
.5	Canary Islands
594	Cape Verde Islands
.5	St. Helena
595	Tristen da Cunha
.5	Falkland Islands
	Indian Ocean Islands
596	Maldive Islands
.5	Seychelles
597	Comoro Islands
.5	Mauritius
598	Reunion
.5	Kerguelen Islands
601-610	Australia
661-670	New Zealand
	Pacific Ocean Islands
681	General works
.5	Trust Territory of the Pacific. Micronesia
	Including Mariana, Caroline and Marshall Islands
	Hawaii, see HC107.H3

1/
    For subarrangement, unless otherwise provided, see tables, p. 23

2/
    For list of topics, see HC79

1/ For subarrangement, unless otherwise provided, see tables, p. 23

2/ For list of topics, see HC79

By region or country 1/
    Africa - Continued
      Southern Africa

900	General works
905	South Africa
910	Rhodesia
	Including Southern Rhodesia
915	Zambia. Northern Rhodesia
920	Lesotho. Basutoland
925	Swaziland
930	Botswana. Bechuanaland
935	Malawi. Nyasaland
940	Namibia. Southwest Africa

      Central Africa. Equatorial Africa

945	General works
950	Angola
955	Zaire. Congo (Democratic Republic)
960	Equatorial Guinea
965	Sao Tome é Príncipe
970	French Equatorial Africa. French Congo
975	Gabon
980	Congo (Brazzaville). Middle Congo
985	Central African Republic. Ubangi-Shari
990	Chad
995	Cameroon

      West Africa. West Coast

1000	General works
1005	French-speaking West Africa
1010	Benin. Dahomey
1015	Togo
1020	Niger
1025	Ivory Coast
1030	Guinea
1035	Mali
1040	Upper Volta
1045	Senegal
1050	Mauritania
1055	Nigeria
1060	Ghana
1065	Sierra Leone
1070	Gambia
1075	Liberia
1080	Guinea-Bissau. Portuguese Guinea
1085	Spanish Sahara

1/
    For subarrangement, unless otherwise provided, see tables, p. 23

PRODUCTION

Organization of production. Management. Industrial
management
    Cf. HB241, Production (Economic theory)
        HD2341+, Corporate organization
        HD3611+, The state and industrial organization
        HD9000+, Special industries
        T554+, Industrial engineering

28	Periodicals. Societies. Serials
29	Congresses
	Collected works (nonserial)
30	Several authors
.12	Individual authors
.15	Dictionaries. Encyclopedias
.17	Terminology. Abbreviations. Notation
	Theory. Method

Class here works of a general nature, or works on
topics of decision-making, forecasting, planning
and related fields. For works on these topics
stressing the quantitative or technical approach,
see T55.4+

.22	Managerial economics
.23	Decision making
.25	Mathematical models
.26	Management games
.27	Forecasting
	Cf. HB3730, Economic forecasting
.28	Planning
.29	Problem solving

Communication in management. Communication of
information
    Cf. HF5549.5.C6, Personnel management
        HF5718+, Business communication
        T58.6, Management information systems

.3	General works
.34	Television in management
	Information services
.35	General works
.36	By region or country, A-Z

Study and teaching. Research
    Cf. HF1101+, Commercial education

.4	General works
.412	Audiovisual aids
.413	Problems, exercises, examinations
.42	By region or country, A-Z

Museums. Exhibitions, see T391+
History

.5	General works
	Special schools
.6	Management by exception
.65	Management by objectives
	Biography
.8	Collective
.85	Individual, A-Z

Production
    Organization of production. Management. Industrial
      management - Continued
      General works, treatises, and advanced textbooks

31	English
33	French
35	German
36	Russian and other Slavic languages
37	Other languages, A-Z
38	General special
.4	Bureaucracy
.7	Business intelligence. Trade secrets

      Capital. Capital investments
          Cf. HB501, Capital (Economic theory)
             HC79.C3, Capital (Economic history)
             HG4028.C4, Capital investments (Finance)

39	General works
.3	Industrial equipment
	Cf. TS191+, Plant engineering
.4	Industrial equipment leases
	Cf. HF5548.6, Computer leases
.5	Industrial procurement
40	Inventory policy
	Cf. HF5484+, Warehousing (Commerce)
	TS160+, Inventory control
.6	Maintenance and repair
	Cf. TS192, Plant maintenance
.7	Surplus property
41	Competition and cooperation. Regulation and restriction of output

    Contracting. Letting of contracts, <u>see</u> HD2365+
    Control of industry. Technological innovations
        Cf. HC79.T4, Economic history
           T173.2+, Technological change
           T175, Industrial research

45	General works
.2	Automation
	Cf. HC79.A8, Economic history
	HD6331+, Machinery in industry (Labor)
	T59.5, Technology

    Costs
        Cf. HC79.C7, Costs (Economic history)
           HF5686.C8, Cost accounting
           TA177+, Engineering economy

47	General works
.25	Break-even analysis
.3	Cost control
	Cf. TS160+, Production management
.4	Cost effectiveness

    Crises and overproduction
        Cf. HB3711, Business cycles and crises

49	General works
.5	Inflation
50	Delegation of authority
51	Division of labor. Specialization

    Industrial equipment, <u>see</u> HD39.3

Handwritten annotations in right margin:

Executives. Executive ability. Cf. HD6054.
Women executive

Biography
Collective see H
Individual See
specific industr
in HD

.2 General works
.25 By region or country, A-Z

Production
    Organization of production. Management. Industrial
       management – Continued
      Industrial procurement, see HD39.5
      Industrial research, see T175+

53	Intellectual work
	Inventory policy, see HD40+
	Industrial productivity
	Cf. HC79.I52, Economic history
	T58.7+, Industrial engineering
56	General works
57	Labor productivity
	Cf. HC79.L3, Economic history
	S564, Farm management
.5	Capital productivity
	Cf. HC79.C3, Economic history
58	Location of industry
	Cf. HC79.D5, Distribution of industry (Economic
	history)
	HD1393.5, Industrial property
.4	Management committees
	Cf. HD6972, Labor–management committees
.7	Organizational behavior
	Cf. HD6951+, Industrial sociology
	HF5548.8, Industrial psychology
.8	Organizational change and development
	Organizational effectiveness
.9	General works
.95	Management audit
	Personnel management, see HF5549+
	Public relations. Industrial publicity
	Cf. HM263, Social psychology
59	General works
.2	Corporate image
	Social responsibilities. Corporate and social policies
	Cf. HG4028.C6, Corporate contributions to charities
60	General works
.5	By region or country, A–Z
	Under each country:
	.x General works
	.x2 Local, A–Z
	Quality control, see TS156+
61	Risk in industry. Risk management
	Cf. HB615, Risk and risk bearing (Economic theory)
	HG8059.B8, Business risk insurance
62	Simplification. Standardization. Waste
	Cf. T59+, Technology
	Management of special enterprises
.2	Branch management
	Corporations (General), see HD2741+
.3	Foreign subsidiaries and branches
.4	International business enterprises
.5	New business enterprises
	Cf. HB615, Entrepreneurship
.6	Nonprofit corporations
.7	Small business
.8	Subsidiary corporations
	Valuation, see HF5681.V3

Production
  Organization of production.   Management.   Industrial
    management – Continued

66	Work groups. Team work in industry
69	Other, A–Z

     .B7   Branded merchandise
     .C3   Capacity
     .C6   Business consultants
           Foreign subsidiaries and branches, see HD62.3
           Industrial design, see TS171
           Industrial promotion, see HC79.I53
           Industrial research, see T175+
           Inflation, see HD49.5
           International business enterprises, see HD62.4
           Inventions, see T212
     .M3   Maintenance and repair, see HD40.6
           Materials management, see TS161
           New business enterprises, see HD62.5
     .N4   New products
     .P6   Pollution control policy
              Cf. HC79.P55, Pollution (Economic history)
                  TD172+, Environmental technology
           Production control, see TS15.7+
     .P75   Project management
              Cf. T56.8, Industrial project management
           Reports to management, see HF5719
           Scheduling, see TS157.5+
     .S5   Size of industries
           Small business, see HD62.7
           Surplus property, see HD40.7
           Technicians, see TA158
    By industry or trade, see HD9000+

70	By region or country, A–Z

  The state and production, see HD3611+
  Economic growth, development, planning
    Cf. HC51+, Modern economic history
        HC59.7, Underdeveloped areas
        HD2329, Industrialization

72	Periodicals. Societies. Serials
73	Congresses
	Collected works (nonserial)
74	Several authors
.5	Individual authors
	Theory. Method. Relation to other subjects
75	General works
.5	Mathematical models
.6	Environmental aspects
	Study and teaching. Research
77	General works
.5	By region or country, A–Z
78	History
	General works
82	English
83	French
84	German
.5	Russian and other Slavic languages
85	Other languages, A–Z

Production
  Economic growth, development, planning – Continued
    Public policy (General)
      For the economic policy of particular countries,
        states, etc., <u>see</u> HC95+

87	General works
.5	Planning
88	Limits to growth

LAND USE

Cf. HB401, Rent
    HB701, Ownership of property
For cadastral mapping, <u>see</u> GA109.5

101	Periodicals. Serials
103	Societies
105	Congresses
	Collected works (nonserial)
107	Several authors
.5	Individual authors
	Theory. Method. Relation to other subjects
108	Classification
.4	Mathematical models
.6	Planning
	Communication of information
109	General works
.5	Information services
	Study and teaching. Research
110	General works
.5	By region or country, A–Z
111	General works
	History
113	General works
	Primitive
115	General works
	Europe
117	General works
118	Celtic
119	Germanic
	Asia
121	India (Indo-Aryan)
	Ancient
125	General works
	Classic Orient
126	General works
127	Assyria-Babylonia
128	Media-Persia
129	Hebrews
130	Egypt
131	Other

Land use
  By region or country
    America
      United States
        History - Continued

196	Local. By province or state, A-Z
	1821-1897
	Including public land policy speeches in Congress, "Homesteading" on United States public lands, etc.
	For homesteads, exemption, etc., see HD1337
197	General works
199	Antirent movement, New York, 1835-1846
201	Granger movement
	For the Patrons of Husbandry, see HD1485
205	1898- By date
	Local
207	South
209	West
210	Other regions, A-Z
211	By state, A-W
	Cf. HD243, Public lands
	By city, see HD268, HD1291
	Public lands
	Documents, see HD171+
216	History
	Including state claims to Federal lands
221	Description, guides, etc.
	Including suggestions to homesteaders
	Indian lands, see E93
239	Town sites, etc.
240	Bounty lands
241	Grazing lands
	Cf. HD1635+, Pasture lands
	Mineral lands
242	General works
.3	Coal lands
.5	Oil and gas lands
	Including oil rights
.9	Rights of way
	Including power transmission, telegraph, etc.
	For railroad rights, see HE1063+
	Railroad land grants, see HE1063+
	School lands, see LB2827
	Swamp lands, see HD1665+
243	By region or state, A-Z
	Cf. HD196, United States history of land (Local)
	By city, see HD1291
	Real estate
	Cf. HD1361+, Real estate business
251	Periodicals. Societies. Serials
253	Yearbooks
254	Congresses

   Land use
    By region or country
     America
      United States
       Real estate - Continued
        Study and teaching of real estate business,
         see HD1381

255	General works
256	Farm property. Rural land use
	Cf. HD1443, Agricultural credit
257	Urban property. Urban land use
	Cf. HT165.5+, City planning
258	Recreational land
259	Residential land. Land subdivision
260	Zoning
	Cf. HD1393.6, Real estate business
	HT69.6+, City planning
266	By region or state, A-Z
	Under each:
	.x General works
	.x2 Individual counties, A-Z
268	By city, A-Z
	Cf. HJ3251+, subdivision (2.9) or (5.Z8)
	HJ9013, Public finance documents
	HJ9191+, Public finance
	For municipal property, see HD1290+
	Under each:
	.xA2 Official tax lists. By date
	.xA3-Z General works
	Companies
275	By city, A-Z
277	By name of project or company, A-Z
	If restricted to a city, see HD275
278	Real estate agents. Brokers. Counselors
279	Real estate agents' lists
	Class here works on land in more than one
	area. For works limited to one
	individual geographical area or
	jurisdiction, see HD266, HD268

Land use
   By region or country – Continued

311–1130.5   Other regions or countries.   Table VII, modified 1/
           Under each country:

10 nos.	5 nos.	1 no.	
(1).A1A–Z	(1)	.A1A–Z	Periodicals. Serials
(1.5)	(1.5)	.A5A–Z	Societies
	(3)	.A6–Z6	History
			Including policy
(3)			General works
(4)			Early
(5)			19th and 20th centuries
(6)	(3.2)	.Z63A–Z	1945–
(8)		.Z7A–Z	Special. Miscellaneous
			Local
			Including real estate
(9)	(4)	.Z8A–Z	By region or state, A–Z
(10)	(5)	.Z9A–Z	By city, etc., A–Z

Note: Great Britain
594.6   Enclosures
  .8   18th century
644.8   France.   18th century

1131	Underdeveloped areas
	Land tenure
	Law, see K
	Policy. Theory of distribution of the land
1241	Periodicals. Societies. Serials
1245	Congresses
1251	General works
	Eminent domain. Expropriation. State domain
	Cf. HD3865+, Public works
1259	Periodicals. Societies. Serials
1261	General works
	By region or country
	United States
1262	Federal
1263	States, A–W
1265	Other regions or countries, A–Z
	Under each country:
	.xA1–29 Periodicals. Societies.
	Serials
	.xA6–Z General works
	.x2 Local, A–Z
	Littoral rights. Riparian rights, see K
	Communal ownership
1286	General works
1289	By region or country, A–Z

1/
For Table VII, see pp. 331–340. Add country number in table to 300

```
                    Land use
                      Land tenure
                        Policy.  Theory of distribution of the
                          land - Continued
                          Municipal ownership
1290                        General works
1291                        By region or country, A-Z
                                Under each country:
                                    .x    General works
                                    .x2  Local, A-Z
                          Taxation
                              Including agriculture and taxation
                              Cf. HJ2250+, Public finance
                                  HJ4151+, Public finance
1294                        General works
1295                        By region or country, A-Z
                          Nationalization (Agrarian socialism)
                              Cf. HD1492+, Collective farms
                                  HX550.L3, Socialism and the land question
1301                        General works
1306                        By region or country, A-Z
                          Single tax
1311                          Works by Henry George
                              Other works
1313.A1-5                       Periodicals.  Societies.  Serials
     .A6-Z                          General works
                          Unearned increment, see HD1389
                          Large holdings
                              Cf. HD1471, Large farms
1326                        General works
1329                        By region or country, A-Z
                          Landlord and peasant
1330                        General works
1331                        By region or country, A-Z
                          Land reform.  Agrarian reform
1332                        General works
1333                        By region or country, A-Z
     .5                       Underdeveloped areas
                          Consolidation of land holdings
1334                        General works
1335                        By region or country, A-Z
                                Under each country:
                                    .x    General works
                                    .x2  Local, A-Z
                          Small holdings.  Peasant proprietors
                          Parcellation
                              Cf. HD1476, Small farms
1336                        General works
1337                        Homesteads, exemption, etc.
1339                        By region or country, A-Z
                              Cf. HD300+, Peasantry
                          Agricultural colonization, see HD1516
                          Homes and house lots, see HD1390, HD7286+
                          By region or country, see HD166+
```

Land use – Continued
    Real estate business
        Cf. HD251+, Real estate (United States)
            HD7286+, Housing
            HF5686.R3, Accounting

1361	Periodicals. Societies. Serials
1363	Congresses
1365	Dictionaries. Encyclopedias
1375	General works
1379	Popular works

        Cf. TH1817.5, Home buyers' guides
Study and teaching. Research

1381	General works
.5	By region or country, A–Z

Real estate agents

1382	General works
.2	Salaries, commissions, etc.
.5	Investment

        Cf. HG2040+, Mortgage credit agencies

.7	Multiple listing

Contracts. Leases

1384	General works
.5	Forms
1386.5	Records and correspondence

Valuation
    Including the appraisal of land and buildings
        Cf. HJ3241, Assessment
            HJ4151, Land tax

1387	General works
1388	Tables
1389	Betterments. Unearned increment
1390	Real estate development. Land subdivision

        Cf. TH350+, Subdivision engineering

.5	Residential property
1391	Urban property
1392	Recreational land
1393	Rural property. Farm land

    Including appraisal of land, buildings, crops,
        etc.

.25	Business enterprises
.5	Industrial property

        Cf. HC79.D5, Distribution of industry
            HD58, Location of industry

.6	Impact of zoning

        Cf. HT169.6, Zoning in city planning

1394	Rental property. Real estate management

        Cf. TX955+, Building operation and housekeeping

1395	Exchange of real property. Trade-in housing

By region or country, <u>see</u> HD166+

AGRICULTURE

Class here works on the economic
aspects of agriculture; for
technical works, see S
Cf. HD9000+, Agricultural industries.
Produce trade

1401	Periodicals. Serials
	Societies, see HD1483+
1405	Congresses
	Collected works (nonserial)
1407	Several authors
1408	Individual authors
1410	Dictionaries. Encyclopedias
	Study and teaching. Research
.5	General works
.6	By region or country, A-Z
	Under each country:
	.x General works
	.x2 Local, A-Z
	General works
1411	Early through 1944
1415	1945-
	By region or country, see HD1751+
1417	Underdeveloped areas
	Statistics
1421	Collections of statistics
1425	Theory
	International cooperation
1428	General works
	International Institute of Agriculture, Rome
	Cf. S401, International Council for Scientific
	Agriculture
	Documents
1429.A1-5	Its publications
.A6	Preliminary documents
.A7-Z	By region or country
1430	Nonofficial
1431	Agricultural assistance
	Including aid by individual countries to several
	countries
	Cf. S, Agriculture
	Theory. Method. Relation to other subjects
1433	General works
1434	Agriculture and business
	Cf. HD9000+, Agribusiness
1436	Agriculture and capital
	Agricultural finance
1437	General works
	Agricultural credit
	Cf. HG2041+, Banking
1439	General works
1440	By region or country, A-Z
	Agricultural mortgages, see HG2041+

```
                    Agriculture
                      Theory.  Method.  Relation to other
                          subjects - Continued
                        Agricultural prices (General)
                            Cf. HD9000+, Agribusiness
         1447                General works
                            By region or country, see HD1700+
                        Agriculture and tariff, see HF2601
                        Agriculture and land tax, see HD1294+
                        Agriculture and taxes on industries, and on
                          consumption, see HD9000+, HJ5635, HJ5703+
                        Agriculture wages, see HD4966
         1459            Farm mechanization
                            Cf. HD9486, Implements and machinery (Agriculture)
                                S671+, Farm machinery and farm engineering
                        Agriculture and transportation, see HE149
                        Agriculture and railroads, see HD1043
                      Size of farms
         1470            General works
           .5            By region or country, A-Z
                        Large farms.  Plantations
                            Cf. HD1326+, Land tenure
                                HD1506, Agricultural classes
         1471.A3A-Z        General works
             .A4-Z         By region or country, A-Z
                        Small farms.  Family farms
                            Cf. HD1336+, Land tenure
                                HD1513, Peasant proprietors
         1476.A3A-Z        General works
             .A4-Z         By region or country, A-Z
                      Sharecropping
         1478.A3A-Z        General works
             .A4-Z         By region or country, A-Z
                      Consolidation of land holdings, see HD1332
                      Agricultural associations, societies, etc.
                          Including cooperative agricultural societies, e. g.
                              creameries, and farmers' societies, e. g. Patrons
                              of Husbandry, Farmers' Alliance, etc.
         1483            General works
                        By region or country
                          United States
                              Cf. HD201, Granger movement
         1484              General works
         1485              By society, A-Z
         1486            Other regions or countries, A-Z
                      Cooperative agriculture
         1491.A1A-Z      Periodicals.  Serials
                        Societies, see HD1483+
             .A3A-Z      General works
             .A5-Z       By region or country, A-Z
                            Under each country:
                              .x    General works
                              .x2   Local, A-Z
           .5          Underdeveloped areas
```

```
                          Agriculture - Continued
        1492                  Collective farms
                                  Subarranged like HD1491
                              Government owned and operated farms.  State farms.
                                  Sovkhozes
        1493.A3A-Z            General works
             .A4-Z            By region or country, A-Z
                              Agricultural classes
                                  History, see HD113+
        1501                  General works
                                  Landlord, see HD1330+
                              Farm tenancy
        1510                      General works
        1511                      By region or country, A-Z
                                  Peasant proprietors, see HD1336+
                              Agricultural colonization
                                      Cf. HD1491+, Cooperative agriculture
        1516.A3A-Z            General works
             .A4-Z            By region or country, A-Z
                              Workingmen's gardens
        1519.A3-Z             General works
             .A4-Z            By region or country, A-Z
                              Agricultural laborers
                                  Including labor supply
                                  For wages, see HD4966
        1521                  General works
        1523                  Medieval
                              By region or country
                                  United States
        1525                      General works
        1527                      By region or state, A-Z
                                      Subarranged like HC107
        1529                      Canada
        1531                      Other American regions or countries, A-Z
                                  Europe
             .5                      General works
                                     Great Britain
        1532                         General works
                                         Medieval, see HD594
        1534                         Modern
        1536                      Other European regions or countries, A-Z
        1537                      Asia.  By region or country, A-Z
        1538                      Africa.  By region or country, A-Z
        1539                      Australia
             .5                   New Zealand
        1540                      Pacific islands, A-Z
                                      Hawaii, see HD1527.H3
                              By region or country, see HD166+
        1549                  Gleaning
                              Melioration and reclamation of agricultural land
                                  Cf. S604.8+, Methods and techniques
        1580                  General works
                              By region or country, see HD1751+
```

      Agriculture - Continued
       Utilization and culture of special classes of lands
        Class here works on economic aspects and public
         policy
        Forest lands, see SD
        Pasture lands
         Cf. HD241, Grazing
          SB199, Plant culture

1635	General works
1641	By region or country, A-Z
	Waste lands
	Cf. TC801+, Reclamation of land
1665	General works
1671	By region or country, A-Z
	Flood control, see TC530+
	Drainage
	Cf. S621, Farmers' manuals
	TC970+, Engineering
1681	General works
1683	By region or country, A-Z
	Water resources development. Water supply
	Cf. HD1269, State domain
	HD1711+, Irrigation
	HD4456, Public works
	TC401+, Hydraulic engineering
	TD201+, Water supply systems
1690	Periodicals. Societies. Serials
.5	Congresses
1691	General works
	By region or country
	United States
1694.A1-15	Periodicals. Serials
	International questions. By date
.A17	General works
.A2	United States and Canada
.A3	United States and Mexico
.A45-47	Federal Power Commission
.A5A-Z	General works
.A51-59	General special. By date
.A6-W	States
1695	Local (other than states), A-Z
	e. g. .A8 Arkansas River
	Rio Grande, see HD1694.A3
	Other American regions or countries
1696	By country, A-Z
	Under each:
	.x General works
	.x2 International questions. By date
	.x3 By state, A-Z
	.x4 Other local, A-Z
.5	Regions (not limited to one country), A-Z
	e. g. .R5 Rio de la Plata region
	Europe
1697.A5	General works
.A6-Z	By country, A-Z
	Subarranged like HD1696
.5	Regions (not limited to one country), A-Z
	e. g. .T3 Tagus Valley

Agriculture
  Utilization and culture of special classes of lands
    Water resources development. Water supply
      By region or country - Continued
        Asia

1698.A1A-Z	General works
.A2-Z	By region or country
	Under each country:
	.x General works
	.x2 Local, A-Z
1699	Africa
	Subarranged like HD1698
	Australia
1700.A1A-Z	General works
.A2-Z	Local, A-Z
1701	New Zealand
	Subarranged like HD1700
1702	Underdeveloped areas

  Irrigation. Reclamation
    Cf. HD1691+, Water resources development
      TC801+, Irrigation engineering
    Periodicals. Societies. Serials, see TC801

1711	Congresses
1714	General works
	By region or country
	United States
1720	Periodicals. Societies. Serials
1735	General works
1736	Public policy. By date
1739	By region or state, A-Z
	e. g. .A15 Rocky Mountains
1740	By place or project, A-Z
1741	Other regions or countries, A-Z
	Under each country:
	.x General works
	.x2 Local, A-Z
	By region or country
	America
1748	General works
	North America
1750	General works
	United States
1751	Periodicals. Societies. Serials
1755	Congresses
	History
	Including policy
1759	Collected works (nonserial)
1761	General works
1765	General special. By date of publication
1769	Statistics

        Class here works on agricultural statistics
          limited to economic aspects, including
          prices, consumption, trade, etc. For
          works on general agricultural statistics,
          including acreage, yield production, etc.,
          see S21+, S419

```
                           Agriculture
                             By region or country
                               America
                                 North America
                                   United States - Continued
                                     By region
        1773.A2                        Atlantic
            .A3                        Central
                                         Including Great Plains
            .A5                        South
            .A6                        Southwest
            .A7                        Rocky Mountains
            .A9                        Pacific
        1775                         Local.  By state, A-W
        1781-2210            Other regions or countries.  Table IX, modified 1/
                             Under each country:
```

10 nos.	5 nos.	1 no.	
(1)	(1)	.A1-5	Periodicals. Societies. Serials
	(2)	.A6-Z7	History and description
(3)			General works
(4)			Medieval
(5)			Modern
(7)	(3)	.Z8A-Z	Policy. By date
(10)	(5)	.Z9A-Z	Local, A-Z

Underdeveloped areas, see HD1417

INDUSTRY

Class here general works only;
for special industries, see HD9000+

```
        2321        History
                      Cf. T37, Industrial archaeology
        2326        Theory.  Relation to other subjects
        2328        General works
        2329        Industrialization
                      Cf. HD72+, Economic development
        2330        Rural industry
                    Decentralization of industry, see HC79.D5
                    House industry
        2331          History
        2333          General works
        2336          By region or country, A-Z
                    Sweating system
        2337          General works
        2339          By region or country, A-Z
                    Size of industry, see HD69.S5
```

1/
  For Table IX, see pp. 331-340. Add country number in table to 1780

Industry - Continued
  Small and medium industry, artisans, handicrafts,
    trades
      Including modern guilds, etc.
     Cf. HD62.7, Small business management
        HD8036, Self-employed
        HD9980+, Service industries
        TT1+, Handicraft
     For pre-modern guilds, see HD6456+

2340.8	History
2341	General works
2346	By region or country, A-Z

      Under each country:
        .x   General works
        .x2   Local, A-Z
  Large industry. Factory system. Big business
     Cf. HD2757+, Industrial concentration

2350.8	History
2351	General works
2356	By region or country, A-Z

      Under each country:
        .x   General works
        .x2   Local, A-Z
  Regulation and restriction of output, see HD41, HD2757+
  Contracting. Letting of contracts
      Including competitive letting of contracts
     Cf. HD3128, State contracts with cooperative
          societies
        HD3858+, Public contracts
        TA180+, Specifications and contracts

2365	General works
	Subcontracting
2381	General works
2385	By region or country, A-Z

  Trade and industrial associations
     Cf. HF294+, Boards of trade

2421	General works
	By region or country
	United States
2425	General works
2428	By region or state
2429	Other regions or countries, A-Z

  Corporations. Cartels. Trusts
     Cf. HD3840+, Government owned corporations
        HG4001+, Corporation finance

2709	Periodicals. Societies. Serials
2711	Congresses
2713	Dictionaries. Encyclopedias
2721	History
	General works
2731	English
2733	French
2734	German
2735	Italian
2736	Other languages, A-Z

Industry
   Corporations. Cartels. Trusts – Continued
      Corporate organization and administration
         Class here general works only. For the
           organization and administration of specific
           kinds of corporations, see the specific
           kind, e. g. HD62.8, Subsidiary corporations
         Cf. HD59+, Public relations

2741	General works
2743	Conduct of meetings, voting, etc.
2745	Board of directors

         Cf. HD5650+, Employees' representation in
           management

.5	Corporation secretaries

      Accounting, see HF5686.C7

2746.5	Consolidations. Mergers

         Cf. HD2755.7+, Diversification

2747	Dissolution. Liquidation

      Taxation of corporations
         Cf. HJ4653.C7, Corporate income taxes

2753.A3A–Z	General works
.A5–Z	By region or country, A–Z

      Regulation, see HD3611+

2755	Franchises. Charters

         Cf. HF5429.23+, Retail trade

.5	International business enterprises. Multinational corporations

         Cf. HD62.4, Management
         For works on foreign corporations located in a
           given country, see HD2770+
      Diversification

.8	General works
2756	Conglomerate corporations

         Cf. HD9503, General companies

.2	By region or country, A–Z

     Industrial concentration
         Cf. HD41, Competition

2757	General works
.2	Monopolies
.3	Oligopolies
.5	Cartels
2758	Holding companies
.5	Trusts

      Trusts and the railroads, see HE1051
      Trusts and the tariff, see HF2591
      Public utilities. Public service commissions.
        Public service corporations
         Cf. HD3840+, State industries and public works

2763.A2A–Z	Periodicals. Societies. Serials
.A5–Z	General works
2765	Valuation

      By region or country
        United States

2766.A3A–Z	Periodicals. Societies. Serials
.A6–Z	General works
2767	By region or state, A–Z

           Under each state:
              .x   Periodicals. Serials
              .x4 General works
              .x5 Local, A–Z

```
                          Industry
                            Corporations.  Cartels.  Trusts
                              Industrial concentration
                                  Public utilities.  Public service commissions.
                                    Public service corporations
                                  By region or country - Continued
         2768                         Other regions or countries, A-Z
                                          Subarranged like HD2767
                              By industry, see HD9000+
                              By region or country
                                America
         2770                     General works
                                  North America
           .5                       General works
                                    United States
         2771                         Periodicals.  Societies.  Serials
         2783                         Congresses
                                      Directories, see HG4057
         2785                         General works
         2795                         Public policy
         2798                         By region or state, A-Z
    2807-2930.7                   Other regions or countries.  Table V, modified 1/
                                    Under each country:
```

4 nos.	1 no.	
(1)	.A1A-Z	Periodicals. Societies. Serials
(3)	.A5-Z7	History
(4)		Public policy
(4.5) 2/	.Z8A-Z	Local, A-Z

```
                              Industrial cooperation.  Mutuality
                                  Cf. HD1491, Cooperative agriculture
                                      HF5431+, Cooperative business
                                      HM131, Mutuality (Social theory)
         2951                     Periodicals.  Serials
                                  Collected works (nonserial)
           .5                       Several authors
           .6                       Individual authors
         2952                     Societies
         2953                     Congresses
         2954                     Dictionaries.  Encyclopedias
                                  Study and teaching.  Research
         2955                       General works
           .5                       By region or country, A-Z
         2956                     History
                                  Statistics
         2958                       Collections of statistics
         2959                       Theory
         2961                     Theory.  Method.  Relation to other subjects
```

1/
     For Table V, see pp. 331-340. Add country number in table to 2800

2/
     If 4.5 is not available, use 4.15

Industry
　　Industrial cooperation.　Mutuality - Continued
2963　　　　　　　General works
2965　　　　　　　Handbooks, manuals, etc.
　　　　　　　　　Profit-sharing
　　　　　　　　　　　Cf. HD5650+, Employee ownership
2970　　　　　　　Congresses
2971　　　　　　　General works
2981-3110.9　　　By region or country.　Table V 1/
　　　　　　　　　　Subarranged like HD3441-3570.7, modified as
　　　　　　　　　　　follows
　　　　　　　　　　Under each country:

　　　　　4 nos.　　　　1 no.

　　　　　(4).A1A-Z　　　.A6A1-19　　By individual company
　　　　　　　　　　　　　　　　　　　(alphabetically)

　　　　　　　　Cooperative production
3120　　　　　　　Congresses
3121　　　　　　　General works
　　　　　　　　　State contracts with cooperative societies
3128.A1-5　　　　General works
　　　.A6-Z　　　　By region or country
　　　　　　　　　　Under each country:
　　　　　　　　　　　.x　　Periodicals.　Societies.　Serials
　　　　　　　　　　　.x2　General works
　　　　　　　　　By industry or trade, see HD9000+
3131-3260.9　　　By region or country.　Table V 1/
　　　　　　　　　　Subarranged like HD3441-3570.9
　　　　　　　　Cooperative distribution
　　　　　　　　　　Including consumers' cooperatives
　　　　　　　　　　Cf.　LB3612, Student cooperatives
3271　　　　　　　General works
3281-3410.9　　　By region or country.　Table V 1/
　　　　　　　　　　Subarranged like HD3441-3570.9
3423　　　　　　　Women's cooperative guilds
　　　　　　　　　Cooperation and socialism, see HX519
3441-3570.9　　　By region or country.　Table V 1/
　　　　　　　　　　Under each country:

　　　4 nos.　　　　1 no.

　　　(1)　　　　　　.A2-39　　　Periodicals.　Societies.　Serials
　　　(2)　　　　　　.A4A-Z　　　General works
　　　(2.5)　　　　　.A45A-Z　　　Biography
　　　(3)　　　　　　.A5A-Z　　　Public policy
　　　(4)　　　　　　　　　　　　Local
　　　　.A1A-Z　　　　.A6A1-19　　General cooperative societies
　　　　.A3A-Z　　　　.A6A2-Z　　　By state, province, etc., A-Z
　　　　.A5-Z4　　　　.A7-Z　　　　By city, A-Z
　　　　　　　　　　　　　　　　　By race or ethnic group, see the race
　　　　　　　　　　　　　　　　　　or ethnic group, e. g. E59.I5,
　　　　　　　　　　　　　　　　　　Indians
3575　　　　　　　Underdeveloped areas

————————
1/
　　For Table V, see pp. 331-340.　Add country number in table to 2980,
3130, 3280, or 3440, as the case requires

Industry - Continued
The state and industrial organization
    Cf. HC79.I52, Industrial promotion

3611	General works
3612	Regulation
3616	By region or country, A-Z

        Under each country:
           .x Periodicals. Societies. Serials
           .x2 History
           .x3 Public policy
           .x4 Local, A-Z

Licensing of occupations and professions
    Cf. HJ5621+, Taxation
    For special occupations and professions,
      see Classes B - Z

3629	General works
3630	By region or country, A-Z

Taxation, see HD2753
Subsidies. Bounties
    Cf. HF1421, Trade adjustment assistance

3641	General works

Special industries, see HD9000+

3646	By region or country, A-Z

Inspection. Factory inspection

3656.A1-5	Periodicals. Societies. Serials
.A6-Z	General works
3661-3790.9	By region or country. Table V 1/

    Under each country:

4 nos.	1 no.	
(1)	.A1-4	Periodicals. Serials
(3)	.A6-Z4	General works
(4)	.Z5A-Z	Local: States, provinces, etc., A-Z

State industries. Public works. Government
ownership
    Including government-owned corporations and
      monopolies
    Cf. HD9000+, Special industries
        TA21+, Public works
    For socialist economies, see HC95+

3840	Periodicals. Societies. Serials
3842	Congresses
	Collected works (nonserial)
3845	Several authors
.4	Individual authors
.6	Theory. Method. Relation to other subjects
3848	Study and teaching. Research
	General works
3850	English
3854	French
3855	German
3856	Other, A-Z

1/
  For Table V, see pp. 331-340. Add country number in table to 3660

	Industry
	The state and industrial organization
	State industries. Public works. Government
	ownership - Continued
	Public contracts
	Cf. JK1661+, Government property (United
	States)
	UC267, Army contracts
3858	General works
.2	Tables
3860	Awards of public contracts
	Cf. HD3128, State contracts with cooperative
	societies
	TA180+, Specifications and contracts
	(Engineering)
	Right of eminent domain, expropriation, condemnation
	proceedings (including "Excess condemnation")
	Class here only works dealing with public
	works. For general works on eminent domain,
	see HD1259+
3865.A1-3	General works
	By region or country
	United States
.A4A-Z	General works
.A45	Special. By date
.A5-Z	By region or state
	Under each state:
	.x General works
	.x2 Special. By date
3866	Other regions or countries, A-Z
	Under each country:
	.x General works
	.x2 Special. By date
	By industry, see HD9000+
	By region or country
	United States
3881	Periodicals. Societies. Serials
3885	General works
3887	Organization and administration
3888	Public policy
3890	By region or state, A-Z
4001-4420.7	Other regions or countries. Table IX 1/
	Under each country:

10 nos.	5 nos.	1 no.	
(1)	(1)	.A1-5	Periodicals. Societies. Serials
(5)	(3)	.A6-Z7	General works
(7)			Organization and administration
(8)	(4)		Public policy
(10)	(5)	.Z8A-Z	Local, A-Z

1/
For Table IX, see pp. 331-340. Add country number in table to 4000

Industry

The state and industrial organization – Continued

Municipal industries. Municipal public works

Cf. HD2763+, Public service corporations

HD9000+, Special industries

For technical and administrative reports

of engineers, boards, etc., see T

4421	Periodicals. Societies. Serials
	Collections
4423	Several authors
.5	Individual authors
4425	Congresses
4431	General works

Waterworks

Cf. TD201+, Water supply systems

4456	General works
	By region or country
	United States
4461	General works
4464	Local, A-Z
4465	Other regions or countries, A-Z

Sewage disposal

Cf. TD511+, Sewage and municipal refuse

(Sanitation engineering)

4475	General works
	By region or country
	United States
4477	General works
4479	Local, A-Z
4480	Other regions or countries, A-Z

Refuse disposal

Cf. TD785+, Environmental technology

4482	General works
	By region or country
	United States
4483	General works
4484	By region or state, A-Z
4485	Other regions or countries, A-Z

Lighting

Cf. HD9685+, Electrical engineering industry

TK4125+, Electric lighting plants

4486	General works
	By region or country
	United States
4491	General works
4493	By region or state, A-Z
4494	Local, A-Z
4495	Other regions or countries, A-Z

Under each country:

.x   General works

.x2 Local, A-Z

Urban transit, see HE305+

Industry

The state and industrial organization

Municipal industries. Municipal public works - Cont.

4501   Other industries, A-Z

              For history, etc., of special industries, general as well as in particular countries, see HE9000+; for technical works, see T

              Under each:

                 .x   General works

                 .x2   Local, A-Z

            .B2-22   Bread supply

            .C6-62   Coal supply

            .H4-42   Heat supply

            .I4-42   Icehouses

            .M5-52   Milk supply

            .S6-62   Slaughterhouses

4601-4730.9   By region or country. Table V 1/

              Under each country:

4 nos.	1 no.	
(1)	.A1-4	Periodicals. Societies. Serials
(3)	.A5A-Z	General works
(4)	.A6-Z	Local, A-Z

1/

    For Table V, see pp. 331-340. Add country number in table to 4600

LABOR

Cf. HF5548.8, Industrial psychology
    HF5549+, Personnel management

Periodicals. Societies. Serials
    Cf. HD6350, Trade union journals
    American (United States and Canada)
4801   Early through 1864
4802   1865–
4805   British
4807   French
4809   German
4811   Other
4813   Congresses
4814   International directories
        Collected works (nonserial)
4815   Several authors
  .3   Individual authors
4821   Museums. Exhibitions
        Study and teaching. Research
4824   General works
  .5   By region or country, A–Z
        Statistics
4826   Collections of statistics
  .5   Theory
4831   Labor bureaus. Departments of labor, etc. (General)
            Cf. HD5860+, Labor exchanges
                HD7801+, International bureaus (Labor and the
                    state)
            For labor bureaus of particular countries, see
                HD8051, and HD8101+, subdivision (1) under each
                country
4839   Dictionaries. Encyclopedias
        History
4841   General works
4843   Primitive
4844   Ancient
4847   Medieval
            Modern
4851   General works
4853   19th century
4854   20th century
            By region or country, see HD8045+
        Labor systems
            Slave labor
                Cf. HT901, Economic aspects of slavery
4861   General works
4865   By region or country, A–Z
            Convict labor, see HV8888+
4869   Labor service
                Cf. HD3840+, Public works
                For compulsory government labor service, see
                    HD4871+
            Contract labor. Peonage. Compulsory labor
                Cf. HD8026+, State labor
4871   General works
4875   By region or country, A–Z

```
                    Labor
                     Labor systems - Continued
                      Compulsory non-military service in wartime,
                        see HD3840+, HD4905.5
                      Apprentice labor, apprenticeship
                       Including individual trades
4881                    General works
4885                     By region or country, A-Z
4889                    Entrance to trades
4895                    Mastership.  Certificate of mastership.
                          Competence
4901                   General works, treatises, and advanced textbooks
4902                   Syllabi, outlines
     .5                Juvenile works
                       Freedom of labor.  Employment discrimination
                           Cf. E185.8, Afro-Americans
                               HD6060+, Sex discrimination
                               HD6300+, and subdivision (18), HD8100+,
                                 Minority and immigrant labor
                               HF5549.5.A34, Affirmative action programs
4903                    General works
     .3                 By industry or trade, A-Z 1/
     .5                 By region or country, A-Z
4904                   Theory.  Method.  Relation to other subjects
     .5                Fatigue
                           Cf. BF482, Psychology of fatigue
                               T59.72, Fatigue aspects of man-machine
                                 systems
                       Leisure, see BJ1498, HD7395.R4
     .7                Human capital
4905                   Ethics.  Dignity of labor, etc.
                           Cf. BJ1498, Ethics
                               HF5387, Business ethics
     .5                Labor in time of war
                         Including compulsory service
                     Wages
                           Cf. HC79.W24, Wage-price policy
                               HF5549.5.C67, Compensation management
4906                    General works
                        Theory
4909                     English
4910                     French
4911                     German
4912                     Other languages, A-Z
                        Statistics
4915                     Theory
4916                     Collections of statistics
                     Minimum wage
                           For individual industries and trades, see HD4966
4917                    General works
                        By region or country
                         America
                          United States
4918                       General works
4919                        By region or state, A-Z
4920                       Other American regions or countries, A-Z
```

<u>1/</u>

For list of industries and trades, <u>see</u> pp. 88-96. Use insofar as applicable

```
                         Labor
                         Wages
                           Minimum wage
                             By region or country - Continued
        4921                   Europe.  By region or country, A-Z
        4922                   Asia.  By region or country, A-Z
                               Africa
          .8                     General works
        4923                     By region or country, A-Z
        4924                   Oceania and other, A-Z
                           Family allowances
        4925                 General works
                             By region or country
                               United States
          .3                     General works
          .4                     By region or state, A-Z
          .5                   Other regions or countries, A-Z

                         Methods of remuneration
                             Cf. HF5549.5.C67, Compensation management
                                 HF5549.5.I5, Incentives
        4926                 General works
        4928                 By method, A-Z
                                 Under each:
                                   .x    General works
                                   .x2  By region or country, A-Z

                                 .A5  Annual wage
                                 .B6  Bonus
                                 .C5  Checkweighing
                                 .C7  Cost-of-living adjustments
                                 .D3  Day work
                                 .D5  Dismissal wage

                                 .E4  Employee discounts
                                 .M3  Maintenance, Employee
                                 .N5  Night labor
                                 .N6  Non-wage payments
                                      Overtime pay, see HD5111

                                 .P4  Paydays
                                 .P5  Piecework
                                 .P6  Portal-to-portal wage
                                 .T5  Tipping
                                 .T7  Travel expenses
                                 .T8  Truck system

                         Wages of state labor
                             For civil service salaries, see JF1661, JK771, etc.
        4938                 General works
        4939                 By region or country, A-Z
                                 Under each country:
                                   .x    General works
                                   .x2  By industry or trade, A-Z 1/
```

1/
  For list of industries and trades, see pp. 88-96. Use insofar as applicable

	Labor
	Wages - Continued
	Relation of wages to production
	Cf. HC79.L3, Labor productivity (Economic history)
	HD57, Labor productivity (Management)
4945	General works
4946	By region or country, A-Z
4961	Comparative tables of wages, etc.
	For individual industries, see HD4966
	For individual countries, see HD4971+
	For tables for calculating wages, see
	HF5705
	Professional salary and fees
	Class here general works only; for
	special professions, see NA2570, R728, etc.
4964	General works
4965	By region or country, A-Z
	Salaries of business and industrial executives
.2	General works
.25	Expense accounts
.3	By industry or trade, A-Z 1/
.5	By region or country, A-Z
4966	By industry or trade, A-Z 1/
	Under each:
	.x General works
	.x2 By region or country, A-Z
4967	Underdeveloped areas
4971-5100.7	By region or country. Table V 2/
	Under each country:

4 nos.	1 no.	
(1)	.A1-5	Periodicals. Societies. Serials
(3)	.A7-Z8	General works
(4)	.Z9-A-Z	Local, A-Z

	Tipping, see HD4928.T5
	Hours
5106	General works
	Staggered hours
5108	General works
.2	By region or country, A-Z
	Under each country:
	.x General works
	.x2 Local, A-Z
	Flexible work hours
5109	General works
.2	By region or country, A-Z
	Under each country:
	.x General works
	.x2 Local, A-Z

1/
   For list of industries and trades, see pp. 88-96. Use insofar as applicable
2/
   For Table V, see pp. 331-340. Add country number in table to 4970

Labor

<u>Hours</u> - Continued

Part-time work

Cf. HD5709+, Underemployment

HD5854+, Temporary employment

For part-time employment of special classes, <u>see</u> HD6050+

5110	General works
.2	By region or country, A-Z

Under each country:

.x   General works

.x2   Local, A-Z

Overtime

Including overtime pay

5111.A3A-Z	General works
.A5-Z	By region or country, A-Z

Shift work

.5	General works
.6	By region or country, A-Z

Under each country:

.x   General works

.x2   Local, A-Z

Rest periods

5112	General works
.2	By region or country, A-Z

Night work

Including night employment of women and children, and night employment in special countries and trades

5113	General works
.2	By region or country, A-Z

Weekly rest day.   Sunday work

5114.A3A-Z	General works
.A5-Z	By region or country, A-Z

Attendance.   Punctuality.   Absenteeism

5115	General works
.2	By region or country, A-Z

Under each country:

.x   General works

.x2   Local, A-Z

Sick leave

.5	General works
.6	By region or country, A-Z

Under each country:

.x   General works

.x2   Local, A-Z

Women labor, <u>see</u> HD6064

5119	By industry or trade, A-Z 1/

Under each:

.x   General works

.x2   By region or country, A-Z

1/

For list of industries and trades, <u>see</u> pp. 88-96.   Use insofar as applicable

Labor
Hours - Continued

5121-5250.7   By region or country. Table V 1/

4 nos.	1 no.	
(1)	.A1-5	Periodicals. Societies. Serials
(2)	.A6-Z8	General works
(4)	.Z9A-Z	Statistics
(4.5) 2/	.Z98A-Z	Local, A-Z

         Note: For United States use:
             (1) Periodicals. Societies. Serials
             (2) General works
             (3) Public policy
             (4) Local, A-Z

        Leave of absence
5255   General works
         Educational leave
5257   General works
   .2   By region or country, A-Z
             Under each country:
                .x   General works
                .x2 Local, A-Z
   .3   By region or country, A-Z

        Vacations
5260   General works
         By region or country
          America
            United States
5261   General works
5262   By region or state, A-Z
5263   Other American regions or countries, A-Z
5264   Europe. By region or country, A-Z
5265   Asia. By region or country, A-Z
5266   Africa. By region or country, A-Z
5267   Oceania and other, A-Z

1/
  For Table V, see pp. 331-340. Add country number in table to 5120

2/
  Substitute (4.15) for (4.5) in case of conflict, HD5220.15, Local (India),
HD5220.5, Pakistan

Labor – Continued

Labor disputes.   Strikes.   Lockouts

Cf. HD6350+, Trade unions

5306	General works
5307	General strikes
5309	Sympathetic strikes
5311	Wildcat strikes
5321–5450.7	By region or country. Table V 1/
	Under each country:

4 nos.	1 no.	
(1)	.A1–5	Periodicals. Societies. Serials
(2)	.A6A–Z	General works
(3)	.A7–Z8	By industry or trade, A–Z 2/
		Under each:
	.x	General works
	.x2	Individual strikes. By date
		For strikes in a particular
		place, assign after date
		a 2d Cutter for place
(4)	.Z9A–Z	Local. By state or other subdivision, A–Z

e. g.   United States, (3) By industry or
trade, A–Z

HD5325.A8–82	Automobile industry
.A8A–Z	General works
.A82	Individual strikes. By date and
	place, A–Z
.A82 1971	Strike, 1971 (General)
.A82 1971L65+	Strike, 1971, Lordstown, Ohio
.A82 1971L658	Weller, The Lordstown struggle,
	1974
.R1–2	Railway disputes and strikes
.R1A–Z	General works
.R12	Particular strikes (before Eastern
	Railways arbitration.) By date
	Eastern Railways arbitration, 1912;
.R14A–Z	Engineers
.R16A–Z	Firemen
.R165A–Z	Conductors, trainmen
.R2	Later disputes and strikes (1913–　　).
	By date and name of company

5461	Boycotts
5466	Blacklisting
5468	Picketing
5471	Lockouts
5472	Restriction of output. Slowdowns
5473	Sabotage
	Cf. HD6477, Syndicalism
5474	Sit-down strikes. Factory occupations

1/

  For Table V, see pp. 331–340.   Add country number in table to 5320

2/

  For list of industries and trades, see pp. 88–96.   Use insofar as
applicable

Labor - Continued
    <u>Arbitration and conciliation</u>

5481	General works
	By industry or trade, <u>see</u> HD5321+
5501-5630.7	By region or country. Table V <u>1</u>/
	For individual arbitrations, <u>see</u> HD5321+
	Under each country:

3 nos.	1 no.	
(1)	.A1-5	Periodicals. Societies. Serials
(2).A3A-Z	.A6A-Z	General works
.A4-Z	.Z7-Z	Local, A-Z
(3)		General special

Employees' representation in management. Shop
    councils. Employee ownership
      Cf. HD2970+, Profitsharing
         HD6961+, Industrial relations

5650	General works
5658	By industry and trade, A-Z <u>2</u>/
	Under each:
	.x General works
	.x2 Local, A-Z
5660	By region or country, A-Z

<u>Labor market. Labor supply and demand</u>
    Cf. HF5549+, Personnel management

5701	Periodicals. Societies. Serials
.3	Congresses
	Collected works (nonserial)
.4	Several authors
.45	Individual authors
	Theory. Method. Relation to other subjects
.5	Employment theory
.55	Forecasting
.6	Mathematical models
.75	Data processing
	Communication of information
.8	General works
.85	Information services
	Study and teaching. Research
5702	General works
.5	By region or country, A-Z
5706	General works, treatises, and advanced textbooks
5707	General special
	Statistics, <u>see</u> HD5711+

<u>1</u>/
    For Table V, <u>see</u> pp. 331-340. Add country number in table to 5500
<u>2</u>/
    For list of industries and trades, <u>see</u> pp. 88-96. Use insofar as
applicable

           Labor
             Labor market.   Labor supply and demand – Continued
               Unemployment
                 Cf. HD6331+, Technological unemployment

5707.5	General works
5708	Social and psychological effects
	Layoffs. Plant shutdowns. Redundancy
	Cf. HF5549.D55, Dismissal of employees
	(Personnel management)
.5	General works
.55	By region or country, A–Z
	Under each country:
	.x General works
	.x2 Local, A–Z
	Seasonal unemployment, see HD5855+
	Disguised unemployment
.7	General works
.75	By region or country, A–Z
	Under each country:
	.x General works
	.x2 Local, A–Z
	Hardcore unemployed
	Cf. HF5549.5.H3, Personnel management
.8	Geneal works
.85	By region or country, A–Z
	Under each country:
	.x General works
	.x2 Local, A–Z
	Underemployment
	Class here works on less than full-time
	employment or utilization of an employed
	worker's talent and/or training
5709	General works
.2	By region or country, A–Z
	Under each country:
	.x General works
	.x2 Local, A–Z
	Unemployment and inflation
5710	General works
.2	Phillip's curve
.5	Job vacancies
	Foreign trade and employment
	Cf. HF1421, Trade adjustment assistance
.7	General works
.75	By region or country, A–Z
	Under each country:
	.x General works
	.x2 Local, A–Z
	Rural employment
	Including rural-manpower policy
	Cf. HD1521+, Agricultural laborers
.8	General works
.85	By region or country, A–Z
	Under each country:
	.x General works
	.x2 Local, A–Z
	Statistics
5711	Theory
5712	Collections of statistics

Labor
   Labor market. Labor supply and demand – Continued
    Manpower policy
      Cf. HC54+, Full employment policies (Economic
         history)
         HF1421, Trade adjustment assistance
         HF5549.5.M3, Manpower planning (Personnel
           management)
      For works on employment agencies, see HD5860+

5713	General works
.2	Employment stabilization

    Public service employment. Public works employment
      Class here works on public sector employment
      as a counter–cyclical policy measure
      intended to provide jobs for the unemployed.
      For works on government enterprise and
      public works undertaken on their own merits,
      see HD3840. For works on government employees
      in general, see HD8001+

.5	General works
.6	By region or country, A–Z

      Under each country:
        .x   General works
        .x2 Local, A–Z

   Occupational training and retraining
      Cf. HD4881, Apprenticeship
         HF5549.5.T7, Employee training (Personnel
           management)

5715	General works
	By region or country
	United States
.2	General works
.3	By region or state, A–Z
.4	By city, A–Z
.5	Other regions or countries, A–Z

      Under each country:
        .x   General works
        .x2 Local, A–Z

   Labor and occupational mobility
      Cf. HB1951+, Population geography
         HB2581+, Professions (Demography)
         HF5549.5.T8, Employee turnover
           (Personnel management)
         HN90.S65, and HN101+, subdivision (20).S65,
           Social mobility, under each country

5717	General works
.2	Commuting
.5	By region or country, A–Z

      Under each country:
        .x   General works
        .x2 Local, A–Z

5718	By industry or trade, A–Z 1/

    For agricultural laborers, see HD1521+
    Under each:
      .x   General works
      .x2 By region or country, A–Z

1/
  For list of industries and trades, see pp. 88–96. Use insofar as
applicable

Labor
Labor market. Labor supply and demand - Continued

5721-5851   By region or country. Table V, modified 1/
          Under each country:

4 nos.	1 no.	
(1)	.A1-5	Periodicals. Societies. Serials
(3)	.A6A-Z	General works
(4)	.A7-Z	Local, A-Z

            Note: For United States use:
                5723   Periodicals. Societies. Serials
                5724   General works
                5725   By region or state, A-Z
                5726   By city, A-Z
                    For Canada use:
                5727   Periodicals. Societies. Serials
                5728   General works
                5729   By province, A-Z

5852   Underdeveloped areas
          Temporary employment
            Cf. HD5110, Part-time work
5854   General works
    .2   By region or country, A-Z
          Seasonal trades. Migrant workers
            Cf. HD1521+, Agricultural laborers
            For emmigration and immigration, see JV6346.M5
5855   General works
           By industry or trade, see HD8039, HD9000+
5856   By region or country, A-Z
          Labor exchanges. Employment agencies. State
          employment bureaus, etc.
            Cf. HD4831+, Departments of labor
5860   Periodicals. Societies. Serials
5861   General works
5870   By industry or trade, A-Z 2/
            Under each:
               .x   General works
               .x2 By region or country, A-Z

5871-6000.7   By region or country. Table V, modified 1/
          Under each country:

4 nos.	1 no.	
(1)	.A1-5	Periodicals. Societies. Serials
(3)	.A6A-Z	General works
(4)	.A7-Z	Local, A-Z

            Note: For Australia use:
                5997   Periodicals. Societies. Serials
                5998   General works
                5999   By state, A-Z

1/
    For Table V, see pp. 331-340. Add country number in table to 5720 or
5870, as the case requires
   2/
    For list of industries and trades, see pp. 88-96. Use insofar as
applicable

```
                      Labor - Continued
                        Classes of labor
                          Woman labor
                            Including works on woman and child labor
                            Cf. HD7268, Industrial hygiene
        6050                Periodicals.  Societies.  Serials
                            Collected works (nonserial)
        6051                  Several authors
          .2                  Individual authors
        6052                Congresses
        6053                General works
                            Employment of special groups
                              Women college graduates
          .5                    General works
          .6                    By region or country, A-Z
                                  Under each country:
                                    .x    General works
                                    .x2  Local, A-Z
                              Married women
        6055                    General works
          .2                    By region or country, A-Z
                                  Subarranged like HD6053.6
                              Middle-aged and older women
        6056                    General works
          .2                    By region or country, A-Z
                                  Subarranged like HD6053.6
                              Minority women
        6057                    General works
          .5                    By region or country, A-Z
                                  Subarranged like HD6053.6

                            Occupations for women
                              Cf. HF5381, Choice of profession
                                  HF5500.2+, Women executives
          .9                    General works
                              By region or country
        6058                    United States
        6059                    Other regions or countries, A-Z
                            Sex discrimination in employment
                              Cf. HD4903, Freedom of labor
        6060                General works
          .5                By region or country, A-Z
                                  Under each country:
                                    .x    General works
                                    .x2  Local, A-Z
                            Wages.  Equal pay for equal work
        6061                General works
          .2                By region or country, A-Z
                                  Subarranged like HD6060.5
                            Hours
        6064                General works
                            Maternity leave
        6065                  General works
          .5                  By region or country, A-Z
        6066                By region or country, A-Z
                                  Subarranged like HD6060.5
                            Health and safety.  Hygiene
        6067                General works
          .2                By region or country, A-Z
                                  Subarranged like HD6060.5
```

```
                      Labor
                        Classes of labor
                          Woman labor - Continued
                            Factory labor
6068                          General works
    .2                          By region or country, A-Z
                                  Subarranged like HD6060.5
                            Retail and service occupations
6070                          General works
    .2                          By region or country, A-Z
                            Domestic service
                              Cf. HD8039.D5, Domestic servants
6072                          General works
    .2                          By region or country, A-Z
                                Under each country:
                                  .x   General works
                                  .x2  Local, A-Z
6073                        Special industries or trades, A-Z 1/
                              Under each:
                                  .x   General works
                                  .x2  By region or country, A-Z
6076                        Women's exchanges
                            Women's lodging houses, see HD7288.5+
                            Women in trade unions
6079                          General works
    .2                          By region or country, A-Z
                                Under each country:
                                  .x   General works
                                  .x2  Local, A-Z
                            Pensions.  Social security
6080                          General works
    .2                          By region or country, A-Z
                                Under each country:
                                  .x   General works
                                  .x2  Local, A-Z
6091-6220.7                 By region or country.  Table V 2/
                              Under each country:
```

4 nos.	1 no.	
(1)	.A1-5	Periodicals. Societies. Serials
(2)	.A6A-Z	Statistics
(3)	.A7-Z5	General works
(4)	.Z6A-Z	Local, A-Z

```
6223                        Underdeveloped areas


                          Child labor
                            Cf. HD5113, Night work
6228                        Periodicals.  Societies.  Serials
6229                        Congresses
                            Collected works (nonserial)
    .3                        Several authors
    .4                        Individual authors
```

1/
    For list of industries and trades, see pp. 88-96. Use insofar as applicable

2/
    For Table V, see pp. 331-340. Add country number in table to 6090

```
                         Labor
                           Classes of labor
                             Child labor - Continued
6231                           General works
6247                           By industry or trade, A-Z 1/
                                 Under each:
                                   .x    General works
                                   .x2   By region or country, A-Z
6250                           By region or country, A-Z
                                 Under each country:
                                   .x    Periodicals.  Societies.  Serials
                                   .x2   General works
                                   .x3   Local, A-Z

                             Youth labor
                                 Cf. HD4881+, Apprenticeship
                                     HD5715+, Occupational training
                                     HD6487.8+, Labor unions
                                     HQ799.9.D7, Dropouts (Social problem)
                                     JK923.S8, Federal employment of college
                                         students
6270                           General works
                               Summer employment
6271                             General works
    .2                           By region or country, A-Z
                                 By region or country
                                   United States
6273                               General works
6274                               By region or state, A-Z
6275                               By city, A-Z
6276                             Other regions or countries, A-Z
                             College students
    .5                           General works
    .52                          By region or country, A-Z
                                   Under each country:
                                     .x    General works
                                     .x2   Local, A-Z
                             College graduates
                                 Cf. HD6053.5+, Employment of women college
                                         graduates
6277                           General works
6278                           By region or country, A-Z
                                 Under each country:
                                   .x    General works
                                   .x2   Local, A-Z
                             Middle-aged and older workers
                                 Cf. HF5549.5.O44, Personnel management
                                     HD6056+, Woman labor
                                     JK723.O4, United States federal service
6279                           General works
                               By region or country
                                 United States
6280                             General works
6281                             By region or state, A-Z
6282                             By city, A-Z
6283                           Other regions or countries, A-Z
```

_____

1/

    For list of industries and trades, see pp. 88-96. Use insofar as applicable

```
                Labor
                Classes of labor - Continued
6300                Immigrant labor (General)
                        Cf. HD8081, Minority labor in the United
                                States
                            HD8101+, subdivisions (18) and (8.5),
                                Immigrant labor in other countries
    .5              Frontier workers
                    Minorities
                        Cf. HD6057, Minority women
                            HD8081, Minority labor in the United
                                States
                            HD8101+, subdivisions (18) and (8.5),
                                Minority labor by region or country
                            HF5549.5.M5, Personnel management
6304                General works
6305                By minority or ethnic group, A-Z
                        Afro-Americans, see E185.8
                    .A8   Asians
                    .B56  Blacks
                            Cf. E185.8, Afro-Americans
                    .J3   Jews

                Labor and machinery.  Technological unemployment
6331                General works
    .18             By industry or trade, A-Z 1/
    .2              By region or country, A-Z
                        Under each country:
                            .x   General works
                            .x2  Local, A-Z
6335            Labor and the trusts
6336            Labor and international business enterprises
                Labor and the church
                        Cf. BR115.E3, Christianity in relation to
                                economics and labor
6338                General works
    .2              By region or country, A-Z
                        Under each country:
                            .x   General works
                            .x2  Local, A-Z
    .3          Labor and Judaism
    .4          Labor and Islam
6339            Labor and the intellectuals
```

1/
    For list of industries and trades, see pp. 88-96. Use insofar as applicable

Labor - Continued
Trade unions. Labor unions. Workingmen's
  associations
    Cf. HD6079+, Women in trade unions
      HD6960+, Industrial relations, collective
        bargaining, etc.
      HD8005+, Government employees' unions
    For general trade union federations, see HD6475,
      HD8055, and HD8101+, subdivisions (3) and (2);
      for unions of individual countries by industry
      and trade, see HD6515, and HD6521+, subdivisions
      (8) and (4)

6350   Periodicals. Serials. By industry or trade, A-Z 1/
                Class here general works only, including
                  official union organs of international unions
                For American periodicals, including official
                  union organs, see HD6500, HD6515
                For foreign periodicals, including official
                  union organs, see HD6521+, subdivision
                  (1) or (8) under each country
              History
6451   General works
6452   Oriental
                  Including Assyrian, Babylonian, Egyptian,
                    Hebrew, Phoenician, etc.
6453   Greek
                  Cf. DF, Greek history
6454   Roman
                  Cf. DG, Roman history
6455   Late Roman and Byzantine
              Medieval (to 1789). Guilds
                Including medieval history of particular
                  crafts
                For modern guilds, see HD2340.8+
              General
6456   General works
6458   By industry or trade, A-Z 1/
              By region or country
              England
6460   General works
6461   By industry or trade, A-Z 1/
                  Including individual guilds
                  Under each:
                    .x   General works
                    .x2 Local, A-Z
6462   Local, A-Z
6464-6466   France
                  Subarranged like HD6460-6462
6467-6469   Germany
                  Subarranged like HD6460-6462
6470-6472   Italy
                  Subarranged like HD6460-6462

1/
  For list of industries and trades, see pp. 88-96. Use insofar as
applicable

Labor

Trade unions. Labor unions. Workingmen's
    associations

    History

      Medieval (to 1789). Guilds

        By region or country - Continued

6473   Other regions or countries, A-Z 1/

            Under each country:

            .xA1-3   Periodicals. Societies.
                      Serials

            .xA6-Z   General works
                      By period

            .x2A3-39   Origins. Earliest history
            .x2A6-Z   Later (16th-18th century)
            .x3A-Z   By industry or trade, A-Z 2/
            .x4A-Z   Local, A-Z

1/

    Special arrangement for Netherlands, Scandinavia, etc. (Medieval to
1789)

	Netherlands (Low Countries)		Scandinavia - Continued
	General	.S37-375	Sweden
.N2	General works		Subarranged like
.N23	Earliest		Denmark
.N25	Later	.S5	By industry or trade A-Z 2/
	Belgium	.S6	Local, A-Z
.N3	General works		
.N33	Earliest		Spain and Portugal
.N35	Later	.S65	General works
		.S66	Earliest
.N4-45	Netherlands (Holland)	.S68	Later
	Subarranged like Belgium	.S7	By industry or trade, A-Z 2/
.N5	By industry or trade, A-Z 2/		
.N6	Local, A-Z	.S73	Local, A-Z
	Scandinavia		Switzerland
	General	.S8	General works
.S1A-Z	General works	.S83	Earliest
.S13	Earliest	.S85	Later
.S15	Later	.S89	By industry or trade, A-Z 2/
	Denmark	.S9	Local, A-Z
.S2	General works		
.S23	Earliest		
.S25	Later		
.S27-275	Norway		
	Subarranged like Denmark		

2/

    For list of industries and trades, see pp. 88-96. Use insofar as
applicable

```
                  Labor
                    Trade unions.  Labor unions.  Workingmen's associations
                      History - Continued
                        Modern (1800-    )
                          Cf. HD2340.8+, Modern guilds
                          Periodicals.  Serials, see HD6350
                          International associations, congresses, etc.
      6475.A1                 General works
         .A2                  Individual associations, etc., A-Z
         .A4-Z                By industry or trade, A-Z 1/
         .2                 Directories
                              For local, see HD6504 and HD6520+,
                                subdivision (3) under each country
      6476                  General works
                          Syndicalism
                            Cf. HX821+, Anarchism
      6477                  General works
                          By region or country, see HD6500+
      6479                Guild socialism
      6481                Catholic labor unionism
                          Trade unions and socialism, see HX544
      6483              General works
                        Special topics
                          Class here special topics applied to individual
                            regions or countries rather than in HD6500+
                          Benefit features
                            Cf. HD7090+, Social insurance
                                HD6490.W38, Welfare funds
      6484                  General works
         .2                 By région or country, A-Z
      6486-6486.2         Finance 2/
                            Including accounting
                            Cf. HG1968+, Trade union banks
      6487-6487.2         Incorporation 2/
                          Political activity, see HD8076+, HD8108, etc.
      6488-6488.2         "Open shop".  "Closed shop" 2/
      6489-6489.2         Union label, etc. 2/
      6490                Other special topics, A-Z
                            Under each:
                              .x   General works
                              .x2  By region or country, A-Z
                              Business agents, see .S5
                          .C4    Central labor unions.  Industrial union
                                   councils
                          .C6    Company unions
                          .C62   Consolidation.  Mergers
                          .C64   Corrupt practices
                          .D5    Discipline
                                   Cf. HF5549.5.L3, Labor discipline
                          .E4    Elections
                                   Cf. HD6490.V6, Voting
                                 Featherbedding, see HD6973.5
                          .F58   Foreign policy
                                   Cf. HD6510 and HD6520+, subdivision
                                       (7), Political activity
```

Labor
    <u>Trade unions. Labor unions. Workingmen's</u>
        <u>associations</u>
        Special topics

6490	Other special topics, A-Z - Continued

            Under each:
                .x   General works
                .x2 By region or country, A-Z
           .F6   Foremen unions. Supervisors' unions
                Grievance procedures, <u>see</u> HD6972.5
           .I6   Independent unions
           .L33 Labor-management committees
           .M4   Meetings
                Mergers, <u>see</u> .C62
           .M5   Middle manager unions

           .O4   Officers
           .O7   Organizing of unions
           .P8   Public relations
           .R2   Race relations. Minority membership
           .R3   Racketeering
           .R4   Recognition
                Restrictive practices, <u>see</u> HD6973
           .S5   Shop stewards. Business agents
           .S6   Social responsibilities
           .U5   Union security
           .V6   Voting
                Cf. HD6490.E4, Elections
           .W38 Welfare funds
           .W4   Welfare work
                Women, <u>see</u> HD6079+
           .Y65 Youth
                Cf. HD6270+, Youth labor

    Professional associations. By region or country,
        A-Z
        Class here general works only; for special
            professions, <u>see</u> L10+, Teachers; NA10+,
            Architects; etc.

6496.5	General works
6497	By region or country, A-Z

    By industry or trade, <u>see</u> HD6475.A4-Z, HD6515,
        HD6668, etc.
    By region or country
        For special topics relating to special regions
            or countries, <u>see</u> the topic, HD6484+
        United States

6500	Periodicals. Serials

           Including official union organs (General)
           For organs of unions of particular
             industries or trades, <u>see</u> HD6515
        Associations, unions, etc., <u>see</u> HD8055, HD6515

6504	Directories

           Including state and local directories

6508	General works

        Biography

.5	Collective
6509	Individual, A-Z
6510	Political activity

Labor
    <u>Trade unions. Labor unions. Workingmen's</u>
        <u>associations</u>
        By region or country
          United States - Continued

6515	By industry or trade, A-Z <u>1/</u>
	For unions of civil service employees, <u>see</u> HD8001+
	Under each:
	.x General works
	.x2 Local, A-Z
6517	By state, A-W
	For unions of particular industries or trades in particular places, <u>see</u> HD6515
	For state branches of the American Federation of Labor, <u>see</u> HD8055
6519	By city, A-Z
	For unions of particular industries or trades in particular places, <u>see</u> HD6515
	Under each:
	.x General works
	.x2 Individual unions
6521-6940.5	Other regions or countries. Table IX, modified <u>2/</u>
	For medieval to 1789, <u>see</u> HD6456+
	Under each country:

10 nos.	5 nos.	1 no.	
(1)	(1)	.A1-5	Periodicals. Serials
			Including official union organs (General). For organs of unions of particular industries or trades, <u>see</u> subdivision (8)
			Associations, unions, etc., <u>see</u> HD8101+, subdivisions (3) and (2); by industry and trade, <u>see</u> HD6521+, subdivisions (8) and (4)
(3)			Directories
(4)	(2)	.A6-Z53	General works
(5)	(2.5)		Biography
.A1-29	.A1-29	.Z54A-Z	Collective
.A3-Z	.A3-Z	.Z55A-Z	Individual, A-Z
(6)	(3)	.Z6A-Z	Trade union literature
(7)	(3.5)	.Z65A-Z	Political activity
(8)	(4)	.Z7	By industry or trade, A-Z <u>1/</u>
			For unions of civil service employees, <u>see</u> HD8001+
			Under each (10 number and 5 number countries only):
			.x General works
			.x2 Individual unions, A-Z
(9)	(5)	.Z8A-Z	Local (General), A-Z
			For special trades, <u>see</u> subdivision (8) and (4) above
6940.7			Underdeveloped areas

<u>1/</u>
    For list of industries and trades, <u>see</u> pp. 88-96. Use insofar as applicable
<u>2/</u>
    For Table IX, <u>see</u> pp. 331-340. Add country number in table to 6520

Labor - Continued
Employers' associations
Class here works on the interests of employers as
distinct from those of the employees
For works on the economic situation, etc., of
particular industries, see HD9000+

6941	Periodicals. Serials
6942	International associations
	Class here general works only
	For special associations, see HD6944+
6943	General works
.5	Strike insurance
6944	By industry or trade, A-Z 1/
	Class here general works only
	For local, see HD6945+
	By region or country
	United States
6945	General works
6946	By region or state, A-Z
	For the associations of particular
	industries of particular places,
	see HD6947
6947	By industry or trade, A-Z 1/
	Under each:
	.x General works
	.x2 Local, A-Z
6948	Other regions or countries, A-Z
	Under each country:
	.x General works
	.x2 By state, province, etc., A-Z
	.x3 By industry or trade, A-Z
	Under each:
	.x General works
	.x2 Local, A-Z

	Industrial sociology. Social conditions of labor
	Cf. HN50+, Social history
6951	Periodicals. Societies. Serials
6952	Congresses
	Study and teaching. Research
6953	General works
6954	By region or country, A-Z
6955	General works
6956	By industry or trade, A-Z 1/
	Under each:
	.x General works
	.x2 By region or country, A-Z
6957	By region or country, A-Z
	Under each country:
	.x General works
	.x2 Local, A-Z

1/
   For list of industries and trades, see pp. 88-96. Use insofar as
applicable

                     Labor - Continued
                       Industrial relations
                           Cf. HF5549+, Personnel management

6958.5	Periodicals. Societies. Serials
6959	Congresses
	Study and teaching. Research
6960	General works
.5	By region or country, A-Z
	Theory. Methodology. Relation to other subjects
6961	General works
.2	Data processing
6971	General works, treatises, and advanced textbooks
	Collective bargaining
.5	General works
	By region or country, see HD6500+
.7	Management rights
6972	Labor-management committees
.5	Grievance procedures
	Restrictive practices
6973	General works
.5	Featherbedding
6974	Factory labor
6976	By industry or trade, A-Z 1/

                             Under each:
                               .x   General works
                               .x2   By region or country, A-Z
                     By region or country, see HD8045+

Wages and cost of living.   Standard of living
                         Class here works specifically on the cost of
                           living
                         Cf. HB231+, Prices (General)
                             TX326, Household budgets

6977	Statistics (Genreal)
6978	General works
6981-7080	By region or country. Table I 2/

                         Under each country (except United States):
                           .A-Z5   General works
                           .Z8A-Z   Local, A-Z

Social insurance.   Social security.   Pensions
                         Cf. HD6080, Women's insurance
                            HG8205+, Government insurance

7088	Periodicals. Societies. Serials
7090	Congresses
.5	Dictionaries. Encyclopedias
7091	General works
	Unemployment
7095	General works
7096	By region or country, A-Z

                            Under each country:
                             .x   General works
                             .x2   Local, A-Z

1/
    For list of industries and trades, see pp. 88-96.   Use insofar as applicable
2/
    For Table I, see pp. 331-340.   Add country number in table to 6980

Labor
  Social insurance. Social security. <u>Pensions</u> - Cont.
    <u>Public health insurance. Accident insurance</u>
      Including public medical care plans for
        the aged
        Cf. HD7260+, Labor hygiene
            HG9301+, Accident insurance
            HG9383+, Health insurance
            HV1451+, Free medical advice for the aged
            RA4137.A4, Private medical care plans
              for the aged

7101	General works
7102	By region or country, A-Z
	Under each country:
	.x General works
	.x2 Local, A-Z
	Mental health insurance
.5	General works
.6	By region or country, A-Z
	Pharmaceutical service
7103	General works
.5	By region or country, A-Z
	Workmen's compensation
	Cf. HG9964, Employer's liability insurance
.6	General works
.65	By region or country, A-Z
	Dental insurance
	Cf. RK58, Dental economics
7104	General works
.5	By region or country, A-Z
	Under each country:
	.x General works
	.x2 Local, A-Z
	Old age pensions. Invalidity. Retirement
	Cf. HD6080+, Pensions for women
7105	General works
.2	Disability insurance
	Cf. HD7103.6, Workmen's compensation
.3	Old age pensions
.4	Pension trusts
7106	By region or country, A-Z
	Family allowances, <u>see</u> HD4925
7116	By industry or trade, A-Z <u>1/</u>
	Under each:
	.x General works
	.x2 Local, A-Z
7121-7250.7	By region or country. Table V <u>2/</u>
	Class here general works only; for special
	industries and trades, <u>see</u> HD7116
	Under each country:

4 nos.	1 no.	
(1)	.A1-5	Periodicals. Societies. Serials
(3)	.A7-Z7	General works
(4)	.Z8A-Z	Local, A-Z

<u>1/</u>
  For list of industries and trades, <u>see</u> pp. 88-96. Use insofar as applicable
<u>2/</u>
  For Table V, <u>see</u> pp. 331-340. Add country number in table to 7120

Labor - Continued

Rehabilitation of the disabled

Cf. HV3000+, Handicapped

RD701+, Medicine

UB360+, Military science

7255.A2A-Z	Periodicals. Societies. Serials
.A3-Z	General works
.5	Rehabilitation counseling
7256	By region or country, A-Z

Under each country:

.x   General works

.x2 Local, A-Z

Industrial hygiene. Welfare work

Class here administrative and statistical aspects
only; for other aspects, see RA, RC, T, etc.

Cf. RC963+, Industrial medicine

T55, Industrial safety

7260	Periodicals. Societies. Serials
.5	Congresses
	Study and teaching. Research
.6	General works
.62	By region or country, A-Z
7261	General works

Dangerous occupations. Accidents

Class here general works only; for special
industries, see HD7269

Cf. HD3611+, State and industrial organization

HD7814+, Workmen's compensation

7262	General works
.25	Investigation
.5	By region or country, A-Z

Industrial poisons and diseases

Class here general works only; for special
industries, see HD7269

Cf. HD3611+, State and industrial organization

RA1190+, Toxicology (Public aspects of
medicine)

7263	General works
7264	Dusts. Vapors. Gases

Cf. RA577, Air pollution by noxious gases

RA1245+, Gaseous poisons

7265.5	By region or country, A-Z
7266	Heat. Cold. Moisture
	Women, see HD6067+, RC963.6.W65
7269	By industry or trade, A-Z 1/

Under each:

.x   General works

.x2 By region or country, A-Z

Safety measures and devices, see T55+

Inspection. Factory inspection, see HD3656+

1/

For list of industries and trades, see pp. 88-96. Use insofar as
applicable

Labor
  Industrial hygiene. Welfare work - Continued
      Housing
          Cf. HD1361+, Real estate business
              HT166+, City planning
              HV4023+, Slums
7285   Periodicals. Societies. Serials
7286   Congresses
   .5   Directories
7287   General works
   .5   General special
   .55   Finance
                  Cf. HG2040, Mortgage loans
   .6   Apartment houses
                  Cf. NA7860, Architecture
                      TH4820, Construction
              .A3A-Z General works
              .A4-Z   By region or country, A-Z
              Condominiums
   .65   General works
   .67   By region or country, A-Z
                      Under each country:
                          .x   General works
                          .x2 Local, A-Z

   .7   Cooperative housing
              .A3A-Z General works
              .A4-Z   By region or country, A-Z
              Home ownership
   .8   General works
   .82   By region or country, A-Z
                      Under each country:
                          .x   General works
                          .x2 Local, A-Z
              Housing for the aged
   .9   General works
   .92   By region or country, A-Z
                      Under each country:
                          .x   General works
                          .x2 Local, A-Z
              Housing for the handicapped, see HV1569+

              Lodging houses
7288.A3A-Z   General works
     .A5-Z   By region or country, A-Z

              Lodging houses for women
   .5   General works
   .6   By region or country, A-Z
              Minority housing
   .7   General works
   .72   By region or country, A-Z
                      Under each country:
                          .x   General works
                          .x2 Local, A-Z

Labor
   Industrial hygiene. Welfare work
      Housing - Continued
         Open housing. Discrimination
            Cf. HG2040.2, Discrimination in mortgage
                loans

7288.75	General works
.76	By region or country, A-Z
	Under each country:
	.x General works
	.x2 Local, A-Z
	Public housing. Housing authorities
.77	General works
.78	By region or country, A-Z
	Under each country:
	.x General works
	.x2 Local, A-Z
	Rental housing
.8	General works
.82	Rent control
.83	Rent subsidies
.84	Rentees strikes
.85	By region or country, A-Z
	Under each country:
	.x General works
	.x2 Local, A-Z
	Residential mobility
	Cf. HB1954, Demography
.9	General works
.92	By region or country, A-Z
	Under each country:
	.x General works
	.x2 Local, A-Z
	Rural housing
7289.A3A-Z	General works
.A4-Z	By region or country, A-Z
	Under each country:
	.x General works
	.x2 Local, A-Z
	Urban homesteading
.4	General works
.42	By region or country, A-Z
	Under each country:
	.x General works
	.x2 Local, A-Z
.5	Industrial housing
	.A2A-Z General works
	.A3A-Z By region or country, A-Z
	.A4-Z By industry, A-Z 1/
	Mobile homes
	Cf. HD9715.7, Trailer homes (Construction
	industry)
	TX1100+, Mobile home living
.6	General works
.62	By region or country, A-Z
7290	Labor camps. Construction camps

1/
   For list of industries and trades, see pp. 88-96. Use insofar as
applicable

Labor
  Industrial hygiene. Welfare work
    Housing - Continued
7291-7390   By region or country. Table I 1/
        Under each country (except United States):
          .A3A-Z   General works
          .A4A-Z   Finance
          .A5-Z   Local, A-Z

        Note: For HD7293 (United States) use:
          .A1A-Z   Periodicals. Societies. Serials
                For United States Department of
                  Housing and Urban Development,
                  see HT167.2
          .A6-Z   General works

7391   Developing countries   ~~Underdeveloped areas~~

7393   Restaurants, lunchrooms, etc.
        Cf. TX945, Home economics
7395   Other special, A-Z
        .C5   Clothing, Protective
        .C6   Company stores
            Counseling service for workers, see
              HF5549.5.C8

            Mobile homes, see HD7289.6+
        .P45   Physical training

        .R4   Recreation
        .R5   Rest homes
            Traffic problems, see HD5717.2

      Model plants and factories
7406   General works
7411-7510   By region or country. Table I 1/
        Under each country:
          .A3A-Z   General works
          .A5-Z   By firm or plant, A-Z
      Public buildings. Government offices, shops, etc.,
        see JK1606+, JN851+, etc.
      Department stores, see HF5461+
      Model communities
        Class here works on model industrial villages;
          for residence cities and suburbs, see HT161+
7526   General works
7531-7630   By region or country. Table I 1/
        Under each country (except the United States;
          for the United States local, apply
          appropriate number from Table I, p. 331):
          .A3A-Z   General works
          .A5-Z   Local, A-Z

1/
  For Table I, see pp. 331-340. Add country number in table to 7290, 7410,
or 7530, as the case requires

Labor
  Industrial hygiene. Welfare work - Continued

7651-7780.7   By region or country. Table V 1/
         Under each country:

4 nos.	1 no.	
(1)	.A1-5	Periodicals. Societies. Serials
(2)	.A6-Z5	General works
(3)	.Z7A-Z	By state, A-Z
(4)	.Z8A-Z	By city, A-Z

7790   Workers' travel programs, study tours, etc.
7791   Labor day. May day
      Labor and the state
        Cf. HD4831+, Labor bureaus
          HD5713+, Manpower policy
          HD5860+, Labor exchanges
7795   General works
7801   International bureaus
      Inspection, see HD3656+
      State labor
        Cf. HD4939, The state and wages
       Administrative (and Industrial)
         Cf. JF1411+, Government and administration
           JK631+, United States Civil Service
           JN-JQ, subdivision Civil service under
             each country
           JS148+, Municipal government
           JS358+, Municipal government (United
             States)
           JS1701+, Municipal government (other
             countries)
8001   General works
      Strikes and lockouts
8004   General works
  .2   By region or country, A-Z
        Under each country:
          .x General works
          .x2 By department or bureau, A-Z
          .x3 Local, A-Z
      Trade unions
8005   General works
  .2   By region or country, A-Z
        Subarranged like HD8004.2
      Collective bargaining
  .5   General works
  .6   By region or country, A-Z
        Subarranged like HD8004.2
      By region or country
       United States
8008.A1A-Z   Periodicals. Societies. Serials
  .A6-Z   General works
8009   By department, bureau, etc., A-Z
        Postal service, see HE6499

1/
  For Table V, see pp. 331-340. Add country number in table to 7650

Labor
 Labor and the state
  State labor
   Administrative (and Industrial)
    By region or country
     United States - Continued
8011   By region or state, A-Z
       Under each state:
        .x General works
        .x2 By county, region, etc., A-Z
8012   By city, A-Z
8013   Other regions or countries, A-Z
      Under each country:
       .x Periodicals. Societies. Serials
       .x4 General works
       .x5 Special departments, A-Z
         Postal service, see table below
          HE6651+, subdivision (9)
         Other, A-Z (.P4 Personnel)

   Industrial
8021   General works
8023   By region or country, A-Z
     Under each country:
      .x General works
      .x2 By industry or trade, A-Z 1/
   Contract labor
    Class here state contracts only
    Cf. HD4871+, Peonage
8026   General works
8027   By region or country, A-Z

  Labor in politics
8031   General works
    By region or country
     United States, see HD8076+
     Other regions or countries, see HD8101+,
      subdivisions (15)-(17) and (8) under
      each country
   Self-employed
8036   General works
8037   By region or country, A-Z
   Professions (General)
    Cf. HD6277, Employment of college graduates
     HT687, The professional class as a social
      group
    For special professions, see the profession,
     e. g. NA1995, Architects
8038.A1A-Z General works
 .A3-Z   By region or country, A-Z

1/
 For list of industries and trades, see pp. 88-96. Use insofar as
applicable

	Labor – Continued	
8039	By industry or trade, A–Z 1/	
		Actors, see PN
.A23		Aeronautics employees (General)
.A25		Aerospace industry workers
.A27		Agricultural industry employees
(.A29)		Agricultural laborers, see HD1521+ 2/
.A32		Agricultural processing industry workers
.A4		Air pilots, etc.
.A425		Air traffic controllers
.A43		Airline flight attendants
.A45		Airplane industry workers
.A47		Airplane maintenance workers
.A48		Airport employees

.A49   Aluminum industry workers
.A5   Amusement industry workers
.A55   Asbestos workers
.A6   Atomic workers
.A76   Automobile drivers
             Cf. HD8039.M795, Motor-truck drivers
                 HD8039.M8, Motorbus employees
                 HD8039.T16, Taxicab drivers
.A8   Automobile industry workers
        Automobile mechanics, see .M34

.B2   Bakers
.B26   Bank employees
             Cf. HG1615.5+, Personnel management in
                 banks
.B3   Barbers
        Bartenders, see .H8
.B35   Battery industry workers
.B4   Beauty shop employees
.B47   Beverage industry workers
.B48   Bicycle workers
.B49   Bill posters
.B5   Blacksmiths
.B58   Blast-furnace workers
.B6   Boiler makers and iron shipbuilders

.B65   Bookbinders
.B67   Bookmakers (Betting)
.B7   Boot and shoe workers
.B73   Bottling workers
.B76   Box makers

1/
    Suggested Cutter numbers are assigned for arranging industries and
trades throughout the Labor scheme. In some instances the Cutter listed here
will be in conflict with those already in use elsewhere and must be modified
accordingly. Under each, subarrange as follows: .x General works, .x2 By
region or country, A–Z, e. g. .C3, Carpenters; .C32U6, Carpenters in the
United States
  2/
    This Cutter is not valid under HD8039; it may, however, be used under other
numbers which refer to this list of industries and trades for subarrangement,
e. g. HD4966

                 Labor

8039   By industry or trade, A-Z 1/ - Continued

.B87	Broom makers
.B89	Building laborers
.B895	Building-service employees
.B9	Building trades

                     Class here works on persons employed
                         in the building trades in general.
                         For works on independent businesses
                         in the building trades, see HD9716.
                         For individual trades, see the
                         trade, e. g. .B78, Bricklayers

.B96	Butchers
.C15	Cabinetmakers
.C258	Canal construction workers
.C265	Candlemakers
.C27	Canners
.C3	Carpenters and joiners
	Carpet industry workers, see .R94
.C33	Carriage and wagon workers
.C34	Cashew nut industry employees
.C35	Caterers
.C38	Cement workers
.C43	Charcoal makers
	Chauffers, see .A76
.C45	Chemical workers
.C48	Chimney-sweeps
.C5	Chocolate workers
	Chorus girls, see PN
.C52	Church maintenance workers
.C54	Cigar makers
	Civil service employees, see HD8001+ and J
.C58	Clay industry workers
	Clerks, see .F4, .M39
	Cloth hat and cap makers, see .H4
.C6	Clothing trades
.C635	Cocktail waiters and waitresses
.C64	Coir industry workers
	Commercial telegraphers, see .T25+
.C65	Commercial travelers
	Conductors, see .R3, .S8
	Confectioners, see .B2
	Construction workers, see .B89, .B9, .R315, .R6
.C6523	Container industry workers
.C653	Coopers
.C654	Copy writers
.C655	Coremakers

1/
   For subarrangement under each, see footnote, p. 88

Labor
8039   By industry or trade, A-Z 1/ - Continued

.C6556   Cork industry workers
.C66   Cotton pickers
           Cotton workers, see .T4
.C77   Cranberry pickers
.C9   Cutlery workers
.D3   Dairy workers

.D37   Data processing personnel
.D4   Diamond cutters
           Distillery workmen, see .L65
.D5   Domestic servants
             Cf. HD6072+, Domestic service
           Dredge men, see .S57

.D7   Drug clerks.   Drugstore employees
.D74   Drug industry employees
.D9   Dyers
           Elastic goring weavers, see .R9
           Electroplaters, see .M5
.E3   Electrical workers
           Electronic data processing personnel,
             see .D37

.E37   Electronic industry workers
.E47   Energy industries employees
           Engineers, see TA157
.E6   Engravers
             Cf. HD8039.P43, Photographers
.E8   Express company employees
           Farm labor, see .A29
.F3   Farmers
             Cf. HD1483+, Agricultural associations

.F35   Fastening industry workers
           Federal employees, see HD8001+ and J
.F42   Fertilizer industry
.F43   Fertilizer workers
.F5   Fire fighters
           Firemen
             Locomotive, see .R34
.F6   Stationary

.F65   Fishermen
           Flight attendants, see .A43
           Flint glass workers, see .G5
           Flour mill employees, see .M56
.F7   Food preparations

.F73   Forging industry workers
.F75   Foundry workers
.F8   Freight handlers
             Cf. HD8039.L8, Longshoremen

1/
For subarrangement under each, see footnote, p. 88

Labor

8039   By industry or trade, A-Z 1/ - Continued

.F9   Furniture workers
.G28   Gardeners
       Garment workers, see .C6
.G3   Gas company workers
       Gas fitters, see .P6
.G43   Gearing industry workers
.G45   Geological survey employees

       Glass blowers, see .G5
.G5   Glass workers
.G58   Glove workers
.G6   Gold beaters
.G7   Goldsmiths
       Government employees, see HD8001+ and J
       Granite cutters, see .S7+
       Green glass workers, see .G5
.G8   Grocers
.H15   Hammock industry employees
.H17   Hardware industry employees
.H2   Harness makers
       Hat finishers, see .H3+
.H3   Hatters
.H4   Cloth hat and cap makers
.H45   Heating plants

       Hod carriers, see .B89
.H6   Horseshoers. Farriers
.H75   Hosiery workers
       Hospital employees, see RA971.35
.H8   Hotel and restaurant employees. Waiters
         Including bartenders
           Cf. HD8039.C635, Cocktail waiters and
                 waitresses
.H84   Housewives. Home management
         Cf. HD6055, Employment of married women

.I2   Ice cream, ices, etc. makers
.I4   Ink makers
       Inland water transportation employees, see
         .S4
.I48   Insurance employees
         Cf. HG8091, Insurance agents
.I5   Iron and steel workers
         For blast-furnace workers, see .B58
.I7   Iron molders
       Iron shipbuilders, see .B6

       Joiners, see .C3
.J5   Jewelers
       Journalists, see PN4699+
.J8   Jute industry workers

1/

For subarrangement under each, see footnote, p. 88

                Labor

8039   By industry or trade, A-Z 1/ - Continued

         .L2   Laborers
         .L22   Lace makers
                Ladies' garment workers, see .C6
         .L25   Lathers
         .L3   Laundry workers
                Law clerks, see K
         .L4   Leather workers
                Leather workers on horse goods, see .H2

                Letter carriers, see Post office employees
         .L5   Liquor trades
             Bartenders, see .H8
         .L6   Brewers
         .L65   Distillery workmen
         .L7   Wine makers
                Cf. HD8039.V5, Vineyards
                Locomotive engineers, see .R32
                Locomotive firemen, see .R34

         .L8   Longshore workers. Stevedores
         .L9   Lumbermen. Loggers
                Machine woodworkers, see .W6
         .M2   Machinists. Machinery industry
                Maintenance-of-way employees, see .R43
                Marble cutters, see .S7+
                Marine engineers, see VM
         .M25   Masons
                Cf. HD8039.B78, Bricklayers
                      HD8039.P5, Plasterers
                      HD8039.S7+, Stonecutters
         .M28   Match industry
                Meat cutters, see .B96
                Meat industries, see .P15
         .M3   Mechanics
         .M34   Automobile mechanics
         .M39   Mercantile clerks. White-collar employees
                Cf. HD8039.C65, Commercial travelers
                      HD8039.O3, Office machine operators
                      HD8039.S58, Stenographers

                Merchant seamen, see .S4
         .M5   Metal workers
         .M56   Millers
         .M58   Milliners
         .M59   Millwrights
         .M6   Miners
         .M615   Coal miners
         .M65   Diamond miners
         .M7   Iron, copper, lead, etc. miners
         .M73   Gold, and silver miners
                Model makers, see .W6
         .M77   Modeling (Fashion)

1/
   For subarrangement under each, see footnote, p. 88

Labor

8039   By industry or trade, A-Z 1/ - Continued

                    Molders, see .I7
                    Mosaic tile layers, see .T53

.M78   Motion-picture industry
.M795   Motor-truck drivers
           Cf. HD8039.A76, Automobile drivers
               HD8039.T7, Transportation
                   workers
.M8   Motorbus employees
           Cf. HD8039.A76, Automobile drivers
               HD8039.S8, Street railway
                   employees
.M84   Motorcycle industry workers
         Motormen, see .S8

.M9   Munition workers
.M95   Mushroom workers
.N29   Nail makers
.O3   Office machine operators
         Office workers, see .M39
.O34   Offshore oil industry workers
         Oil and gas well workers, see .P4
.O5   Oil industry workers
           Cf. HD8039.O34, Offshore oil workers
               HD8039.P4, Petroleum workers
.P15   Packing industries
.P24   Paint makers
.P26   Painters and paper hangers
.P3   Paper box makers
         Paper hangers, see .P26
.P33   Paper makers
.P35   Pattern makers

.P36   Pavers
.P375   Peat industry
.P385   Pecan shellers
         Pedicab drivers, see .R5
.P39   Perfumers
.P4   Petroleum workers

.P43   Photographers. Photographic industry
           workers
.P45   Piano and organ workers
.P46   Picture frame industry workers
.P5   Plasterers
.P54   Plastic workers
         Plate printers, see Z243

.P6   Plumbers
.P62   Plywood industry
.P65   Poldermen
         Police, see HV7551+
.P655   Polishes industry workers
.P659   Porters
         Porters, Railroad, see .R36

1/
   For subarrangement under each, see footnote, p. 88

Labor

8039   By industry or trade, A-Z 1/ - Continued

                  Post-office employees
                     For United States, see HE6499; for other
                        countries, see table below HE6651+,
                        subdivision (9) Other, A-Z (.P4 Per-
                        sonnel)
.P8   Potters
           Printing trades, see Z243
              Type founders, see .T95
.P86   Public bath employees
.P88   Public utility workers
.P9   Publishing trade
           Quarrymen, see .S7
           Radio operators, see .T25+

           Radio station employees, see .T38
           Railroad employees
.R1   General works
.R2   Brakemen
.R23   Bridgemen
.R25   Carmen
.R28   Clerks
.R3   Conductors
.R315   Construction workers
.R317   Dining-car employees
.R318   Dispatchers
.R32   Engineers
.R34   Firemen
.R36   Porters
             Including Redcaps
.R38   Shopmen
.R39   Signalmen
.R4   Switchmen
           Telegraphers, see .T27
.R43   Trackmen
.R45   Trainmen

           Rapid transit employees, see .S8
.R46   Refuse collectors
.R469   Repairing trades
           Restaurant employees, see .H8
           Retail clerks, see .M39
.R48   Rice workers
.R5   Rickshaw men. Pedicab drivers

.R6   Road construction workers
.R65   Road maintenance workers
.R7   Roofers
.R8   Rope makers
.R9   Rubber workers
.R94   Rug and carpet industry workers
           Sailors, see .S4
           Salesmen, see HF5438+

1/

For subarrangement under each, see footnote, p. 88

Labor

8039   By industry or trade, A-Z 1/ - Continued

.S2   Salt workers
.S25   Sand and gravel industry workers
.S257   Sanitation workers
.S3   Sawmill workers
        School employees, see LB
.S36   Scientific instrument industry workers
.S37   Screen process printers

.S4   Seamen
        Servants, Domestic, see .D5
.S45   Service industries
          For works on specific industries, see
              the industry, e. g. .L3, Laundry
              workers
        Sheet metal workers, see .M5
.S48   Shellac workers
.S49   Shingle industry workers
.S5   Shipbuilders. Shipwrights
        Shipbuilders, Iron, see .B6

        Shirtwaist laundry workers, see .L3
        Shoe workers, see .B7
        Silk workers, see .T4
.S52   Silversmiths
.S55   Soapmakers
.S555   Soy sauce workers
        Spinners, see .T4

.S56   Sporting goods industry
        Stationary engineers, see TJ
        Stationary firemen, see .F6
        Steam engineers, see .R1+
        Steam fitters, see .P6
.S57   Steam shovel men
        Steel workers, see .I5
.S58   Stenographers

        Stevedores, see .L8
        Stewards, see .H8
        Stone cutters
.S7   General works
.S73   Granite
.S75   Marble
.S78   Stove workers
.S8   Street railway employees. Rapid transit
       employees
        Structural-iron workers, see .B82

.S85   Sugar workers
        Switchmen, see .R4
        Tailors, see .C6

1/
   For subarrangement under each, see footnote, p. 88

Labor
8039   By industry or trade, A-Z 1/ - Continued

             Tanners, see .L4
.T16   Taxicab drivers
.T2   Teamsters
.T24   Telecommunication workers
        Telegraphers
.T25   Commercial
.T27   Railroad
.T3   Telephone employees

.T38   Television station employees. Radio
           station employees
.T4   Textile workers
        Theatrical employees, see PN
.T53   Tile layers
        Tin workers, see .I5
        Tin plate workers, see .M5

.T57   Tinkers
.T58   Tire industry workers
.T6   Tobacco workers
.T64   Tourist trade employees
.T67   Toy makers. Toy industry workers
        Trackmen, see .R43
.T7   Transportation workers
            Cf. HD8039.M795, Motor-truck drivers

        Traveling sales personnel, see .C65
        Truck drivers, see .M795
.T8   Turpentine industry workers
.T95   Type founders
        Typographical unions, see Z120
.U5   Undertakers

.U6   Upholsterers
.V5   Vineyard laborers
            Cf. HD8039.L7, Wine makers
        Wagon workers, see .C33
        Waiters, see .H8
        Warehouse men, see .F8
.W2   Watchmakers
        Weavers, see .T4

.W4   Welders
.W48   Whip makers
        Wine makers, see .L7
.W5   Wood carvers
.W6   Woodworkers
        Woolen workers, see .T4
.W8   Wreckers

1/
   For subarrangement under each, see footnote, p. 88

Labor - Continued
By region or country
America
8045   General works
     United States
8051   Periodicals. Serials
8055   Associations, unions, etc.
Class here works about particular general trade unions. For official organs of general trade unions, see HD6500; for unions belonging to individual industries and trades, including their official organs, see HD6515
Under each:
.xA1-5 Periodicals. Serials
.xA6-Z General works
.x2A-W State branches. By state, A-W
For American Federation of Labor, use .A5-6

8057   Congresses
8059   Yearbooks
8061   Directories
     Statistics
8064   Collections of statistics
.2   Theory
8066   History (General)

     General works and history. By period
8068   Colonial
8070   1776-1865
8072   1865-1945
.5   1945-
     Biography
8073.A1A-Z   Collective
.A2-Z   Individual, A-Z

     Labor in politics
     Cf. HD6510, Trade unions
8076   General works
8079   Local, A-Z

     Minority labor
8081.A1-49   Periodicals. Societies. Serials
.A5A-Z   General works
.A6-Z   By race or ethnic origin, A-Z
Under each:
.xA1-5 Periodicals. Societies. Serials
.xA6-Z General works
Afro-Americans, see E185.8
8083   By region or state, A-Z
8085   By city, A-Z
Under each:
.x Associations, unions, etc. (General)
.x2 Directories
.x3 General works

Labor
  By region or country - Continued

8101-8942.5   Other regions or countries. Table VIII, modified 1/
      Under each country:

20 nos.	10 nos.	5 nos.	1 no.	
(1)	(1)	(1)	.A1-4	Periodicals. Societies. Serials
(3)	(2)	(2)	.A5A-Z	Associations, unions, etc.

				Class here works about partic-
				  ular general trade unions.
				  For official organs of general
				  trade unions, see HD6521+,
				  subdivision (1); for unions
				  belonging to individual in-
				  dustries and trades, including
				  their official organs, see
				  HD6521+, subdivision (8) and
				  (4)

(4)				Congresses
(5)	(3)			Yearbooks
(6)				Directories
(7)				Statistics
(8)	(4)	(3)	.A6-Z7	History (General)
				General works and history. By period
(9)	(5)			Early through 1848
(10)	(6)			1849-1945
(11)	(6.5)	(3.5)		1945-
(13)	(7)			Biography, A-Z
				.A1A-Z Collective
				.A2-Z Individual, A-Z
	(8)			Labor in politics
(15)				General works
(16)				Chartists movement (Great Britain)
(17)				Local, A-Z
(18)	(8.5)			Minority labor. By race or ethnic origin, A-Z
				e. g. .A2 General works
				.B55 Blacks
(19)	(9)	(4)	.Z8A-Z	By region or state, A-Z
				Under each state:
				.x Periodicals. Societies. Serials
				.x2 General works. History
				.x3 General special
(20)	(10)	(5)		By city, A-Z
				Under each:
				.x Early to 1848
				.x2 1848-

8943   Underdeveloped areas

1/
 For Table VIII, see pp. 331-340. Add country number in table to 8100

SPECIAL INDUSTRIES AND TRADES

Class here economic aspects of individual industries
and trades including management, finance, marketing,
governmental policy, etc. For the labor of
individual industries and trades, see HD8039.
For technical considerations, including management
at the plant or factory level, see the appropriate
topic in Classes R, S, and T

<u>Agricultural and other plant and animal products. Food
products 1/</u>

9000–9019	Produce and provisions (General)
	Cf. UC700+, Provisioning of armies
9000.9	Inspection
	Including government inspection, policy on
	adulteration, etc.
	Cf. TX563, Food adulteration
	.A1A–Z General works
	.A5–Z By region or country, A–Z

                    e. g.   United States

	.U5A1–19	Periodicals.
		Societies. Serials
	A6–69	Congresses
	A7–Z	General works
	.U6A–Z	By region or
		state, A–Z
	.U7–8	Cold storage
		Cf. TP372.2,
		Technique
		Subarranged like
		.U5–6 above

9019	Special products, A–Z	
	.B66–662	Borassus sundaica
	.C65–652	Coromandel ebony leaves
	.G55–552	Ginseng
		Cf. HD9675.G5, Drugs
	.H7–72	Hops
	.I3–32	Indigo
	.O39–4	Olive oil
		Cf. HD9259.O3+, Olives
	.P75–753	Protein products
	.S43–432	Seeds
	.T76–763	Tropical crops

9030–9049	Grain and hay	
9049	Special products, A–Z	
	.A4–5	Alfalfa
	.B3–4	Barley
	.B7–8	Buckwheat
	.C5–52	Chick-pea
	.C7–8	Corn
	.H2–3	Hay
	.M5–6	Millet

1/

   For subarrangement, see tables, pp. 122–124

Special industries and trades
Agricultural and other plant and animal products. Food
products 1/
Grain and hay

9049	Special products, A-Z - Continued

           .019-2   Oats
           .Q55-552 Quinoa
           .R8-9   Rye
           .S59-6   Sorghum
           .S8-82   Straw
                   Cf. HD9156.S9+, Straw industries
           .W3-5   Wheat

9052	Feeds

     Flour and meal. Prepared cereals

9056	General works
9057	Bakeries

     Rice

9066	General works
9067	Special products, A-Z

        .R53-532 Rice crackers

9070-9089	Cotton

     For cotton manufacture, see HD9870+; cotton
        speculation, see HG6047

9089	Special products, A-Z

     .B3-4 Bagging

9093	Cotton-seed. Cotton-seed oil
9100-9119	Sugar
9119	Special products, A-Z

        .B3-4   Bagasse
        .C5-6   Corn sugar

        .G6-7   Glucose
        .M3-32   Maple sugar
        .M65-66 Molasses

        .S29-3   Saccharin

9120	Honey
9130-9149	Tobacco
9149	Special products, A-Z

        .C4-43 Cigarettes
        .C49-5 Cigars
        .S6-62 Snuff

9155	Fibers (General)

     Including flax and hemp

9156	Other fibers, A-Z

        .A2   General works on minor fibers
        .C6-63   Coir
        .J7-8   Jute
        .K6-63   Kapok
        .M35-352 Manila hemp

        .R2-4   Ramie
        .S6-8   Sisal
        .S9-92   Straw
                Cf. HD9049.S8+, Straw (Field crop)

1/
  For subarrangement, see tables, pp. 122-124

Special industries and trades
Agricultural and other plant and animal products. Food
products 1/ - Continued

9161	Rubber
	Cf. TS1870+, Rubber manufacture
	SB289+, Rubber culture
	Tea and coffee
9195	General works
9198	Tea
	Cf. SB271+, Agricultural aspects
9199	Coffee
	Cf. SB269+, Agricultural aspects
9200	Cocoa and chocolate
	Cf. SB267+, Agricultural aspects
	Spices
	Cf. SB305, Plant culture
9210	General works
9211	Special products, A-Z
	.C55-554 Cinnamon
	.C56-564 Citronella grass. Citronella oil
	.C57-574 Cloves
	.N88-884 Nutmeg
	Cf. SB307.N8, Plant culture
	.P45-454 Pepper
	Cf. SB307.P4, Plant culture
	.P46-464 Peppermint
	Flavoring extracts
9212	General works
.5	Special products, A-Z
	.V34-344 Vanilla
9213	Salt
	Vegetables
	Cf. SB320+, Agricultural aspects
9220	General works
9225	Fresh vegetables
9227	Frozen vegetables
9230	Canned vegetables
	For special varieties of canned vegetables
	as groceries, see HD9330
9235	Particular vegetables, A-Z
	.A7-72 Artichokes
	.A8-82 Asparagus
	.B4-42 Beans
	.B76-762 Broccoli
	.C3-32 Cabbage
	.C34-342 Carrots
	.C36-362 Cassava
	.C37-372 Cauliflower
	.C44-442 Celery
	.C5-52 Chicory
	.C83-832 Cucumbers
	.G36-362 Garlic
	.G8-82 Guar
	.L4-42 Lettuce
	.M95-952 Mushrooms
	.O6-62 Onions
	.P3-32 Peanuts

1/
  For subarrangement, see tables, pp. 122-124

Special industries and trades
Agricultural and other plant and animal
products. Food products 1/
Vegetables

9235   Particular vegetables, A-Z - Continued
                .P4-42   Peas
                .P8-82   Potatoes
                .R3-32   Rapeseed

                .S4-42   Sesame
                .S6-62   Soybeans
                .S9-92   Sweet potatoes
                .T6-62   Tomatoes

9240-9259   Fruits and nuts
9259   Special products, A-Z
                .A45-47 Almonds
                .A5-6   Apples
                              Cf. SB363.6, Marketing
                .A95-954 Avocado

                .B2-3   Bananas
                .B46-464 Betel nuts
                .B52-524 Blueberries
                .B7-74   Brazil nuts
                .C3-33   Cashew nuts
                .C45-47 Cherries

                .C5-54   Citrus fruits
                .C58-6   Coconuts
                .C7-73   Cranberries
                .C78-8   Currants
                .D3-33   Dates

                .F45-47 Figs
                .F5-53   Filberts
                .G68-7   Grapes
                .G75-77 Grapefruit
                .G8-83   Guava

                .L4-43   Lemons
                .L5-53   Limes
                .M28-284 Mango
                .N68-7   Nuts
                .O3-4   Olives
                .O7-8   Oranges

                .P23-234 Papaya
                .P25-254 Passion fruit
                .P298-3 Peaches
                .P33-333 Pears
                .P35-37 Pecans
                .P5-53   Pineapples

                .P63-634 Plums
                .P7-73   Prunes

1/
    For subarrangement, see tables, pp. 122-124

Special industries and trades
  Agricultural and other plant and animal
    products. Food products 1/
    Fruits and nuts

9259		Special products, A-Z - Continued
	.R1-3	Raisins
	.S8-84	Strawberries
	.T3-34	Tangerines
	.W35-354	Watermelons

Cut flower and ornamental plant industries,
  see SB442.8
Dairy products
  Cf. SF221+, Dairying

9275	General works
9278	Butter
9280	Cheese
9281	Ice cream
9282	Milk
9284	Eggs

      Cf. HD9437, Poultry industry
          SF502, Marketing

9320-9330	Groceries

  Including canned goods
  Cf. HD9230, Canned vegetable industry
      HD9240+, Fruit and nuts industry
      HF5469, Supermarkets
      HF5469.5, Convenience stores
      TP368+, Food processing and manufacture

9330		Special products, A-Z
	.A8-83	Asparagus
	.B2-23	Baking powder
	.B32-323	Bean curd industry
	.C65-654	Confectionary. Candy
	.M32-324	Macaroni
	.M37-374	Margarine and other butter substitutes
		Cf. TP684.M3, Margarine (Chemical
		technology)
	.M57-573	Miso industry
	.P6-63	Pineapples (Canned)
	.S24-26	Salad dressing
	.S3-33	Salmon (Canned)
	.S65-653	Soy sauce
	.S73-734	Starch
	.S87-874	Syrup
	.T7-73	Tomatoes (Canned)
	.V55-554	Vinegar
	.Y4-43	Yeast

1/

For subarrangement, see tables, pp. 122-124

	Special industries and trades
	Agricultural and other plant and animal
	products. Food products 1/ - Continued
9333	Ethnic food industry
9340	Pet food industry
	Beverages
	Including nonalcoholic drinks (General)
	Cf. HD9195+, Tea, coffee, and cocoa
9348	General works
.5	Fruit juices
	.A1-3 General works
	.A5-Z Special juices, A-Z
	.C52-524 Citrus juice (General)
	.G72-724 Grape juice
	.O72-724 Orange juice
9349	Other nonalcoholic beverages, A-Z
9350-9369	Liquors
	Cf. HJ5001+, Excise
	HV5001+, Alcoholism
9369	Special topics, A-Z
	.A4-6 Absinthe
	.B5-7 Bottling
9370-9389	Wines
	Including viticulture; for technical
	works, see SB387+ and TP544+
	Distilled liquors
9390	General works
9391	Alcohol
9393	Brandy
9394	Rum
9395	Whisky
9397	Malted liquors
9398	Cider and perry
9399	Denatured alcohol
9410-9429	Animal industry
	Including meat packing industries and
	butchering business
	Cf. HD9996, Veterinary supplies
	SF, Animal culture
	TS1950+, Technology
	For hides and skins, see HD9780
9429	Special (non-edible products), A-Z
	.B6-62 Bone products
	.B7-72 Bristles
	.F4-42 Feathers. Down
	.G4-43 Gelatine
	.G8-82 Gut industries
	.I86-864 Ivory, horn, bone, etc.
9433	Cattle. Beef. Veal. Oxen
9434	Horses
9435	Hogs. Pork
9436	Sheep. Mutton. Lamb
9437	Poultry
	Cf. HD9284, Eggs
	SF481+, Poultry culture

1/
  For subarrangement, see tables, pp. 122-124

	Special industries and trades
	<u>Agricultural and other plant and animal products.</u>
	Food products 1/
	Animal industry - Continued
9438	Other, A-Z
	.R3-4 Rabbits
	.V4-5 Venison
9440	Meat products
9450-9469	Fishery products
	Cf. SH334, Economic aspects of fisheries
9469	Special products, A-Z
	.A52-522 Anchovies
	.B8-812 Buffalo fish
	.C38-382 Catfish
	.C39-392 Caviar
	.C6-63 Cod-liver oil
	.F5-512 Fish meal
	.F76-762 Frog legs
	.H4-43 Herring
	.K4-412 Kelp
	.N65-652 Nori
	.O5-53 Oil, Fish
	.S2-23 Salmon
	.S3-321 Sardines
	.S5-53 Sharks
	.S8-83 Swordfish
	.T8-83 Tuna
	Shellfish industry
9471	General works
9472	Particular shellfish, A-Z
	.C5-53 Clams
	.C7-73 Crabs
	.C74-743 Crayfish
	.L6-63 Lobsters
	.M8-83 Mussels
	.O8-83 Oysters
	.S34-343 Scallops
	.S6-63 Shrimps
	<u>Agricultural supply industries. Accessory industries</u>
9475	General works
9481	Ice
	Refrigeration, cold storage, <u>see</u> TP490+, HD9000.9
	Fertilizers
	Cf. HD9650+, Chemical industry
	S631+, Agriculture
	TP963+, Chemical technology
9483	General works
9484	Special products, A-Z
	.B6-62 Bone meal
	.C65-652 Compost
	.G8-9 Guano

1/

For subarrangement, <u>see</u> tables, pp. 122-124

	Special industries and trades
	Agricultural and other plant and animal products.
	Food products 1/
	Agricultural supply industries. Accessory industries
	Fertilizers
9484	Special products, A-Z - Continued
	.N5-6 Nitrates
	Cf. HD9660.N3+, Chemical industries
	.P4-5 Phosphate
	Potash, see HD9660.P68+
	Saltpeter, see .N5+, HD9585.S14
	Implements and machinery (Agricultural)
	Cf. S671+, Use
	TJ1480+, Manufacture
9486	General works
.5	Gardening equipment
	Cf. SB454.8, Gardening
	Forest products, see HD9750+
	Fishing equipment industry
	Cf. SB344+, Fisheries
	SH447+, Angling
9488	General works
9489	Special industries, A-Z
	.T33-334 Tackle
9490	Oils, fats, and waxes
	For cottonseed oil, see HD9093; for petroleum,
	see HD9560+
9502	Energy industries (General). Energy policy
	Cf. TJ163.3+, Energy conservation
	Industries in general (other than agricultural)
	For technical works on manufacturing processes,
	etc., see T
	General works, see HC
	General companies
	Cf. HD2756, Conglomerate corporations
9503	United States
9505	Other regions or countries, A-Z
	Mineral and metal industries 1/
9506	General works
	Particular metals
9510-9529	Iron and steel
9529	Special products, A-Z
	.A48-5 Alloys
	.B28-3 Barrels
	.B58-6 Boilers
	.B7-73 Bridges
	.C8-9 Cutlery
	.D5-53 Die castings
	.F4-43 Ferrosilicon
	.H6-63 Hoops
	.M3-34 Magnet steel
	.N32-324 Nails and spikes
	.P5-54 Pipes
	.R5-53 Rivets
	.S59-594 Springs
	.S62-623 Stainless steel

1/

For subarrangement, see tables, pp. 122-124

Special industries and trades
   Mineral and metal industries 1/
      Particular metals
        Iron and steel

9529		Special products, A-Z - Continued
	.S67-673	Steel castings
	.S7-73	Steel shafts for golf clubs
	.S75-753	Steel straps
	.T6-63	Tinplate
	.T82-823	Tubes
		Umbrella parts, see HD9970.5.U53+
	.V3-33	Valves
	.W5-53	Wire
	.W58-583	Wire netting
9536		Gold and silver
		Other nonferrous metals
9539.A1A-Z		Periodicals. Societies. Serials
.A2A-Z		General works
.A3A-Z		By region or country, A-Z
.A4-Z		Particular metals, A-Z
		Subarrange each metal like Table A(19), B(10), p. 124
	.A6-64	Aluminum
	.A82-83	Antimony
	.B45-454	Beryllium
	.B57-574	Bismuth
	.B7-8	Brass
	.B86-87	Bronze
	.C3-34	Cadmium
	.C4-42	Chromium
	.C46-464	Cobalt
	.C5-7	Copper
	.L38-43	Lead
	.L58-584	Lithium
	.M23-234	Magnesite
	.M25-28	Magnesium
	.M3-34	Manganese
	.M4-44	Mercury
	.M6-64	Molybdenum
	.N5-52	Nickel
	.P5-52	Platinum
	.R3-34	Rare earths
	.T34-344	Tantalum
	.T5-6	Tin
	.T7-74	Titanium
	.T8-82	Tungsten
	.U69-73	Uranium
	.Z49-62	Zinc

1/
  For subarrangement, see tables, pp. 122-124

Special industries and trades
   Mineral and metal industries 1/ - Continued

9540-9559	Coal
9559	Special products, A-Z
	.B7-74 Briquets (Fuel)
	.C43-45 Charcoal
	.C68-7 Coke
	.L4-6 Lignite
	.P3-5 Peat
9560-9579	Petroleum
	Including motor fuel (General)
	Cf. HD242.5, Public oil and gas lands
9560.9	Inspection
	.A1A-Z General works
	.A2-Z By region or country, A-Z
	Under each country:
	.x General works
	.x2 Local, A-Z
9579	Special products, A-Z
	.C3-34 Chemicals
	.D5-54 Diesel fuels
	.E84-844 Ethylene
	.G3-5 Gasoline
	.L8-84 Lubricants
	.M4-44 Methane
	.N3-5 Naphtha
	.P4-44 Liquefied petroleum gas
	.P76-764 Propane
9580	Pipe lines
9581	Natural gas
9582	Other carbons and hydrocarbons, A-Z
	.A68-7 Asphalt
	.B5-53 Bituminous materials
	.M5-54 Mineral oils
	.T3-33 Tar
	Other non-metallic minerals
9585.A1A-Z	Periodicals. Societies. Serials
.A2A-Z	General works
.A3A-Z	By region or country, A-Z
.A4-Z	Particular minerals, A-Z
	Each mineral subarranged like Table A(19),
	B(10), p. 124
	Cf. HD9621, Building stones
	TN799.5+, Technology
	.A522-5224 Alum
	.A53-56 Apatite
	.A64-66 Asbestos
	.B36-39 Barite
	.C8-83 Cyanite
	.F4-43 Feldspar
	.F5-54 Flint
	.F57-574 Fluorspar
	.G5-53 Gilsonite
	.G9-93 Gypsum

1/
  For subarrangement, see table, pp. 122-124

Special industries and trades
Mineral and metal industries 1/
Other non-metallic minerals

9585.A4-Z		Particular minerals, A-Z - Continued
	.L49-52	Lime
	.M5-53	Mica
	.M6-64	Mineral waters
	.O3-33	Ocher
	.P46-464	Perlite
	.P8-83	Pumice
	.P9-94	Pyrites
	.Q3-33	Quartz
	.S14-143	Saltpeter
	.S15-17	Sand
	.S18-2	Sandstone
	.S4-43	Shale
	.S47-474	Silicon
	.S8-84	Sulphur
	.T3-33	Talc
9590-9600	Clay industries	
9600	Special products, A-Z	
	.K3-33	Kaolin
	.R4-43	Refractory materials
	.S27-3	Sewer pipe
9605	Brick and tile	
9607	Terra cotta	
9610-9620	Pottery and porcelain	
9620.5	Special products, A-Z	
	.E53-534	Enameled ware
	.H65-654	Hollow ware
9621	Building stones	
	Including granite, marble, slate, etc.	
	Cf. TN950+, Technology	
9622	Cement. Concrete	
	Glass	
9623	General works	
9624	Special products, A-Z	
	.B67-673	Bottles
	.G55-553	Glassware
	.M55-553	Mirrors
9650-9660	Chemical industries 1/	
9660	Special products, A-Z	
	.A4-45	Alkalies
	.A48-483	Ammonia
	.A5-53	Ammonium sulphate
	.C29-32	Calcium carbide
	.C33-333	Calcium cyanamide
	.C35-37	Carbides
	.C38-383	Carbon black
	.C39-393	Carbon dioxide
	.C4-43	Cellulose
	.C5-53	Chlorine
	.C6-63	Coal tar products

1/
   For subarrangement, see tables, pp. 122-124

Special industries and trades
    Chemical industries 1/ - Continued

9660   Special products, A-Z

.D4-43	Detergents, Synthetic
.D84-844	Dyestuffs
.E58-584	Enzymes
.F48-484	Fermentation products
	Fertilizers, see HD9438+
.F56	Fluorocarbon
.F85-854	Furaldehyde
.G37-373	Gases
.G58-6	Glycerine
.H4-43	Helium
	Insecticides, see .P3+
.L33-334	Lacquer
.L5-53	Lithium hydroxide
.L57-574	Lithopane
.M47-474	Matches
.N3-5	Nitrates
	Cf. HD9484.N5+, Fertilizers
.N6-8	Nitrogen industries
.P25-254	Paint
.P3-33	Pesticides. Insecticides
.P68-7	Potash
.R4-44	Resins
.S6-7	Soda
.S724-7244	Sodium carbonate
.S73-734	Solvents
.S78-8	Sulphuric acid
.S85-853	Surface active agents
.T3-33	Tar
.U72-724	Urea
.U73-734	Urethane
.Z5-53	Zinc oxide

         Plastics

9661   General works
9662   Special products, A-Z

.A25-27	Acrylic plastics
.G5-53	Glass reinforced plastics
.P5-53	Plastic foams
.P6-63	Polyvinyl chloride

9663   Explosives
9665-9675   Drugs 1/
           Cf. HV5800+, Opium, etc.
             RS68, Pharmaceutical companies
9675   Special products, A-Z

.A5-54	Animal extracts
.A6-64	Antibiotics
.A7-74	Aspirin
.C24-25	Camphor
.G5-7	Ginseng
.I45-47	Insulin
.I52-54	Iodine
.Q5-7	Quinine
.V5-53	Vitamins

1/
   For subarrangement, see tables, pp. 122-124

	Special industries and trades – Continued
	<u>Precious stones</u> 1/
9676	General works
9677	Diamonds
9678	Other, A–Z
	.E57–6 Emeralds
	.O52–524 Onyx
	.P39–43 Pearls
	.T52–524 Tiger's eyes
	<u>Mechanical industries</u> 1/
	Cf. TA217, General engineering companies, consulting engineers, etc.
9680	General works
9681	Solar energy industries
9682	Geothermal industries
9683	Heating industries
9684	Lighting industries
	Class here lighting industries in general; for electricity, <u>see</u> HD9685; for gas, <u>see</u> TP751.3
	Cf. HD4486+, Municipal lighting
	HJ5635.L4, Taxation
	<u>Electric utilities and industries</u>
9685	General works
9688	Rural electrification
	Cf. TK4018, Agriculture and the farm
9695	Machinery and supplies
	Including electrical contracting
	Electronic industries
9696.A1A–Z	Collected works (nonserial)
.A2A–Z	General works
.A3A–Z	By region or country
.A4–Z	Particular equipment, A–Z
	Subarrange each like Table A(19), B(10), p. 124
	.A92–924 Audio equipment industry
	.A96–964 Automatic control equipment
	.C6–64 Computers
	.E5–54 Electron tubes
	.E56–564 Electronic alarm systems
	.E57–574 Electronic funds transfer equipment
	.I58–584 Integrated circuits industry
	Lasers, <u>see</u> HD9999.L32+
	Medical electronic equipment, <u>see</u> HD9995.E4
	.M53–534 Microwave equipment
	.N3–34 Navigation equipment
	.P76–764 Process control equipment
	.R34–344 Radar
	.R36–364 Radio
	.S4–44 Semiconductors
	.T44–444 Telecommunication equipment
	.T46–464 Television
	.T7–74 Traffic control equipment
	.V3–34 Vacuum tubes
	Electric industries
9697.A1A–Z	Periodicals. Societies. Serials
.A2A–Z	General works
.A3A–Z	By region or country

1/

For subarrangement, <u>see</u> tables, pp. 122–124

Special industries and trades
Mechanical industries 1/
Electric utilities and industries
Electric industries – Continued

9697.A4–Z   Particular appliances and equipment, A–Z
                    Subarrange each like Table A(19), B(10), p. 124
    .A84–844   Audiovisual materials and equipment
                        Cf. HD9810+, Educational technology
                            industries
    .B32–324   Batteries
    .C33–334   Cables
                    Household, see HD9971.5.E54+
    .L33–334   Lamps

    .M68–684   Motion-picture equipment
    .P56–564   Phonograph records
    .T45–454   Telephone equipment

    .T73–734   Trucks, Electric
    .V54–544   Video tapes
    .W43–434   Welding equipment

                 Nuclear power industry. Table C, modified 1/
9698   General works
    .4   European Atomic Energy Community. EURATOM
    .5   International Atomic Energy Agency
9700   Machine shops
                 Cf. TJ1125+, Technology
9703   Machine tools
                 Cf. TJ1180+, Technology
             Machinery
                 Class here general works on machinery applicable
                     to several industries
                 For machinery limited in application to a specific
                     industry, see the industry, e. g. HD9486,
                     Agricultural machinery; HD9506, Mining machinery;
                     HD9695, Electric machinery
9705   General works
    .5   Special products, A–Z
                 .B43–434   Bearings
                 .F87–874   Furnaces
                 .O55–554   Oil burners
                 .P85–854   Pumps
             Instrumentation industries
9706   General works
    .2   Measuring instruments
    .4   Physical instruments
    .5   Recording instruments
    .6   Scientific apparatus and instruments
9707   Optical goods
             Photographic equipment
9708   General works
    .5   Special equipment, A–Z
                 .C35–354   Cameras

─────────────
1/
    For subarrangement, see tables, pp. 122–124

Special industries and trades
   Mechanical industries 1/ - Continued
      Transportation vehicles and equipment
         Class here works on the production of vehicles
           and equipment used for transportation. For
           works on transportation economics, see HE

9709	General works
.5	Carriages and wagons
	Automobiles. Motor vehicles
	Cf. HD9715.7, Trailer homes
9710	General works
.3	Automobile supplies, parts and accessories industry
.5	Motorcycle industry
.6	Moped industry
9711	Airplanes
	Cf. TL500+, Aeronautical engineering
	TL671.28, Airplanes (Manufacturing. Factory
	equipment and methods)
	TL724+, Airplane industries (Technical aspects)
.3	Lighter-than-air craft
	Cf. TL667+, Technology
.5	Aerospace industry
	Cf. TL780+, Rocket propulsion
	TL787+, Astronautics
9712	Railroad rolling stock, equipment, etc.
9714	Snowmobiles
	Shipbuilding, see VM

   Construction industry and materials 1/
      Cf. HD9621, Building stones
         TH434+, Estimates, etc.

9715	General works
.5	Prefabricated buildings
.7	Trailer homes
	Cf. HD7289.6, Mobile homes
	Building supplies
.8	General works
.9	Special products, A-Z
	For works on particular materials used in
	construction, see the material, e. g. HD9605+,
	Brick and tile
	.P56-564 Pipe
	Cf. HD9529.P5+, Steel pipe
	.P68-684 Plumbing supplies
9716	Particular trades, A-Z
	Class here works on independent business in the
	building trades. For works on persons employed
	in the building trades, see HD8039.B9
	.C3-33 Carpentry
	.P16-163 Painting, Industrial
	.P2-23 Paperhanging
	.P46-47 Plumbing
	Cf. HD9715.9.P68+, Plumbing supplies
	.S75-78 Stonemasonry
	.R66-664 Roof construction

1/
  For subarrangement, see tables, pp. 122-124

```
                        Special industries and trades
                          Construction industry and materials 1/ - Continued
        9717                  Hydraulic structures
            .5                Other enterprises, A-Z
                                .R6  Road construction
                                        Cf. HE333, Traffic engineering.  Roads
                                              and highways
                          Environmental engineering industries
        9718                  General works
            .5                Particular industries, A-Z
                                .A57-574  Air pollution control equipment
                                .W36-364  Water pollution control
                                .W38-384  Water purification equipment
    9720-9739             Manufacturing industries
                            Metal
        9743                  Munitions.  Arms and ammunition
                                  Cf. JX5390, Munitions export and neutrality
                                        UF530+, Manufacture of ordnance and small arms
        9745                  Hardware
                                  Including hardware store merchandise (General)
        9747                  Jewelry
                                Musical instruments, see ML
    9750-9769             Forest products.  Lumber
        9769                  Special products, A-Z
                                .A2         By-products
                                .B3-34      Balsa wood
                                .C5-7       Chestnut
                                .C72-74     Cork
                                .C9-93      Cypress
                                .D6-63      Douglas fir
                                .E9-94      Excelsior
                                .F6-63      Flooring
                                            Gums, see .R4+
                                .K3-33      Kauri gum
                                .L3-33      Lac.  Shellac
                                .M3-33      Mahogany
                                .N3-33      Naval stores
                                .O2-23      Oak
                                .P3-33      Particle board
                                .P5-53      Pine
                                .P56-59     Pit-wood
                                .P6-63      Plywood
                                .R25-253    Railroad ties
                                .R4-44      Gums and resins
                                .S3-33      Sandalwood
                                            Shellac, see .L3+
                                .S5-53      Shingles
                                .S6-63      Spruce
                                .S815-818   Staves and stave trade
                                .T4-43      Teak
                                .T7-9       Turpentine
                                .V4-43      Veneers
                                .W4-43      Wood floor
                                .W5-53      Woodpulp
                                                Cf. HD9820+, Paper
                                .Y8-83      Yucca
```

1/
  For subarrangement, see tables, pp. 122-124

Special industries and trades
  Manufacturing industries 1/
    Forest products. Lumber - Continued

9773	Furniture. Cabinet-making. Woodcarving
9778	Hides and skins
9779	Tanning materials
	Leather and leather goods
	Including hides and leather (General)
	Cf. HD9941, Belts (Clothing)
	HD9947, Gloves
	HD9970.5.L85+, Luggage
9780	General works
9787	Footwear. Shoes
	Including machinery
	Graphic and artists' supplies
9790	General works
9791	Artists materials
9792	Ink
9793	Marking devices
9794	Pencils
9795	Pens
	Office equipment and supplies
	Cf. HF5546+, Office organization
9800	General works
9801	Business machines
	Cf. HD9696.C6+, Computer industry
9802	Typewriter and supplies
	Educational supplies. Instructional materials
	Cf. HD9697.A84+, Audiovisual materials and
	equipment
	LB1042.5, Audiovisual education
9810	General works
9811	Educational technology industries
	Cf. LB1028.3, Educational technology
9820-9839	Paper. Stationery
	Cf. HD9750+, Forest products
	TS1080+, Paper manufacture
9839	Special products, A-Z
	.B5-53 Blank books
	.F4-44 Papermaking felts
	.G7-73 Greeting cards
	.N4-44 Newsprint
	.P28-284 Paper bags
	.P3-34 Paperboard industry
	.T3-34 Toilet paper
	.W3-34 Waste paper
9843	Wallpaper
9850-9869	Textile industries
9869	Special products, A-Z
	Cordage, see HD9999.C75+
	.F3-33 Fabrics (General)
	.N64-643 Nonwoven fabrics
	.P6-63 Poplin
	.R6-63 Rope
	.T5-53 Thread
	.T8-83 Tufted textiles
	.T9-93 Twine

1/
  For subarrangement, see tables, pp. 122-124

Special industries and trades
Manufacturing industries 1/
Textile industries - Continued

9870-9889	Cotton
	Cf. HD9070+, Cotton growing
9890-9909	Wool
	Including wool growing
	Cf. SF371+, Sheep (Animal culture)
9909	Special products, A-Z
	.R28-3 Rags
	.S58-6 Shoddy
	.T9-93 Tweed
	.Y28-3 Yarns
9910-9929	Silk
9929	Special products, A-Z
	.C7-73 Crepe
	.R4-6 Ribbon
	.T5-53 Thread
	Synthetic textile fibers
9929.2	General works
.5	Special fibers, materials, A-Z
	.N9 Nylon
	.O7 Orlon
	.P3 Paper thread
	.R3 Rayon. Artificial silk
9930	Linen
9933	Lace
9935	Embroidery
9936	Tapestry
.5	Needlework
9937	Floor coverings. Carpets, rugs, etc.
9938	Canvas, bagging, burlap, etc.
	Cf. HD9089.B3, Cotton
9939	Drapery. Curtains
	Clothing
9940	General works
9941	Belts
.5	Corsets
9942	Dresses
9944	Furs
9947	Gloves
9948	Hats. Millinery
9949	Uniforms
9950-9969	Dry goods
9969	Special products, A-Z
	.B55-553 Blouses
	.B88-9 Buttons
	.F65-653 Foundation garments
	.H3-33 Handkerchiefs
	.H5-53 Hooks and eyes
	.H6-8 Hosiery

1/
For subarrangement, see tables, pp. 122-124

<u>Special industries and trades</u>
    <u>Manufacturing industries 1/</u>
        Dry goods

9969   Special products, A-Z - Continued
             .H83-833 Household linens. White goods
             .K5-7   Knit goods

             .S3-33   Scarves
             .S5-7   Shirts
             .T67-673 Towels
             .U5-6   Underwear
                        White goods, <u>see</u> .H83+
             .Z5-6   Zippers

        Personal consumption goods
9970   General works
  .5   Special products, A-Z
             .C45-454 Chewing gum. Chicle
             .C65-654 Combs
             .C67-674 Cosmetics

             .I54-544 Infants' supplies
             .L85-854 Luggage
             .N68-684 Novelties

             .P57-574 Pipes. Tobacco
             .T65-654 Toilet preparations
             .U53-534 Umbrellas

        Household goods and appliances
9971   General works
  .5   Special products, A-Z
             .B76-764 Brooms
             .C56-564 Clothespins
             .E54-544 Electrical appliances (General)

             .M38-384 Mattresses
             .R44-444 Refrigerators
             .S48-484 Sewing machines

             .S76-764 Stoves
             .W37-374 Washing machines
             .W56-564 Window shades

9975   Waste products (General) 1/
           Including consumer and industrial waste products,
             e. g. rag-picking, junk, scrap metal
9980-9990   Service industries (General)
           Cf. HD2340.8+, Small industry
               HD8039.S45, Employees
           For special service industries, <u>see</u> the industry,
             e. g. HD9999.L38, Laundries; TT950+,
             Hairdressing

1/
  For subarrangement, <u>see</u> table, pp. 122-124

Special industries and trades - Continued
Recreational equipment. Sporting goods
Cf. GV743+, Use
TS2301.S7, Manufacture
9992   General works
9993   Special products, A-Z
.A58-584   Amusement rides
.B54   Bicycles
.B63   Boats. Boat equipment
.C35-354   Camping equipment
.C74-744   Cricket equipment
.G35-354   Games
.G65-654   Golf equipment
Moped industry, see HD9710.6
.P53-534   Playing cards
.S53   Skates
.S95-954   Swimming pool industry
.T46   Tennis supplies
.T69-694   Toys
.T76-764   Trophies

Medical instrument and apparatus industry 1/
Cf. HD9665+, Drug industry
9994   General works
9995   Special industries, A-Z
.C6   Contraceptives
.D4   Dental equipment
.E4   Electronic equipment

.H6   Hospital equipment
.O7   Orthopedic apparatus and equipment
.P75   Prosthesis
.S2   Sanitary supply
.S9   Surgical instruments
.U74   Urinary incontinence products
9996   Veterinary supplies
9999   Miscellaneous industries and trades, A-Z
Subarrange each industry or trade like Table A(19)
and Table B(10), p. 124
.A2-24   Abrasives
.A4-44   Adhesives
.A5-54   Air conditioning equipment

.A82-824   Artificial flowers
.A83-834   Artificial leather
Bagging, see HD9938
.B14   Barbers' supplies
.B16-164   Baskets
Bearings (Machinery), see HD9705.5.B43+
.B25   Beauty shop supplies
.B3   Belts and belting
Cf. HD9941, Belts (Clothing)
.B45-454   Bleaching
.B46   Blueprinting
.B7   Box

_____
1/
For subarrangement, see tables, pp. 122-124

Special industries and trades

9999   Miscellaneous industries and trades, A-Z - Continued

	Brooms, see HD9971.5.B76+
.B84	Brushes
	Business machines, see HD9801
	Camping equipment and suppplies, see HD9993.C35+
.C25	Cans
.C27-274	Car wash
	Carriages and wagons, see HD9709.5
	Caskets, see .C65
	Chewing gum. Chicle, see HD9970.5.C45+
.C48-484	Cleaning and dyeing
.C486-4864	Cleaning compounds
.C58	Clocks and watches
	Clothespins, see HD9971.5.C56+
.C646-6464	Coatings industry
.C65	Coffins and caskets
	Combs, see HD9970.5.C65+
.C715-7154	Composite materials
	Confectionaries. Candy, see HD9330.C65+
.C74	Containers
.C746-7464	Cookware
	Copying processs, see Z48; HF5541.C8
.C75	Cordage
.C78-784	Corrosion control
	Cosmetics, see HD9970.5.C67+
.C945-9454	Crucibles
.D62-624	Do-it-yourself products
	Dyeing, see .C48+
	Dyestuffs, see HD9660.D84+
	Educational technology industries, see HD9810+
	Electric batteries, see HD9697.B32+
	Enameled ware, see HD9620.5.E53+
.E5	Engraving
.E78	Essences and essential oils
.F3	Fastenings
	Feathers. Down, see HD9429.F4
.F5	Fire-fighting equipment
.F55-554	Fireproofing
	Furnaces, see HD9705.5.F87+
	Games, see HD9993.G35+
	Gardening equipment, see HD9486.5
.G43-434	Gear industry
.G48-484	Gift shops
.G6	Glue
	Hollow ware, see HD9620.5.H65+
	Household appliances, see HD9971+
	Houseplants, see SB419.3
.I43-434	Industrial safety equipment
	Infants' supplies, see HD9970.5.I54+
	Ink, see HD9792
	Instructional materials, see HD9810+
	Instruments, see HD9706+
	Ivory, horn, bone, etc., see HD9429.I86+

	Special industries and trades
9999	Miscellaneous industries and trades, A-Z - Continued
	Lacquer, see HD9660.L33+
.L32-324	Lasers
.L38-384	Laundries
	Cf. TT890+, Technology
.L418	Laundry machinery
	Cf. HD9971.5.W37+, Washing machine industry
.L436	Lease and rental services
.L46	Linoleum
.L5	Linseed oil
	Lithopone, see HD9660.L57+
	Luggage, see HD9970.5.L85+
	Marking devices, see HD9793
.M2-24	Matches
.M2613	Mats
	Mattresses, see HD9971.5.M38+
	Measuring instruments, see HD9706.2
	Millinery, see HD9948
.M64-644	Modeling agencies, schools, etc.
	Motion-picture equipment, see HD9697.M68+
.M8	Musical instruments
	Cf. ML, Literature of music
	Needlework industry and trade, see HD9936.5
	Novelties, see HD9970.5.N68+
	Office equipment and supplies, see HD9800+
	Oil burners, see HD9705.5.O55+
	Optical goods, see HD9707
	Paint, see HD9660.P25+
.P2	Patterns (Metalwork)
	Pencils, see HD9794
	Pens, see HD9795
.P393-3934	Perfumes
	Phonograph records, see HD9697.P56+
	Photographic apparatus, see HD9708+
	Physical instruments, see HD9706.4
.P6	Pins, needles, etc.
	Pipe, see HD9715.9.P56+
	Pipes, Tobacco, see HD9970.5.P57+
	Plumbing supplies, see HD9715.9.P68+
.P69	Polishes
	Pumps, see HD9705.5.P85+
	Radio, see HD9696.R36+
.R3-34	Razor industry
	Refrigerators, see HD9971.5.R44+
	Rental services, see .L436
.R54	Restaurant equipment
.S29	Safes
	Scientific apparatus and instruments, see HD9706.6
.S44-444	Screw machine products industry
.S45-454	Security systems

Special industries and trades
9999   Miscellaneous industries and trades, A-Z - Continued
Sewing machines, see HD9971.5.S48+
.S52   Shellcraft
.S7   Soap
.S914   Sponges

Springs (Mechanism), see HD9529.S59+
Stoves, see HD9971.5.U76+
Telephone equipment, see HD9697.T45+
Television, see HD9696.T46+
Tires, see HD9161
Toilet preparations, see HD9970.5.T65+

Toys, see HD9993.T69+
Typewriters and supplies, see HD9802
Umbrellas, see HD9970.5.U53+
.U5-54   Undertaking

Video tapes, see HD9697.V54+
Washing machines, see HD9971.5.W37+
Watches, see .C58

.W37-374 Wedding supplies and services
Window shades, see HD9971.5.W56+
Wire, see HD9529.W5+

Special industries and trades

TABLES OF SUBDIVISIONS UNDER INDUSTRIES AND TRADES
(HD9000-9999)

Under each:

A (20 nos.)	B (11 nos.)	
0.1	0.1	Periodicals. Societies. Serials
		For manufacturers' associations formed
		with particular reference to labor
		questions, <u>see</u> HD6941+
.2	.2	Yearbooks
.3	.3	Directories
		For directories of manufacturers and
		their products, <u>see</u> T
.4	.4	Statistics, prices, etc.
.5	.5	General works. History
		Including biography
.6	.6	Public policy
.65	.65	Handbooks, manuals, etc.
		Taxation
		Cf. HD2753+, Taxation of corporations
		HF2651, Tariff
.8A1A-Z	.8A1A-Z	General works
.8A2-Z	.8A2-Z	By region or country, A-Z
		Under each country:
		.x Periodicals. Societies. Serials
		.x2 General works
.9	.9	Inspection
		Subarranged like .8
		Class here works on the state inspection
		of specific industries; for factory
		inspection in general, <u>see</u> HD3656+
		By region or country
	1	United States
1	.1	Periodicals. Societies. Serials
2	.2	Yearbooks
3	.3	Directories
		For directories of manufacturers and
		their products, <u>see</u> T
4	.4	Statistics, prices, etc.
5	.5	General works. History
6	.6	Public policy
7	.7	By region or state, A-Z
8	.8	By city, A-Z
9	.9	By firm, etc., A-Z
		Biography
.8	.94	Collective
10	.95	Individual, A-Z

Special industries and trades

TABLES OF SUBDIVISIONS UNDER INDUSTRIES AND TRADES

(HD9000-9999)

Under each:

A (20 nos.)	B (11 nos.)	
		By region or country - Continued
11	2	Great Britain
.1	.1	Periodicals. Societies. Serials
.2	.2	Yearbooks
.3	.3	Directories
		For directories of manufacturers and their products, <u>see</u> T
.4	.4	Statistics, prices, etc.
.5	.5	General works. History
		Including biography
.6	.6	Public policy
.7	.7	By region or constituent country, A-Z
.8	.8	By city, A-Z
.9	.9	By firm, etc., A-Z
12	3	France
		Subarranged like Great Britain
13	4	Germany
		Subarranged like Great Britain
		Other regions or countries
		Under each country:
		.x Periodicals. Societies. Serials
		.x2 General works. History
		Including biography
		.x3 Local, A-Z
		.x4 Firms, etc., A-Z
14	5	America. By region or country, A-Z
15	6	Europe. By region or country, A-Z
16	7	Asia. By region or country, A-Z
17	8	Africa. By region or country, A-Z
18	9	Other. By region or country, A-Z
		.A55 Arab countries (General)
		.C6 Communist countries (General)

Special industries and trades

TABLES OF SUBDIVISIONS UNDER INDUSTRIES AND TRADES
(HD9000-9999)

Under each:

A (20 nos.)	B (11 nos.)	
19	10	Special products, A-Z

Under each (using successive Cutter
numbers):

Four numbers:
.x   Periodicals. Societies. Serials
.x2 General works. History
        Including biography
.x3 Local, A-Z
.x4 Firms, A-Z
Three numbers:
.x   Periodicals. Societies. Serials
.x2 General works. History
        Including biography
.x3 Local, A-Z
Two numbers:
.x   General works. History
        Including biography
.x2 Local, A-Z
In case only two or three numbers are
indicated, others may be established.
If desired, "Local" may include "Firms."
The practice of omitting Cutter numbers
ending in "one" is generally observed
at the Library of Congress. For
example HD9019.H7-72, Hops, is read:
.H7, General works; .H72, Local; .H71
is not used; .H69 may be established
for "Periodicals" and .H73 for "Firms"

C (One number)
.A1A-Z Periodicals. Societies. Serials
.A2A-Z General works
.A4-Z   By region or country, A-Z
        Under each country:
          .x   Periodicals. Societies. Serials
          .x2 General works. History
               Including biography
          .x3 Local, A-Z
          .x4 Firms, etc., A-Z

D (Cutter number), see note under (19) and (10) in tables A and B above

Including roads, waterways, railways, postal service,
    telecommunication, telegraph, telephone, broad-
    casting, commercial aviation, etc.
Cf. HF, Commerce
    P87+, Communication. Mass media
    TA1001+, Transportation engineering

	Periodicals. Societies. Serials. By language of publication
1	English
3	French
5	German
7	Other languages (not A-Z)
8	Yearbooks
	Shippers' guides. Directories. Timetables, etc.
	Cf. G153+, Travelers' guides
.9	General works
9	By region or country, A-Z
11	Congresses
	Museums. Exhibitions
13	General
.2	By region or country, A-Z
	Under each country:
	.x General works
	.x2 Special. By city, A-Z
16-115	Official documents. By country. Table I 1/
	For United States Interstate Commerce Commission, see HE2708; Department of Transportation, see HE206.3
	For United States use:
	17-29 United States
	17 Serials
	28 States, A-W
	29 Cities, A-Z
	For HE30-115 use:
	.A3A-Z General works
	.A5-Z Local, A-Z
	Collected works (nonserial)
131	Several authors
136	Individual authors
141	Dictionaries. Encyclopedias
147	Terminology. Abbreviations. Notation
	Theory. Method. Relation to other subjects
.5	General works
.6	Electronic data processing
.7	Mathematical models
148	Transportation and community development
.5	Transportation and underdeveloped areas
149	Transportation and agriculture
	Cf. HE1043, Railways and farming interests
151	General works

1/   For Table I, see pp. 331-340. Add country number in table to 15

Biography
151.4	Collective
.5	Individual, A-Z
152	Juvenile works
.5	General special (Special aspects of the subject as a whole)
.6	Addresses, essays, lectures
153	Use of animals for transportation

Cf. SF180, Draft animals

History

(155)	Primitive, see GN438+

Ancient

159	General works
161	Egypt
163	Phoenicia
167	Assyro-Babylonian Empire. Persia
169	Other Oriental

Greece and Rome

171	General works
173	Greece
175	Rome
177	Other, A-Z

Middle Ages
Including works treating the ancient period and
Middle Ages combined

181	General works

By region or country, see HE201+
Modern, see HE151

Statistics

191.4	Collections of statistics
.5	Theory

Information services

.8	General works
.82	By region or country, A-Z

Study and teaching

.9	General works
192	By region or country, A-Z

Research

.5	General works
.55	By region or country, A-Z
193	Public policy (General)

Rate making
Including costs

195.4	General works
.5	By region or country, A-Z
196	Concessions
.5	Finance

Taxation, tolls, etc.
Cf. HE384+, Tolls on waterways
HJ5951+, Road taxes

.9	General works
197	By region or country, A-Z
198	State ownership (General)

For state ownership related to a subject, see the subject
Freight (General)
For freight related to a special form of transportation,
see the form

199.A2A-Z	General works
.A3-Z	By region or country, A-Z

For the freight of a special commodity in a special
place, see HE199.5

Freight (General) - Continued
199.5   Special commodities, A-Z   .B8 *Bulk solids*
       .B7   Bricks
       .C5   Chlorine
       .C6   Coal
       .C63 Coffee

       .D3   Dangerous goods
       .F3   Farm produce
       .F6   Food
       .F8   Fuel
       .G3   Natural gas
       .G7   Grain

       .L45 Liquids
       .L5   Livestock
       .M4   Metal products
       .M5   Milk

       .O7   Ores
       .P4   Petroleum
       .R3   Radioactive substances
       .W5   Wheat

.9   Passenger traffic (General)
      Cf. LB2864, School children
          HQ1063.5, Aged
          HV554, Evacuation of civilians in disasters
          HV3005.5, Mentally handicapped
          HV3022, Physically handicapped
      For passenger traffic by special forms of
         transportation, see the form, e. g. HE2561+,
         Railroads
    By region or country
201   America
    North America
202   General works
    United States
203   General works
    Public policy
204   To 1860
205   1860-1900
206   1900-1967
    1967-
.2   General works
.3   Department of Transportation
207   New England and Middle Atlantic States
208   South
209   Central States
    The West
210   General works
.5   The Southwest
.7   Rocky Mountain States
211   Pacific Coast
212   Outlying territories (General)
213   States, A-W
    Cities, see HE310

By region or country - Continued

215-300   Other regions or countries. Table I 1/
                       Under each country:
                          .A1A-Z General works   ; A15 Period. Societies. Serials.
                          .A3A-Z Ancient
                          .A5A-Z Medieval   . A2A-Z Gen. wks.
                          .A7-Z5 Modern
                          .Z7A-Z Local
                                      For urban transportation, see
                                      HE311.x2
                    Urban transportation
                          Cf. HE331+, Traffic engineering
                              TA1205, Transportation engineering
305   General works
                    By region or country
                       United States
308   General works
309   By region or state, A-Z
310   By city or metropolitan area, A-Z
311   Other regions or countries, A-Z
                          Under each country:
                             .x   General works
                             .x2 Local, A-Z
                    Geography. Trade routes
                          Cf. HF403, Trade routes (Middle Ages)
                              HF1021+, Commercial geography
                              UA985+, Military geography
323   General works
                    Overland transport
325   General works
326   Special routes
                    Ocean routes
327   Steam lanes
                             Cf. VK813, Pilot guides
328   Sailing vessels

                TRAFFIC ENGINEERING. ROADS AND HIGHWAYS. STREETS

                    Cf. HD9717.5.R6, Road construction
                           industry
                        HE5601+, Automotive transportation
                        TE, Highway engineering

331   Periodicals. Societies. Serials
332   Congresses
   .3   Dictionaries. Encyclopedias
   .5   Study and teaching. Research
333   General works
335   General special (Special aspects of the subject
                       as a whole)
336   By subject, A-Z
                       .A32 Access roads to airports
                       .A33 Access roads to ferries

1/
  For Table I, see pp. 331-340. Add country number in table to 200

Traffic engineering. Roads and highways.
  Streets

336   By subject, A-Z - Continued
              Accidents, see HE5614.2+
       .A8 Automatic data processing. Electronic
             data processing
       .B8 Bus lanes

       .C5 Choice of transportation. Modal split
       .C58 Citizen participation in highway planning
       .C67 Country roads
       .E3 Economic aspects
             Electronic data processing, see .A8
       .H5 Highway relocation
             Pedestrian facilities design, see TE279.5
       .P43 Pedestrians. Pedestrian areas
             Safety devices, see TE228
       .S5 Shopping center traffic
       .S7 Statistical methods
       .T64 Toll roads
       .T68 Traffic assignment
             Traffic control devices, see TE228
       .T7 Traffic flow
       .T76 Travel time
       .U74 Use of rights of way and airspace
       .U8 Utilities

     History
341   General works
       Biography
  .8   Collective
342   Individual, A-Z
       Ancient
343   General works
343   Orient
345   Greece
347   Rome
349   Other, A-Z
351   Medieval
       Medieval and modern
353   General works
       By region or country
         Under each country (unless otherwise provided for):

1 no.	Cutter no.	
.A1-3	.x	Periodicals. Serials
.A4-Z54	.x2	General works
.Z55A-Z	.x3	Special topics, A-Z
		For list of topics, see HE336
.Z6A-Z	.x4	By region or province, A-Z
		Including special roads
.Z7A-Z	.x5	By city, A-Z

         United States
355.A3A1-29   Periodicals. Serials
  .A5-Z   General works
  .3   Special topics, A-Z
          For list of topics, see HE336; for special topics
            applicable to special places, see HE356+

Traffic engineering. Roads and highways.
  Streets
  History
    By region or country
      United States - Continued
356   By region or state, A-Z
                Including interstate roads, e. g.
                  .C4, Capital Beltway; .C8, Cumberland
                  Road; .L4, Lee Highway; .L7, Lincoln
                  Highway
                For intrastate roads, see the state, e. g.
                  .N5, Garden State Parkway, New Jersey
  .5   By city, A-Z
357   Canada
          Other American regions or countries
              Including Latin America (General)
358   General works
359   By region or country, A-Z
          Europe
361   General works
363   By region or country, A-Z
365   Asia. By region or country, A-Z
          Africa
366.5   General works
367   By region or country, A-Z
368   Australia
  .2   New Zealand
  .5   Pacific islands, A-Z
            Hawaii, see HE356.H3

  Traffic surveys (General)
        Cf. HE5601+, Automotive transportation
            HV8079.5, HV8130+, Traffic police
369   General works
370   Special topics, A-Z

          .M68 Motorcycles
          .O75 Origin and destination of traffic
                  surveys

          .P44 Pedestrians
          .S35 School safety patrols
          .T74 Travel time

        By region or country
          United States
371.A2A-Z   Periodicals. Societies. Serials
   .A3A-Z   General works
   .A4-Z   By region or state, A-Z
372   By city, A-Z
373   Other regions or countries, A-Z
                Under each country:
                  .x   General works
                  .x2 By region, state, etc., A-Z
                  .x3 By city, A-Z
                  e. g. Soviet Union: .R9, General works;
                  .R92A-Z, Provinces, etc., A-Z; .R93A-Z,
                  Cities

```
                    Traffic engineering.  Roads and highways.
                      Streets - Continued
                    Bridges
                        Cf. TG, Bridge engineering
     374                General works
                        By region or country
                          United States
     375                    General works
     376.A2A-Z               By region or state, A-Z
        .A4-Z                Special places and special bridges, A-Z
     377                  Other regions or countries, A-Z
                              .x   General works
                              .x2  Local, A-Z
                    Vehicular tunnels
                        Cf. TA800+, Engineering
     379                General works
     380                By region or country, A-Z
                          Under each country:
                            .x   General works
                            .x2  By region or state, A-Z
                            .x3  Special tunnels.  By place, A-Z
```

WATER TRANSPORTATION

```
                  Waterways
                      Class here the economic aspects of waterways.  For
                        engineering and construction, see TC; for commerce
                        see HF; for hydrography, see GB651+
     380.8            Periodicals.  Societies.  Serials
     381              General works
     383              Waterways in relation to other forms of transportation
                        For railroads and waterways, see HE1049
                      Control, taxation, tolls, etc.
     384                General works
                        International waterways
                            Cf. JX4122+, Waterways as natural boundaries
     385                  General works
     386                  Harbors, straits, etc., A-Z
                            For harbors, straits, etc. of an individual
                              country, see HE389, subdivision (3)
                            e. g.  .S7 Sound duties (The Sound, Öresund)
                          Rivers
                            General works, see JX4150
     387                    Special, A-Z
                              e. g.  .D2  Danube
     388                Inland
     389                By region or country, A-Z
                          Under each country:
                            .x   General works
                            .x2  Inland
                            .x3  Ports
                            .x4  Special waterways, rivers whose course
                                   is entirely within the limits of one
                                   country, A-Z
```

```
                    Water transportation
                      Waterways - Continued
                        By region or country
                          United States
    392.8                   Periodicals.  Societies.  Serials
                            Collected works (nonserial)
    393.A3A-Z                 Several authors
       .A32A-Z                Individual authors
       .A4                  Congresses
       .A5-Z                General works
       .5                   By region or state, A-Z
    394                     River improvement.  By name of river, A-Z
                              Under each:
                                .x   Periodicals.  Serials
                                .x3  General works
                                .x4  General special
                            Canals
    395.A1A-Z                 Periodicals.  Serials
       .A3A-Z                 General works
       .A4-Z                  By region or state, A-Z
                                Under each state:
                                  .x   Periodicals.  Serials
                                  .x3  Guides, tables, etc.
                                  .x4  General works
    396                     Special canals.  By name, A-Z
    398                     Great Lakes
    399-401             Canada
    401.5               Latin America
    402                   Mexico
    403-520.9           Other regions or countries.  Table V 1/
```

	4 nos.	1 no.	
	(1).A1	.A1	Periodicals. Societies
	.A5-Z	.A4-Z3	General works
	(2)	.Z4A-Z	Regions or states, A-Z
	(3)	.Z5A-Z	Rivers or canals, A-Z
	(4)	.Z7A-Z	Companies, A-Z

```
                    By type of waterway
                      The oceans, see HE327+
    524               Arms of the sea.  Bays, straits, channels
                        Class here general works only; for the
                          special waterways of particular countries,
                          see HE391+
                        Cf. HE385+, Control, taxation, tolls, etc.
    525               Rivers and lakes
                        Class here general works only; for the special
                          rivers and lakes of particular countries,
                          see HE391+
    526               Inland canals
                        Cf. TC601+, Inland navigation (Hydraulic
                          engineering)
                        Class here general works only; for the special
                          canals of particular countries, see HE391+
```

1/
  For Table V, see pp. 331-340. Add country number in table to 390

```
                    Water transportation
                      Waterways
                        By type of waterway - Continued
                          Interoceanic canals
                              Including traffic statistics
                              For engineering materials, see TC770+
        528             Periodicals.  Societies.  Serials
                        General works
        530.A2A-Z         Through 1800
           .A5-Z          1801-1843
        531                1844-
        532             Darien
        534             Tehuantepec Canal
        535             Tehuantepec Ship Railway
                            Cf. HE2819.T3, Tehuantepec Railway
        536             Nicaragua Canal
                        Panama Canal
                            Cf. TC774+, Construction and operation of
                                the Panama Canal
        537             General works
           .1           History through 1876
                        Compagnie universelle
           .3             General works
                          Annual reports.  Directories
           .33              General
           .35              Other
           .36            Special (chronologically)
           .37            Charter.  Bylaws, etc.
           .39            Other
           .4-.49       Compagnie nouvelle
                            Subarranged like HE537.3-.39
           .5           History, 1876-1903
                        United States, 1903-1978
           .6             Periodicals.  Serials
           .8             General works
           .9             Special, A-Z

                          .E3  Economic conditions
                          .L3  Land titles
                               Toll question, see HE538.R3
           .95          Panama, 1978-
                        Administration
        538.A1-5          Periodicals.  Serials
           .A6A-Z          General works
           .A7-Z           Special topics, A-Z

                          .A8  Accounting
                          .M5  Measurement of vessels
                          .P5  Pensions
                          .R3  Rates and tolls

                          .S8  Supplies

        539             Other American projects, A-Z
        543             Suez Canal
        545             Other, A-Z
```

Water transportation
Waterways
By type of waterway – Continued
Ports. Harbors, docks, wharves, etc.
Cf. HE951+, Port guides, regulations,
charges, etc.
TC353+, Harbor engineering
VK321+, Navigation

550	Periodicals. Societies. Serials
551	General works
552	List of harbors, gazetteers, etc.

North America. United States. Canada

553	General works
554	By place, A–Z

.A3   Atlantic ports
.A4   Gulf ports
.A6   Pacific ports
.A7   River ports
.A8–Z   Individual ports, A–Z

Latin America
Including the West Indies

555.A3A–Z	General works
.A4–Z	By country, A–Z
556	By place, A–Z

Europe

557.A3A–Z	General works
.A4–Z	By country, A–Z
558	By place, A–Z
559	Other countries, A–Z
.5	Underdeveloped countries
560	Individual ports (Africa, Asia, Australia, Oceania), A–Z

e. g. .M3 Manila
.R4 Rangoon

Shipping
Cf. HF, Commerce
VK, Navigation. Merchant marine

561	Periodicals. Societies. Serials
.5	Intergovernmental Maritime Consultative Organization
562	Congresses

Navigation statistics
Cf. HE617.5, Interior navigation

.8	General works
563	By region or country, A–Z

Association of ship owners

564.A1A–Z	General works
.A2–Z	International

United States

.A3A–Z	National associations
.A4A–Z	Local associations. By city, A–Z

e. g. .A4N5 New York. Ship Owners'
Association of the State
of New York

Canada and British America

.B3A–Z	National associations
.B4A–Z	Local associations. By city, A–Z

```
                      Water transportation
                        Shipping
                          Associations of ship owners - Continued
                            Other regions or countries
                                Under each country:
                                  .x   By country, A-Z
                                  .x2  Local associations.  By city, A-Z
                                e. g. .E3G6-79, Great Britain; .E4L4-59,
                                  Liverpool
     564.C3-4                   Latin America.  South America
        .E3-4                   Europe
        .F3-4                   Asia
        .H3-4                   Africa
        .K3-4                   Australasia and Pacific islands
                          Lists of vessels.  Tonnage, etc.  Lloyd's register
                            Cf. HE968, Marine insurance
                            For lists of naval vessels of individual
                              countries, see the country in VA; for
                              lists of vessels by class of vessel,
                              see HE566; for lists of vessels owned by
                              a specific company, see HE943
     565.A3                   General works
        .A5-Z                 By country
                                e. g.             United States
                                      .U5A1-4     Periodicals.  Serials
                                      .U5A5-Z9    General works
                                      .U7         Atlantic
                                      .U71        Lakes and inland (General)
                                      .U73        Gulf
                                      .U75        Pacific
     566                     Special classes of vessels, A-Z
                               Including lists of vessels

                               .C6   Container ships
                               .E9   Excursion boats
                               .F7   Freighters
                               .M3   Mail steamers

                               .O25  Ocean liners
                               .O7   Ore carriers
                               .P3   Paddle steamers
                               .S3   Sailing ships
                               .T3   Tank vessels
                               .T7   Tramp steamers
                               .T8   Tugboats
                               .W6   Work boats

     567                     Dictionaries.  Encyclopedias
     568                     Guides, timetables, etc. (General)
                             Biography
        .9                     Collective
     569                       Individual, A-Z
     570                     Study and teaching.  Research
                               For training of shipping crews, see VK401+
     571                     General works
     573                     Handbooks, manuals, etc.
     581                     Public policy (General)
     582                     Maritime economics
```

Water transportation
Shipping - Continued
Taxation
Cf. HE951+, Port guides
587.5   Periodicals. Societies. Serials
.6   Early works to 1800
.7   General works
588   Special topics, A-Z

.T6   Tonnage fees
Registration. Inspection
Cf. HJ6605+, Customs administration
Including guides, rules, etc.
.7   General works
589   By region or country, A-Z
592   Accidents (Statistics, etc.)
Traffic
Class here theory and general works; for
statistics, see HE563
Freight
593   General works
594   Rates
For special countries, see HE597
For special commodities, see HE595
595   Special commodities, A-Z
.A8   Automobiles
.C45 Chemicals
.C6   Coal
.D3   Dangerous goods
.E8   Explosives
.F3   Farm products
.F6   Food
.F7   Fruit
.G8   Grain

.I7   Iron ores
.L5   Livestock
.L8   Lumber

.P4   Petroleum
.P48 Phosphate rock
.R25 Radioactive substances
.R3   Raw materials
.S8   Sugar
.W54 Wheat

596   Charters
Containerization, see TA1215
Bills of lading, see HE606
597   By region or country, A-Z
.B3   Baltic sea
Passenger
599   General works
601   By region or country, A-Z
Under each country:
.x   General works
.x2 Special
.x3 By company, A-Z

		Water transportation

Water transportation
   <u>Shipping</u> - Continued
     Finance

603	General works
604	General special
605	Accounting
606	Bills of lading

     Ship brokers

610.A3A-Z	General works
.A4-Z	By region or country, A-Z
613	Transportation agencies

       Cf. HE945, Navigation companies

     Interior navigation

617	General works
.5	Statistics
619	International rivers, A-Z

       Cf. HE387, International control, tolls, etc.
      .D2   Danube River
     By region or country
      United States

623	Periodicals. Serials
627	General works
629	General special
630	By river, etc., A-Z
631	By region or state, A-Z
633	By company, A-Z

        Under each company:
          .x   Charter, etc.
          .x2 Regular reports
          .x3 Special reports
          .x4 Registers
          .x5 Other

635-720	Other regions or countries. Table I 1/

       Under each country:
     <u>1 no.</u>

.A1-3	Periodicals. Serials
.A5-Z6	General works
.Z7	Local. By region, place, river, etc., A-Z
.Z9	By company, A-Z

<u>Merchant marine</u>
   Cf. VK, Naval science

730	Periodicals. Societies. Serials

   Collected works (nonserial)

731	Several authors
.5	Individual authors
735	General works
736	General special

   Handbooks, manuals, etc.

737	General
738	Tonnage, etc., tables

     Including measurement of packages, etc.
     Cf. HE588.T6, Tonnage tables
       VM153, Naval science

1/
  For Table I, <u>see</u> pp. 331-340. Add country number in table to 620

```
                    Water transportation
                      Shipping
                        Merchant marine - Continued
                          Subsidies
      740                   Periodicals.  Serials
      741                   General works
      743                   By region or country, A-Z
                              Under each country:
                                .x   General works
                                .x2  By company, A-Z
                                        Subarranged by date
                          By region or country
                            United States
      745                     General works
      751                     Coastwise shipping.  Intercoastal shipping
      752                     By region or state, A-Z
      753                     By company, A-Z
                                Under each:
                                  .x   Charters, etc.
                                  .x2  Regular reports
                                  .x4  Registers
                                  .x5  Other
      767                     Individual ports, A-Z
   769-937                    Other regions or countries.  Table II 1/
                                Under each country:


                            2 nos.      1 no.


                              (1)       .A1-Z5      General works
                              (2)       .Z5         Special


      942                   Communist countries
      943                   Underdeveloped countries
                          Navigation companies.  Ocean steamship companies
                              Cf. HE633, American companies (Interior
                                    navigation)
                                  HE753, American companies (Merchant marine)
   945.A2                   General works
      .A3-Z                 By company, A-Z
                          Port guides, charges, etc.
                              Cf. HE384+, Taxation tolls
                                  HE551+, Ports, harbors
                                  TC203+, Engineering works
                                  VK361+, Docking facilities
      951                   General works
      952                   By region or country, A-Z
      953                   Individual ports, A-Z
                          Marine insurance
                              For inland marine insurance, see HG9903
      961                   Periodicals.  Societies.  Serials
                          History
      964                     General works
        .5                    By region or country, A-Z
                                Class here works of purely local interest
      965                   General works
      966                   War risks
```

```
                    Water transportation
                      Shipping
                        Marine insurance - Continued
967                       General special
968                       Lists of vessels.  Classification.  Rating.
                            By region or country, A-Z
                              Cf. HE565, Shipping
                              e. g.            United States
                                    .U5          General works
                                    .U6          Atlantic
                                    .U63         Gulf
                                    .U65         Pacific
                                    .U7          Inland waters, lakes, etc.
969                       Companies, registers, etc., A-Z
970                       Average
                            i. e. damage to goods in shipping
971                       Salvage
                              Cf. JX4436, International law
                                  VK1491, Naval science



                           RAILWAYS

1001            Periodicals.  Serials
1003            Societies
1005            Congresses
1007            Museums.  Exhibitions
1009            Directories
                Collected works (nonserial)
1011              Several authors
1013              Individual authors
                Dictionaries and encyclopedias, see TF9
1021            History
1031            General works
1035            General special
                Relation to other subjects
1041              Railways and civilization
                  Railways and farming interests
1042.8              General works
                    By region or country
1043                  United States
    .5                Other regions or countries, A-Z
                  Railways and industries
1044                General works
1045                Railways and coal interests
1049              Railways and other carriers
                      Including waterways, airplanes, and automobiles
1050              Railways and foreign trade
                Public policy (General).  Government control
                    For United States, see HE2757; for other countries,
                      see HE2801+, subdivision (7) or (3) Public policy,
                      under each country
1051            General works
                  State aid
1059.8            General works
1061              United States
1062              The Pacific railroads
```

Railways
    Public policy (General). Government control
       State aid - Continued
         Land grants
           United States

1063.A6	By name of railroad, A-Z
.A7-Z	General works
1064	By region or state, A-Z

        Use in war, <u>see</u> UC310+

1067	Postal service

           Cf. HE6175, Railway mail service
                HE6475, Parcel post
        Taxation, valuation, depreciation, etc.
           For individual railroads, <u>see</u> HE2791

1070.8	General works

         By region or country
           United States

1071	General works
1075	By region or state, A-Z
1076	Other regions or countries, A-Z
1081	Government ownership

           For particular countries, <u>see</u>
                HE2758; HE2651+

    Railway administration
       For administration and operation of the
         physical plant, <u>see</u> TF501+

1601	General works

       Projection. Promotion

1611	General works

       Location, right of way, tracks, terminals
         Cf. TF190, Technical aspects of location
        United States

1613.A15A-Z	General works
.A2A-W	States, A-W
.A4-Z	Cities, A-Z
1614	
	Other regions or countries, A-Z
1616	Special projects

       Grade crossings

1617	General works

       United States

1618.A2A-Z	General works
.A3A-W	States, A-W
.A4-Z	Cities, A-Z

       Management, personnel, etc.
        Management of railway companies

1621	General works

         Regulations (Service), <u>see</u> TF520+
         Office organization, <u>see</u> TF510+

1739	Publicity departments. Railways and the public

Railways
  Railway administration
    Management, personnel, etc. - Continued
    Personnel management
      Cf. HD6350.R1+, Trade unions and workingmen's
        associations
      HD8039.R1+, Economic history

1741	General works
	Wages, see HD4966.R1+
	Hours, see HD5119.R1
	Pensions, see HD7105+; HD7116.R118+
	Training, education, see TF518
1759	Employees and the public
	Including courtesy, etc.
	Safety measures, see TF610
1771	Inspection. Police
	Trespassing, etc.
1775	General works
1776	By region or country, A-Z

    Accidents

1779	General works
	By region or country
	United States
1780	General works
.5	By state, A-W
1781	By city, A-Z
1783	Other regions or countries, A-Z
	Under each country:
	.A1-5 Official reports
	.A6-Z Nonofficial works
	Liability for injuries to passengers, freight,
	etc., see K
1795	Claim departments

    Trains and station service
      Cf. TF550+, Railway operation and management

1801	General works
	Schedules, see TF565
1811	Conductors
1813	Station agents
	Dispatching, see TF563

    Traffic
      Cf. HE2301+, Freight, baggage, etc.

1821	General works
1825	General special
1826	Demurrage
1827	Private car lines
1828	Sale or lease of rolling stock and equipment
1829	Pooling
	Car service
	Interchange and accounting, see TF605+
	Supply of cars
1830	General works
	Freight cars, see HE2331+
	Passenger cars, see HE2573+

```
                    Railways
                      Railway administration
                        Traffic - Continued
                          Rates.  Tariff
                            Cf. HE2301+, Freight
        1831                General works
        1836                General special
   1841-1940                By region or country.  Table I 1/
                          Passenger tariff
                              Including schedules
        1951                General works
        1953                Adjustable.  Sliding
        1957                Zone system
                            Reduced rates, commutation rates, etc.
        1959                  General works
        1960                  Rates for special classes of passengers, A-Z
                                .B5   Blind
                                .C5   Civil Service employees

                                .T6   Tourists
                                .W7   Workingmen
        1961                Passes
        1965                Transportation in exchange for advertising
        1971                Ticket brokerage
        1976                Tickets
   2001-2100                By region or country.  Table I 1/
                          Freight tariff
                              Including schedules
        2101                General works
                            Calculators, see TF664+
                            Premium tables, see TF664+
        2116                Rates on particular articles, A-Z
                              For rates on articles in a particular
                                country, see HE2121+
   2121-2220                By region or country.  Table I 1/

                          Finance
        2231                General works
        2236                General special
        2241                Accounting
        2242                Bills of lading
        2243                Collecting
        2245                Disbursements
        2246                Auditing
        2251                Receiverships and reorganization
        2261                Clearinghouse
                          Statistics
        2271                Theory.  Method
        2273                General works
                            By region or country, see HE2713, HE2751,
                              and HE2801+, subdivisions (1) and (8)
                              under each country
```

1/
    For Table I, see pp. 341-340. Add country number in table to 1840, 2000, or
2120, as the case requires

Railways
  <u>Railway administration</u>
    <u>Traffic</u> – Continued
      <u>Freight</u>

2301	General works
2311	General special
2315	Weighing of freight
	Refrigerator service, <u>see</u> TF667
2321	Special commodities, products, etc., A–Z

        .A48   Aggregates
        .A5   Agricultural machinery
        .A6   Alcohol
        .A8   Automobiles

        .B35   Berries
        .B4   Beverages
        .B7   Brick
        .C25   Canned food
        .C35   Cement
        .C45   Chemicals
        .C5   Citrus fruits
        .C6   Coal
               Corn, <u>see</u> .M3
        .C7   Corpses
        .C75   Cotton

        .D25   Dairy products
        .D3   Dangerous goods
        .E5   Eggs
        .E8   Explosives
        .F3   Farm produce
        .F4   Fertilizers
        .F7   Fruit
        .F8   Fuel
        .G4   Glass
        .G7   Grain

        .I5   Insecticides
        .I7   Iron
        .L4   Leather
        .L5   Lime
        .L7   Livestock
        .L8   Lumber

        .M3   Maize
        .M4   Meat
        .M45   Metals
        .M6   Mineral products
        .N3   Naval stores
        .P3   Paper
        .P4   Petroleum
        .P5   Plaster
        .P6   Potatoes

        .R44   Refuse
        .R5   Rice
        .R8   Rubber
        .S3   Salt
        .S6   Soap

Railways
   Railway administration
     Traffic
       Freight

2321		Special commodities, products, etc., A-Z - Cont.
	.S7	Steel
	.S75	Stone
	.S8	Sugar
	.S9	Syrups
	.T4	Textiles
	.T6	Tobacco
	.V4	Vegetables
	.W5	Wheat
	.W6	Wood products
	.W65	Wool

Car service
      Cf. HE2573+, Passenger car
          TF605+, Car interchange

2330	General works
2331	Supply of cars
	Car shortage
2332	General works
	By region or country
	United States
2333.A1-29	Periodicals. Serials
.A4-Z	General works
2334	Other regions or countries, A-Z
	Delays in transit
2341	General works
	By region or country
2342.A1-5	International delays
.A6-Z	By region or country, A-Z
2345	Tracers
2351-2547	By region or country. Table II 1/

Under each country:

2 nos.	1 no.	
(1)	.A3A-Z	General works
(2)	.A5-Z	Local, A-Z

2556	Baggage, parcel and mail traffic
	Cf. HE1067, Railway postal service
	HE6175, Railway mail service

Passengers
2561	General works
	Car service
2573	Supply of cars
2575	Car shortage
	By region or country
2583	United States
2591	Other regions or countries, A-Z

1/ For Table II, see pp. 331-340. Add country number in table to 2350

Railways – Continued
By region or country
Class here works on individual companies and
companies of particular places. Works limited
to the discussion of the physical plant of
railways, including the history, operation,
etc., of individual lines, see TF21+
America
2701   General works
United States
Official documents
2704   Periodicals. Serials
2705   Special documents. By date
For reports of ICC and other commissions,
see HE2708
Under each year:
House of Representatives
Committee on Interstate Commerce
Hearings, see KF27.I55
Reports, see KF32.I55
.B1+   Other documents
Senate
Committee on Interstate Commerce
Hearings, see KF26.I55
Reports, see KF31.I55
.D1+   Other reports
.E+   Other (departmental) documents
.F+   Presidential messages
National Convention of Railway Commissioners,
see HE2715
Commerce Court, 1910–1913, see KF2184
2708   Permanent government commissions, A–Z
e. g.   .C7+ Commissioner of Railroads
.I4+ Interstate Commerce Commission
.R3+ U.S. Railroad Administration
State commissions. State railway departments,
see HE2771
2713   Statistics
Class here works which are mainly serial
tabular; for descriptive and historical
works, see HE2751
2714   Periodicals. Serials
2715   Societies
2717   Congresses
2721   Directories of railroads
Cf. HE1009, Annuals, directories, etc.
2723   Directories of officials
2725   Directories of stations
Guides for travelers, time tables
2727   General works
2728   By railroad, A–Z
2729   By city, A–Z
Guides for shippers
2731   General works
2733   By railroad, A–Z
2735   By city, A–Z
2737   Special kinds of freight
Including lumber, etc.
2741   General works

145

<pre>
                    Railways
                      By region or country
                        America
                          United States - Continued
      2751   History. Statistics, etc.
                                  Class here historical and descriptive works
                                  For serial tabular works, see HE2713
                              Biography
                                  Cf. HE2723, Directories of officials
      2752   Collective
      2754   Individual, A-Z
      2757   Public policy. Railways and the state
                                  For state aid, see HE1061+
                              By region
      2761   Atlantic to Mississippi. By date
      2763   Mississippi to Pacific. By date
      2765   To Canada. By date
      2767   To Mexico. By name of railroad
      2771.A1-199   Other regions 1/
          .A2-Z   By state, A-W
      2781   By city, A-Z
      2791   By railroad company, A-Z
                                  Under each:
                                      .x1-29 Periodicals. Serials
                                      .x3A-Z General works
                        Other regions or countries
                          Under each country:
</pre>

10 nos.	5 nos.	1 no.	Cutter no.	
(1)	(1)	.A1-5	.xA-Z	Periodicals. Societies Serials
(4)	(2)			Directories. Guides. Tables
(5)	(3)	.A5-Z6	.x2A-Z	General works
(6)				Administration
(7)				Public policy
				History. Statistics. Description Including preliminary surveys
(8)				General works
				Biography
(8.1)				Collective
(8.2)				Individual, A-Z
(9)	(4)	.Z7A-Z	.x3A-Z	Local, A-Z
(10)	(5)	.Z8A-Z	.x4A-Z	Special railroad companies, A-Z

<pre>
2801-2810   Canada
   2810.5   Latin America
2811-2820   Mexico
2821-2825   Central America
   2824.B7   Belize
2826-2830   Panama
2831-2835   Costa Rica
</pre>

1/
 For Table of Regions of the United States, see p. 343

Railways
  By region or country
    Other regions or countries
      Latin America
        Central America - Continued

2836-2840	Guatemala
2841-2845	Honduras
2846-2850	Nicaragua
2851-2855	El Salvador
2856-2860	West Indies
2861-2865	Bahamas. Lucayos
2866-2870	Cuba
2871-2875	Haiti
2876-2880	Jamaica
2881-2885	Puerto Rico
2889	Other, A-Z
2891-2900	South America
2901-2910	Argentina
2911-2920	Bolivia
2921-2930	Brazil
2931-2940	Chile
2941-2950	Colombia
2951-2960	Ecuador
2961	Guianas
2962	Guyana. British Guiana
2963	Surinam. Dutch Guiana
2964	French Guiana
2965	Special companies, A-Z
2966-2970	Paraguay
2971-2980	Peru
2981-2990	Uruguay
2991-3000	Venezuela
3001-3010	Europe
3011-3020	Great Britain
	Including works on the British Empire, "Greater Britain," etc.
	England, see HE3011+
3031-3040	Scotland
3041-3050	Ireland
3051-3059.2	Austria
3059.2	Special railroads or companies, A-Z
.3	Czechoslovakia
.5	Hungary
3060.5	Poland
3061-3070	France
3071-3080	Germany
	Including West Germany
3080.5	East Germany
3081-3090	Greece
3091-3100	Italy
3100.5	Benelux countries. Low countries
3111-3120	Belgium
3121-3130	Netherlands
3130.5	Luxemburg
3131-3140	Soviet Union
	Including the Soviet Union in Asia
3141-3150	Scandinavia
3151-3160	Denmark
3161-3170	Iceland
3171-3180	Norway
3181-3190	Sweden

Railways
  By region or country
    Other regions or countries
      Europe - Continued

3190.5	Finland
3191-3200	Spain
3201-3210	Portugal
3211-3220	Switzerland
3221-3230	Balkan States
3231-3240	Bulgaria
3241-3245	Yugoslavia
3251-3260	Romania
	Turkey, see HE3371+
3271-3280	Asia
	For the Soviet Union in Asia, see HE3131+
3281-3290	China
3290.5	Taiwan
3291-3300	India
3300.3	Sri Lanka
.5	Pakistan
.6	Bangladesh
3301-3310	Southeast Asia. Indochina
3320.2	Cambodia
.3	Vietnam
.4	Laos
3321-3330	Malaysia
3331-3340	Indonesia
3341-3350	Philippine Islands
3351-3360	Japan
3360.5	Korea
3361-3370	Iran
3371-3380	Turkey
3380.5	Other divisions of Asia, A-Z
3390	Other special companies, A-Z
3391-3400	Africa
	North Africa
3400.5	General works
3401-3410	Egypt. United Arab Republic
3411	Morocco
3412	Algeria
3413	Tunisia
3414	Libya
3415	Sudan
	Northeast Africa
.5	General works
3416	Ethiopia
3417	Somalia
	Including British and Italian Somaliland
3418	French Territory of the Afars and Issas
	Southeast Africa
.5	General works
3419	Kenya
3420	Uganda
3421	Rwanda
3422	Burundi
3423	Tanzania
3424	Mozambique
3425	Madagascar

```
                    Railways
                      By region or country
                        Other regions or countries
                          Africa - Continued
                            Southern Africa
3425.5                        General works
3426                          South Africa
3427                          Rhodesia
                                  Including Southern Rhodesia
3428                          Zambia
3429                          Lesotho.  Basutoland
3430                          Swaziland
3431                          Botswana.  Bechuanaland
3432                          Malawi.  Nyasaland
    .3                        Namibia
                            Central Africa.  Equatorial Africa
    .5                        General works
3433                          Angola
3434                          Zaire
3435                          Equatorial Guinea
3436                          Sao Tome e Principe
3437                          French Equatorial Africa.  French Congo
3438                          Gabon
3439                          Congo (Brazzaville).  Middle Congo
3440                          Central African Republic.  Ubangi-Shari
3441                          Chad
3442                          Cameroon
                            West Africa.  West Coast
    .5                        General works
3443                          French-speaking West Africa
3444                          Benin.  Dahomey
3445                          Togo
3446                          Niger
3447                          Ivory Coast
3448                          Guinea
3449                          Mali
3450                          Upper Volta
3451                          Senegal
3452                          Mauritania
3453                          Nigeria
3454                          Ghana
3455                          Sierra Leone
3456                          Gambia
3457                          Liberia
3458                          Guinea-Bissau.  Portuguese Guinea
    .2                        Spanish Sahara
3460                        Other special railroads, A-Z

3461-3470               Australia
3471-3480                 New South Wales
3491-3500                 North Australia
3501-3510                 Queensland
3511-3520                 South Australia
3521-3530                 Tasmania
3531-3540                 Victoria
3541-3550                 Western Australia
    3550.5             New Zealand
3351-3560             Pacific islands
```

Railways - Continued
    Local and light railways. Narrow gauge,
      industrial, etc. railways
        Including urban and interurban railways
          treated in combination with light railways

3601	Periodicals. Societies. Serials
	Collected works (nonserial)
3603	Several authors
3604	Individual authors
3611	General works
3621	General special
3651-4043	By region or country. Table IV 1/
	Under each country:

3 nos.	2 nos.	1 no.	
(1)	(1)	.A1-4	Periodicals. Serials
(2)	(2)	.A5-Z8	General works
(3)	(2.5)	.Z9A-Z	Particular companies, A-Z

Mountain railways
    Cf. TF680, Technology

4051	General works
4071	By region or country, A-Z
	Under each country:
	.x General works
	.x2 Special companies, A-Z

Street railways. Subways. Rapid transit systems
    Including city and suburban traffic
    Cf. HE310+, Interurban electric railways
        TF701+, TF920+, Engineering

4201	Periodicals. Societies. Serials
4202	Congresses
	Collected works (nonserial)
4207	Several authors
4208	Individual authors
4211	General works
	Public policy (General)
	For the policy of individual countries, see
	the country, e. g. HE4461, United States
4221	General works
4231	Franchises
	Cf. HE4491, Charters, etc.
4241	Municipalization
4251	Taxation
4261	Government use. Transportation of mails, etc.
	For postal service, see HE6159
4291	Freight service
	Administration
4301	General works
4311	Personnel. Management
4321	Car service

1/
  For Table IV, see pp. 341-340. Add country number in table to 3650

Railways
    Street railways. Subways. Rapid transit
        systems
        Administration - Continued
           Fares

4341	General works
4345	Special, A-Z
	.S3 School children
	.W7 Workmen
4347	Transfers
4351	Finance. Accounting. Auditing
	Cf. HG4771, Industrial securities
	HG4991+, Street railroad securities
4371	Forms, time-tables, etc.
4381	Accidents
4391	Claim departments

        By region or country
           Class here works on individual companies and
              companies of particular places. Works limited
              to the discussion of the physical plant of
              particular places and systems, including
              history, operation, etc., see TF721+
           United States

4401	Periodicals. Serials
	Directories
4421	General works
4426	States, regions, etc., A-Z
	For cities, see HE4491, subdivision (3)
	Collected works (nonserial)
4441	Several authors
4442	Individual authors
4451	General works
4456	Administration
4461	Public policy
	Including taxation and valuation
4471	History
4487	By region or state, A-Z
4491	By city, A-Z

              For suburbs and metropolitan areas of
                individual cities, see the city
              Under each city:
                .x1-19 Periodicals. Societies. Serials
                .x2A-Z General works
                .x3A-Z Particular companies, A-Z

Railways
    <u>Street railways. Subways. Rapid transit systems</u>
       By region or country - Continued
        Other regions or countries
          Under each country:

10 nos.	5 nos.	1 no.	Cutter no.	
(1)	(1)	.A1-5	.xA-Z	Periodicals. Societies. Serials
(3)	(2)			Directories. Guides. Tables
(4)	(3)	.A5-Z6	.x2A-Z	General works
(5)				Public policty
(7)				History
(8)	(4)	.Z7A-Z	.x3A-Z	By state, A-Z
(9)	(5)	.Z8A-Z	.x4A-Z	By city, A-Z

4501-4510	Canada
4510.5	Latin America
4511-4520	Mexico
4521-4525	Central America
4524.B7	Belize
4526-4530	Panama
4531-4535	Costa Rica
4536-4540	Guatemala
4541-4545	Honduras
4546-4550	Nicaragua
4551-4555	El Salvador
4556-4560	West Indies
4561-4565	Bahamas. Lucayos
4566-4570	Cuba
4571-4575	Haiti
4576-4580	Jamaica
4581-4585	Puerto Rico
4589	Other, A-Z
4591-4600	South America
4601-4610	Argentina
4611-4620	Bolivia
4621-4630	Brazil
4631-4640	Chile
4641-4650	Columbia
4651-4660	Ecuador
	Guianas
4661	General works
4662	Guyana. British Guiana
4663	Surinam. Dutch Guiana
4664	French Guiana
4666-4670	Paraguay
4671-4680	Peru
4681-4690	Uruguay
4691-4700	Venezuela
4701-4710	Europe
4711-4720	Great Britain
	Including works on the British Empire
	England, <u>see</u> HE4711+
4731-4740	Scotland
4741-4750	Ireland
4751-4759.2	Austria
4759.2	Special railroads or companies, A-Z

Railways
   <u>Street railways. Subways. Rapid transit systems</u>
      By region or country
        Other regions or countries
          Europe – Continued

4759.3	Czechoslovakia
.5	Hungary
4760.5	Poland
4761–4770	France
4771–4780	Germany
	Including West Germany
4780.5	East Germany
4781–4790	Greece
4791–4800	Italy
4800.5	Benelux countries. Low countries
4811–4820	Belgium
4821–4830	Netherlands
4830.5	Luxemburg
4831–4840	Soviet Union
	Including the Soviet Union in Asia
4841–4850	Scandinavia
4851–4866	Denmark
4861–4870	Iceland
4871–4880	Norway
4881–4890	Sweden
4890.5	Finland
4891–4900	Spain
4901–4910	Portugal
4911–4920	Switzerland
4921–4930	Balkan States
4931–4940	Bulgaria
4941–4945	Yugoslavia
4951–4960	Romania
	Turkey, <u>see</u> HE5071+
4971–4980	Asia
4981–4990	China
4990.5	Taiwan
4991–5000	India
5000.3	Sri Lanka
.5	Pakistan
.6	Bangladesh
5001–5010	Southeast Asia. Indochina
5020.2	Cambodia
.3	Vietnam
.4	Laos
5021–5030	Malaysia
5031–5040	Indonesia
5041–5050	Philippines
5051–5060	Japan
5060.5	Korea
5061–5070	Iran
5071–5080	Turkey
5080.5	Other divisions of Asia, A–Z
5091–5100	Africa
	North Africa
5100.5	General works
5101–5110	Egypt
5111	Morocco
5112	Algeria
5113	Tunisia

Railways
    Street railways.   Subways.   Rapid transit systems
      By region or country
        Other regions or countries
          Africa
            North Africa - Continued

5114	Libya
5115	Sudan
.5	Northeast Africa
5116	Ethiopia
5117	Somalia
	Including British and Italian Somaliland
5118	French Territory of the Afars and Issas
.5	Southeast Africa
5119	Kenya
5120	Uganda
5121	Rwanda
5122	Burundi
5123	Tanzania
5124	Mozambique
5125	Madagascar
.5	Southern Africa
5126	South Africa
5127	Rhodesia
	Including Southern Rhodesia
5128	Zambia
5129	Lesotho. Basutoland
5130	Swaziland
5131	Botswana. Bechuanaland
5132	Malawi. Nyasaland
.5	Namibia
.7	Central Africa. Equatorial Africa
5133	Angola
5134	Zaire
5135	Equatorial Guinea
5136	Sao Tome e Principe
5137	French Equatorial Africa. French Congo
5138	Gabon
5139	Congo (Brazzaville). Middle Congo
5140	Central African Republic. Ubangi-Shari
5141	Chad
5142	Cameroon
.5	West Africa. West Coast
5143	French-speaking West Africa
5144	Benin. Dahomey
5145	Togo
5146	Niger
5147	Ivory Coast
5148	Guinea
5149	Mali
5150	Upper Volta
5151	Senegal
5152	Mauritania
5153	Nigeria
5154	Ghana
5155	Sierra Leone
5156	Gambia
5157	Liberia
5158	Guinea-Bissau. Portuguese Guinea
.3	Spanish Sahara

Railways
    Street railways. Subways. Rapid transit systems
        By region or country
          Other regions or countries - Continued

5161-5170	Australia
5171-5180	New South Wales
5181-5190	North Australia
5201-5210	Queensland
5211-5220	South Australia
5221-5230	Tasmania
5231-5240	Victoria
5241-5250	Western Australia
5250.5	New Zealand
5251-5260	Pacific islands

Interurban, electric, and other railways
    For rapid transit within cities and immediate
      suburbs, see HE4201+

5351	General works
5361	General special
5401-5600	By region or country. Table II 1/

      For United States, see Table II, nos. 5-27
      Under other countries:

2 nos.	1 no.	
(1)	.A3A-Z	General works
(2)	.A5-Z	Local, A-Z

AUTOMOTIVE TRANSPORTATION

Including trucking, motor-bus lines, and
  taxicab service
Cf. HD9710+, Automobile industry
    HE369+, Traffic surveys
    GV1021+, Motoring
    TL1+, Motor vehicles

5601	Periodicals. Societies. Serials
5606	Congresses
5611	General works
5613	General special
	Traffic accidents

      Cf. HV8079.55, Traffic accident investigation
        RA772.T7, Public health
        RC1040+, Automotive medicine

5614	General works
	By region or country
	United States
.2	General works
.3	By region or state, A-Z
.4	By city, A-Z
.5	Other regions or countries, A-Z

1/
  For Table II, see pp. 331-340. Add country number in table to 5400

```
                      Automotive transportation - Continued
                        Traffic signs and signals, see TE228
          5616          Truck trailers
                            Cf. GV198.5+, Trailer camping
                                TF582, Piggyback trains


            .5         Motorcycles
          5617         Tariffs.  Rates
                            For local, see HE5621+
          5618         Finance, accounting, etc.
          5620         Special, A-Z


                       .C3   Car pools
                       .D4   Deaf drivers
                             Drivers and driving, see TL152.3+

                       .D65  Drugs and driving
                                Cf. RC1045.D7, Drugs in automotive
                                             medicine
                       .D7   Drunken driving

                       .J8   Juvenile drivers
                       .L5   License plates
                       .S6   Speed regulations

                    By region or country
                      United States
                        General and collective
       5623.A1-3          Periodicals.   Serials
           .A45           Directories.  Guides.  Tables
           .A52-Z5        General works
           .Z7A-Z         Lines and companies (not local), A-Z
                        By region
          5624            New England
          5625            Middle Atlantic States
          5626            South
          5627            North Central
          5628            Mississippi Valley
          5629            West
          5630            Southwest, New
          5631            Pacific coast states
          5632            Other, A-Z
          5633          By state, A-W
          5634          By city, A-Z
```

Automotive transportation
    By region or country – Continued

5635-5720	Other regions or countries. Table I 1/

        Under each country:
            1 no.

.A1-3	Periodicals. Serials
.A45	Directories. Guides. Tables
.A6A-Z	General works
.A7-Z5	Local
.Z6	Transportation of special commodities, A-Z
.Z6B8	Building materials
.Z6F3	Farm produce
.Z6F4	Fertilizers and manures
.Z6G7	Grain
.Z6H39	Hazardous substances
.Z6L5	Livestock
.Z6S9	Sugarcane
.Z7A-Z	Lines. Companies

STAGE LINES

5746	General works
	By region or country
	United States
5747	General works
5748	By region or state, A-Z
5749	Other regions or countries, A-Z

FERRIES

Cf. VM421, Ferry boats

5751	General works
5761	Special (Other than boats)
	e. g. Aerial cableway
	Cf. TG435, Ferry bridges
5771-5870	By region or country. Table I 1/

        Under each country:
          .A3A-Z   General works
          .A5-Z   Local, A-Z

EXPRESS SERVICE

Cf. HF5761+, Shipping (of merchandise, etc.)

5880	Periodicals. Societies. Serials
5881	General works

1/
    For Table I, see pp. 331-340. Add country number in table to 5620 or 5770, as the case requires

	Express service - Continued
5886	Public policy (General)
5889	Rates
	By region or country
	United States
5893	Periodicals. Serials
5895	Directories
5896	General works
5898	Public policy
5900	Administration. Operation. The express business
	For comparative express and parcel post rates, see HE6473
5902	Finance. Accounting
5903	Individual companies, A-Z
	Under each:
	.x1-49 Periodicals. Serials
	.x5A-Z General works
5904	By state, A-Z
.5	By city, A-Z
5905-5990	Other regions or countries. Table I 1/
	Under each country:
	.A1-39 Periodicals. Societies. Serials
	.A4 General works
	.A5-Z7 Individual companies, A-Z

TRANSFER AND FORWARDING AGENTS

5999.A3	General works
	By region or country
.A5-Z5	United States
.Z7A-Z	Other regions or countries, A-Z

POSTAL SERVICE

	Periodicals. Societies. Serials
6000	International associations
6001	American
6003	English
6005	French
6007	German
6009	Other languages, A-Z
6011	Congresses
6015	Exhibitions. Museums
	Collected works (nonserial)
6021	Several authors
6025	Individual authors
6031	Guides. Directories
	For local, see HE6300+
6035	Encyclopedias. Dictionaries

1/ For Table I, see pp. 331-340. Add country number in table to 5890

	Postal service – Continued
6036	Study and teaching. Research
6037	Geography. Post routes
	History
6041	General works
	Ancient
6043	General works
6044	Greece
6045	Rome
6047	Other, A–Z
6051	Medieval
	For local, <u>see</u> HE6300+
6055	Modern
	For local, <u>see</u> HE6300+
	Biography
6061	Collective
	Individual, <u>see</u> HE6300+
6071	General works
6076	General special
	Special topics
	Class here general works only: for special
	countries, <u>see</u> HE6300+
6101	Accounts
6106	Auditing
6111	Budget. Appropriations. Deficit
	Classification. Rates
6123	General works
6124	Non-mailable matter
	For fraudulent use of mails, <u>see</u> K
	Rates
6125	General works
	Classes
6131	First class
6132	Second class
6141	Letter post
6143	Articles, A–Z
6145	International
6147	"Penny"
6148	Franking
6149	Dead letters
	Free delivery
	For special arrangement for United States,
	<u>see</u> HE6451+
6151	General works
6155	Rural
6159	Local transportation
6161	Mail carriers
	Money: Transmission, payment, collection by post
	Money orders (Payment of money)
6165	General works
6166	International
6167	By region or country, A–Z
	For United States, <u>see</u> HE6465+
6168	Special topics, A–Z
	Postal checkes, <u>see</u> HG1953.C6
.P7	Postal notes
6169	Forms

Special topics
  Money: Transmission, payment, collection
      by post - Continued
    Collection
      C.O.D. parcels, see HE6172.C7
      Collection of bills, drafts, etc.

6170.A2A-Z	General works
.A5-Z	By region or country, A-Z

Parcel post

6171	General works
6172	Special subjects, A-Z
	.C7 C.O.D. parcels
	Parcel-post stamps, see HE6184.P35
6173	By region or country, A-Z
	For United States, see HE6471+

Postal savings banks, see HG1951+
Railway mail service
    Cf. HE1067, State aid

6175	General works
.5	Weighing of mails
	For United States, see HE6475.5
6176	Registered mail

Stamps. Postmarks
  History and description

6182	General works
6183	Postage stamps. By topic, A-Z

      .A3   Aeronautics
      .A35   Afro-Americans
      .A45   American Revolution Bicentennial
      .A5   Animals
      .A55   Antiquities
      .A64   Apollo 11
      .A67   Arctic regions
      .A7   Art
      .A8   Astronautics
      .A85   Atomic energy
      .B3   Basketball
      .B5   Bible
      .B53   Birds
      .B6   Bolivar, Simon
             Botany, see .F6, .M4, .P55, or .T7

      .B63   Boy Scouts
      .B64   Boys' Brigade
      .C26   California
      .C34   Catholica

      .C43   Chicago. World's Columbian Exposition
      .C45   Children
      .C47   Christianity
      .C48   Christmas
      .C49   Churchill, Winston

      .C67   Crossbows
      .C68   Crowns
      .C7   Crustacea

Postal service
  Special topics
    <u>Stamps. Postmarks</u>
      <u>History and description</u>

6183   Postage stamps. By topic, A-Z - Continued

.D5	Dimitrov, Georgi
.D7	Dragons
.E35	Edward VIII
.E4	Elizabeth II
.E5	Engravings
.F52	Fire departments
.F6	Flowers
.F7	Franciscans
.F73	Freemasons
.G25	Gandhi, M.K.
.G34	Gaulle, Charles de
.G4	George V
.G42	George VI
.G45	George, Saint
.G5	Girl Scouts
.G88	Gutenberg, Johann
.H3	Hammarskjöld, Dag
.H446	Heraldry
.H5	History (General)
.H6	Horses
.I48	Insects
.I5	International cooperation
.J4	Jews
.K4	Kennedy, John F.
.K6	Knights of Malta
.L4	Lenin, V.I.
.L5	Librarians
.L56	Lincoln, Abraham
.L57	Lindbergh, Charles
.L59	Literature
.L63	Locomotives
.L8	Luther, Martin
	Mammals, <u>see</u> .A5
.M3	Maps
.M33	Mary, Virgin
.M4	Medical botany
.M42	Medicine
.M47	Methodists
.M65	Moscow
.M85	Music
.M9	Mythology
.N3	National parks and reserves
.N35	Natural history
.O4	Olympic games
.O95	Outer space

```
                    Postal service
                      Special topics
                        Stamps.  Postmarks
                          History and description
6183                        Postage stamps.  By topic, A-Z - Continued
                              .P52  Physics
                              .S36  Science
                              .S55  Soccer
                                    Space, Outer, see .O95
                              .S58  Spiritualism

                              .V8   Vsesoiuznyĭ leninskiĭ kommunisticheskiĭ
                                       soiuz molodezhi
                              .W3   Washington, George
                              .W47  The West
                              .W6   Woman

6184                        Other aspects of postage stamps, A-Z

                              .A3   Adhesive
                              .C3   Cancellations (Postmarks)
                              .C6   Color
                              .C63  Conservation and restoration
                              .C65  Covers

                              .D4   Design
                              .E3   Education, Postage stamps in
                              .E4   Emergency currency, Use of stamps as
                              .E7   Errors
                              .F6   Forgeries
                              .I5   Investments
                              .L8   Luminescence
                              .P3   Paper
                              .P35  Parcel-post stamps
                              .P4   Perforations
                              .P5   Plate numbers
                              .P7   Printing
                              .P8   Publicity
                              .R3   Rare stamps
                                    Restoration, see .C63

                              .S6   Souvenir sheets
                                    Telegraph stamps, see HJ5315; HE5321+
                              .W3   Watermarks

6185                        By region or country, A-Z
                                For special topics and aspects, see HE6183, HE6184
                                Under each country:
                                   .x   General works
                                   .x2  Catalogs, lists, etc.
                                   .x3  Local, A-Z

                          Stamp collecting.  Philately
6187                          Periodicals.  Serials
6188                          Societies
6189                          Congresses
6191                          Exhibitions.  Museums.  Public collections
                                  Including their catalogs
                              Private collections, see HE6207
6194                          Yearbooks.  Almanacs
```

Postal service
  Special topics
    Stamp collecting. Philately - Continued
6196   Dictionaries. Encyclopedias
                Collected works (nonserial)
6199   Several authors
6200   Individual authors
                History of philately
6203   General works
6204   By region or country, A-Z
                Biography (Collectors and collections)
6206   Collective
6207   Individual collectors and collections, A-Z
6209   Directories. Lists of collectors and dealers
6213   General works
6215   Handbooks, manuals, etc.
6217   Addresses, essays, lectures
6221   Albums
                Catalogs. Price lists. Exchange lists
                    Class here general trade catalogs; for
                      catalogs for individual countries, see
                      HE6185; for catalogs of museums, see
                      HE6191; for private collections, see
                      HE6207
6224   General catalogs
6226   Price lists (Commercial and dealers'
                      catalogs)
6228   Exchange lists
6230   Catalogs, not otherwise specified, A-Z
                      For catalogs for special countries,
                        see HE6185

                  .A4   Airmail
                  .L6   Local post

                  .M4   Metered mail
                  .M48   Miniature sheets

            Revenue stamps, see HJ5315; HJ5321+

6233   Steam packet. Ocean mail
6235   Subsidies
6237   Mail handling equipment, supplies, etc.
              Including their use
6238   Airmail service
6239   Other special topics, A-Z
              .E54   Electronic mail systems
              .H6   Hovermail
              .P5   Pigeons
              .R6   Rocket mail
              .S8   Sunday mails

6241   Civil service. Appointments. Personnel.
              Compensation
                For the economic and social condition of post
                  office employees, including trade unions, of
                  individual countries, see HE6499, and HE6651+
                  subdivision (9), etc., under individual countries

	Postal service – Continued
	International postal service
6246	General works
	Universal Postal Union
6251	Periodicals. Serials
6261	General works
6271	General special
	Pan American Postal Union
6275	Periodicals. Serials
6276	General works
6277	General special
6278	Other unions, A–Z
	e. g. .A4 African Postal Union
	By region or country
	United States
6300	Periodicals. Societies. Serials
6309	Statistics
	Post Office Department. United States
	Postal Service
	Cf. HE6371+, History of the Service
	HE6499, Employees of the Service
6311	Periodicals. Serials
6313	Annual report of Postmaster General
6326	Nonserial publications. By date
	Collected works (nonserial)
6340	Several authors
6341	Individual authors
	Guides. Directories
6361	General
6363	By state, A–W
	Including state subdivision schemes
6365	Officials
6366	Lists of post offices
	Cf. HE6455.A4, Rural free delivery
	Local post-office guides, see HE6376
	Maps, see G3692.P8
6368	Other special topics
	Including street directory of the principal
	cities
	History
	Including general works on the United States
	Postal Service
	For history of the Confederate States of
	America, see HE6500; for the military
	postal service, see UH80+
6371	General works
6375	Special topics, A–Z
	e. g. .O84 Overland express
	.P65 Pony express

```
                         Postal service
                          By region or country
                           United States
                            History - Continued
                             Local
                                Including guides, etc.
6376.A1A-Z                      Regions or states
     .A2-Z                      Cities
                             Biography
6381                            Collective
6385                            Individual, A-Z
                             Special
6401                            Accounts
6406                            Auditing
6411                            Budget.  Appropriations.  Deficit
                             Classification.  Rates
6423                              General works
6424                              Non-mailable matter
                                     For fraudulent use of the mails, see K
                                  Rates
6425                                General works
                                    Classes
6431                                  First class
6432                                  Second class
6441                                Letter post
6443                                Articles, A-Z
6445                                International
6447                                "Penny"
6448                                Franking
6449                              Dead letters

                             Free delivery
6451                              General works
                                  Rural
6455.A1-4                         Directories: Lists of free delivery
                                     offices
     .A5-Z                        General works
6456                              By state, A-W
                                     Under each:
                                       .x   General works
                                       .x2  Local: Counties, etc., A-Z
                             Money orders
6465                              General works
6467                              Between United States and other countries, A-Z
6468                              Special topics, A-Z

                                  .P7  Postal notes

6469                              Forms
                             Parcel post
6471                              General works
6472                              Special topics, A-Z
                                  .B6  Book rates

                                  Rates, tables, etc.
                                     Including comparative parcel post and
                                        express rates
6473.A3A-Z                        General works
     .A5-Z                        Local, A-Z
```

                    Postal service
                      By region or country
                        United States
                          Special – Continued
                            Railway mail service
6475   General works
    .3   Guides: Routes, offices, etc.
    .5   Weighing of mails
6476   Registered mail. Certified mail
                            Stamps, see HE6181+
6477   Steam packet. Ocean mail

6485   Mail transportation by automotive carriers
6491   Star routes
                              Including contracts for carrying mail in
                                general, other than HE6455, Rural free
                                delivery; HE6459, Local transportation;
                                and HE6475, Railway mail service
6493   Subsidies
                              Cf. HE740+, Merchant marine
6495   Supplies
6496   Airmail service

6497   Other special topics, A–Z

            .A8   Automation
            .D35   Damaged mail
            .F6   Foreign mail
                    Fraud orders, see HE6096

            .K4   Keys, identification tags, etc.

            .M3   Mailboxes
            .M4   Metered mail
                    Military mail, see UH83+
                    Navy mail, see VG63
                    Non-mailable matter, see HE6424

            .P35   Periodical statements
            .P4   Permit privilege
                    Postage-due mail, see .S5
            .R4   Reply letters and postal cards

            .S4   Sea post offices
            .S5   Short-paid mail. Postage-due mail

            .S6   Special delivery
            .S8   Sunday mails
                    Telegraphy codes, see HE7677.P78

6499   Civil service. Appointments. Personnel.
                            Compensation
                              Including employees of the United States
                                Postal Service
                              Cf. HE6161, Mail carriers
                                  HE6475, Railway mail service

6500   Confederate States

166

Postal service
By region or country - Continued
6651-7496   Other regions or countries. Table X, modified 1/
Under each country:

10 nos.	5 nos.	2 nos.	1 no.	
(1)	(1)		.A1-3	Serial documents
				Including reports and statistics of Post Office Department
				For local documents, guides, etc., see subdivision (6) or .Z7
				For documents on general topics, e. g. Classification, employees, see the topic in subdivision (9), (5), or in HE6100+
(2)	(2)			Special documents
.A1				Separate documents. By date
(3)	(3)		.A4A-Z	Guides. Directories
(4)	(4)			Biography
.A1-4	.A1-4		.A5A-Z	Collective
.A5-Z7	.A5A-Z		.A6A-Z	Individual, A-Z
(5)	.A6-Z5	(1)	.A7-Z6	General works
(6)				
.A-Z7	.Z7A-Z	(2)		Local, A-Z
				Colonies
.Z8A-Z	.Z8A-Z			General works
.Z9A-Z	.Z9A-Z			By colony, A-Z
				Class here works concerned with postal communications with individual colonies
	(5)			Technical works
(8)	.Z8A-Z			Classification of mail matter, rates, etc.
(9)	.Z9A-Z		.Z9A-Z	Other special topics, A-Z
				.A3 Accounting
				.A4 Air service
				.F6 Foreign mail
				.M3 Mail steamers
				.M4 Metered mail
				.P4 Personnel
				.P5 Pigeon post
				.R2 Railway mail service
				.S5 Short paid mail
				.S7 Statistics

1/
For Table X, see pp. 331-340. Add country number in table to 6500

PNEUMATIC SERVICE

CF. TJ1015, Mechanical engineering

7511	Periodicals. Societies. Serials
7513	Directories
7516	General works
	By region or country
	United States
7521	Periodicals. Serials
7525	General works
7527	Administration
7529	Finance. Accounting
7531	By state, A-W
7533	By city, A-Z
7535	By company, A-Z
	Other regions or countries
	Under each country:
	.x General works
	.x2 By place, A-Z
	.x3 By company, A-Z
7541	Other American countries, A-Z
7545	Europe, A-Z
7549	Other, A-Z

TELECOMMUNICATION INDUSTRY. TELEGRAPH

Class here telegraph, telephone, and broadcasting; for
  postal service and telegraphy combined, see HE6000+
Cf. HD9696, Electronic industries
    TK5101+, Electric engineering

7601	Periodicals. Serials
7603	Societies
	Collected works
7611	Several authors
7616	Individual authors
7621	Directories. Guides
	For special countries, see HE7771+
7631	General works
	Biography, see TK5241+
7645	Public policy (General)
7647	Taxation
7651	Relation to other institutions and interests
	Administration
	Cf. TK5283, Technical management of telegraphic
	enterprises
7661	General works
	Office organization, see TK5285+
	Personnel, officers and employees, see HD8039.T24+

Telecommunication industry. Telegraph – Continued
<u>Codes</u>
Class wireless codes with ordinary codes

7669	General works
7671	General (blank) codes
7673	Codes for general use
	e. g. Travelers
7675	Number codes
	Commercial codes
7676	General works
7677	Special, A-Z

.A4	Aeronautics
.A8	Automobiles
.B15	Bakers
.B2	Bankers and brokers

Cf. HE7677.I5, Insurance
Bonding companies, <u>see</u> .I5

.B7	Boots and shoes
.B8	Bullion
.B85	Business schools
.B9	Butter, cheese
.C2	Canned goods
.C4	Chemicals
.C5	Clothing
.C6	Coal
.C65	Coffee

Cf. HE7677.T2, Tea and coffee

.C7	Cooperage
.C75	Cordage
.C8	Cotton
.C82	Cotton seed
.C9	Credit
.C95	Crockery
.D35	Dentists' supplies
.D4	Detectives
.D7	Drugs
.D8	Dry goods
.E3	Electric supplies
.E5	Engineering, Civil

Epidemics, <u>see</u> RA652

.F45	Fireworks
.F5	Fish
.F55	Flax and flaxseed
.F6	Flour
.F9	Fruit

Cf. HE7677.P9, Produce and provisions

.F93	Fur
.F95	Furniture
.G7	Grain
.G8	Groceries
.H15	Hardware
.H2	Harness
.H6	Hides

Telecommunication industry. Telegraph
  Codes
    Commercial codes
7677   Special, A-Z - Continued

.H7	Hops
.I4	Income tax
.I45	Ink
.I5	Insurance
.I7	Iron
.J6	Jewelry
.L3	Laundry
.L35	Law
.L38	Lead
.L4	Leather
.L7	Lime
.L75	Liquors
.L78	Livestock
.L8	Locomotives
.L9	Lumber
.M2	Machinery
.M4	Medicine
.M5	Melons
	Meteorology, see QC872
.M55	Millinery
.M6	Mining
	Motion pictures, see .T4
.O3	Oil
.O7	Oriental products
.P2	Packers
.P22	Paint
.P26	Paper
.P3	Peanuts
.P5	Phonograph
.P57	Photography
.P76	Police
.P78	Postal service
.P8	Potato
.P9	Produce and provisions
.R2	Railroad
.R3	Real estate
.R5	Rice
.R85	Rubber goods
.S2	Sash, door, and blind
.S25	Sausage
.S3	Saws
.S45	Seeds
.S5	Ship brokers
.S53	Shipping
.S6	Smelting
.S78	Steam and gas fittings
.S79	Steam boats
.S8	Steam engine

Telecommunication industry. Telegraph
  Codes
    Commercial codes
7677	Special, A–Z – Continued

        .S82 Steel
              Stock brokers, see .B2
        .S9 Sugar
              Surety and bonding companies, see .I5
        .T12 Tailors
        .T16 Tanners
        .T2 Tea and coffee
                Cf. HE7677.C65, Coffee
        .T3 Textiles

        .T4 Theatrical
        .T5 Ticket brokers
        .T6 Tobacco
        .T75 Transportation

        .W2 Wagons
        .W3 Wall paper
        .W4 Waste trade
        .W6 Wine
        .W9 Wool
        .Y2 Yarn

7678	Codes in foreign languages, A–Z
7679	Other special codes, A–Z

      .A8 Axisa
      .B4 Bentley
      .G8 Greening

  Rates
      For individual countries, see HE7761+
7681	General works
7685	Special (other than local)

        Including night rates
7691	Individual companies, A–Z

  Finance
7693	General works
7695	Accounting
7700	International communications

      Including international agencies

  Submarine telegraph. Ocean cables
7709	Periodicals. Societies. Serials
7710	Directories
7711	General works
7713	By region or country, A–Z

    Special regions
      Class here general works only; for special
        cables, see TK5611+
7725	Atlantic cables
7731	Pacific cables
7741	Other, A–Z
7742	Teletype services

  Radio, see HE8660+
  Signaling, see HE9723

Telecommunication industry. Telegraph - Continued
　　By region or country
　　　United States

7761	Periodicals. Serials
7771	Directories. Guides
7775	General works
7781	Public policy
7783	Taxation
7785	Administration
7787	Rates
7791	By state, A-W
7797	By company, A-Z

　　　　　　　Under each:
　　　　　　　　.x1-49 Periodicals. Serials
　　　　　　　　.x5A-Z General works

7798	Confederate states
7811-8630.7	Other regions or countries. Table VII 1/

　　　　　Under each country:

10 nos.	5 nos.	2 nos.	1 no.	
(1)	(1)		.A1-4	Periodicals. Serials
(3)			.A5-59	Directories. Guides
(4)	(2)	(1)	.A6-Z4	General works
(5)	(3)		.Z5A-Z	Public policy. Taxation
(6)	(4)		.Z6A-Z	Administration
(7)				Rates
(8)				States, provinces, A-Z
				Under each:
				.A1-3 Periodicals.
				Serials
				.A5-Z General works
(9)	(5)	(2)	.Z8A-Z	Local, A-Z
(10)				By company, A-Z
				Under each:
				.x1-49 Periodicals.
				Serials
				.x5A-Z General works

Radio. Wireless telegraph
　　　Cf. HD9999.R15, Radio industry
　　　　TK5700+, Technology
　　　　UG610, Military radio
　　　　VG76+, Naval radio

8660	Periodicals. Societies. Serials
8662	Congresses
	Directories
8663	General works
	By region or country
8664	United States
8665	Other regions or countries, A-Z

1/
　For Table VII, see pp. 331-340. Add country number in table to 7800

```
                        Telecommunication industry.  Telegraph
                        Radio.  Wireless telegraph - Continued
    8675                    General works
                            By region or country
                               United States
    8677                       Periodicals.  Societies.  Serials
    8678                       General works
    8679                    Other American regions or countries, A-Z
    8680                    Europe.  By region or country, A-Z
    8681                    Asia.  By region or country, A-Z
    8682                    Africa.  By region or country, A-Z
    8683                    Other, A-Z
    8688                 By company, A-Z
                        Radio and television broadcasting
                            Cf. HD9999.R15, Radio industry
                                HD9999.T37, Television industry
                                LB1044.8, Educational broadcasting
                                PN1991+, Production and direction
    8689                 Periodicals.  Societies.  Serials
      .2                 Congresses
      .4                 General works
      .6                 General special
      .7                 Special topics, A-Z
                            .A8   Audiences
                            .C55  Citizen participation in broadcast policy
                            .F34  Fairness doctrine
                            .P6   Political broadcasts

                         By region or country
      .8                    United States
      .9                    Other regions or countries, A-Z
                         Radio broadcasting
    8690                    Periodicals.  Societies.  Serials
    8691                    Congresses
    8694                    General works
    8696                    General special
    8697                    Special topics, A-Z
                            .A8   Audiences
                            .L5   Liberty of speech
                            .P57  Pirate radio broadcasting.  Offshore
                                    radio broadcasting
                            .P6   Political broadcasts
                         By region or country, A-Z
    8698                    United States
    8699                    Other regions or countries, A-Z
                         Television broadcasting
    8700                    Periodicals.  Societies.  Serials
      .2                 Congresses
      .4                 General works
      .6                 General special
      .7                 Special topics, A-Z
                            .A8  Audiences
                                 Cable TV, see .C6
                            .C6  Community antenna television.  Subscription
                                   television.  Cable TV
                                      Cf. TK6675, Technology
                            .P6  Political broadcasts
                         By region or country
      .8                    United States
      .9                    Other regions or countries, A-Z
```

TELEPHONE INDUSTRY

CF. HE9999.T35, Telephone equipment
        industry
        TK6001+, Technology

8701	Periodicals. Societies. Serials
	Collected works (nonserial)
8711	Several authors
8712	Individual authors
8721	Directories and buyers' guides (General)
	For special countries, see HE8801+
8728	Statistics
	For special countries, see HE8815, etc.
8731	General works
8735	General special
8741	Public policy (General)
	Administration
	Cf. TK6183, Management of telephone enterprises
8761	General works
	Office organization, see TK6185+
	Personnel: Officers and employees, see HD8039.T3
	Rates
8777	General works
8779	Special (other than local)
	Including long distance
	Finance
8783	General works
8785	Accounting
	By region or country
	United States
8801	Periodicals. Societies. Serials
8811	Directories. Buyers' guides
	For local, see HE8841
8815	General works
8817	General special
8819	Public policy
	Administration
8821	General works
8825	Rates
8829	Local, A-Z
8840	By state, A-W
8841	By city, A-Z
	Under each:
	.x Periodicals. Serials
	.x2 Directories and buyers' guides
	.x3 General works
	.x4 By company, A-Z
8846	By company (other than municipal), A-Z
	Under each:
	.x1-49 Periodicals. Serials
	.x5A-Z General works

Telephone industry
By region or country – Continued
8861–9680.7   Other regions or countries. Table VII 1/
Under each country:

10 nos.	5 nos.	1 no.	
(1)	(1)	.A1–4	Periodicals. Societies. Serials
(3)	(2) 2/	.A5–59	Directories. Buyers' guides
(4)		.A6–Z4	General works
(5)		.Z5A–Z	Public policy
(6)		.Z6A–Z	Administration
(7)			Rates
(8)	(3)	.Z8A–Z	By state, province, department, etc., A–Z
(9)	(4)		By city, A–Z
(10)	(5)		By company, A–Z

Under each:
.x1–49 Periodicals. Serials
.x5A–Z General works

Wireless telephone industry
9713   General works
9715   By region or country, A–Z
Artificial satellite telecommunications
Cf. TK5104+, Engineering
9719   General works
9721   By region or country, A–Z

Signaling
Cf. UG570+, Military signaling
V280+, Naval signaling
VK373, VK381+, Marine signaling (General)
9723   General works
9735   Special systems
9737   Codes
9739   Leaflets, etc. dropped from aircraft
Messenger service
9751   General works
United States
9753   General works
9755   Local, A–Z

1/
For Table VII, see pp. 331–340. Add country number in table to 8850
2/
Includes subdivisions (3) – (7) of 10 number table

AIR TRANSPORTATION

Cf. GV750+, Air sports
  HD9711, Airplane industry
  HD9711.5, Aerospace industry
  TL500+, Aeronautics. Aeronautical
    engineering. Air navigation.
    Astronautics
  TL552, Civil aviation (Technology)
  UG630+, Military aeronautics. Air
    warfare
  VG90+, Naval aeronautics. Naval air
    warfare

	Periodicals. Serials. By language
9761	Polyglot
.1	English
.2	French
.3	German
.4	Russian and other Slavic
.5	Spanish and Portuguese
.6	Arabic
.7	Chinese
.8	Japanese
.9	Other, A-Z

Societies

Cf. TL500+, Aeronautical engineering societies,
      aero clubs, and societies of air pilots

	International
9762	General works
.5	International Civil Aviation Organization

Class here administrative material only. For
  technical material and general collections
  published by the organization which include
  material of technical nature, see TL500.5

	By region or country
9763	United States
9764.1	Canada
.2	Latin America. By region or country, A-Z
	Europe
.3	Great Britain
.35	France
.4	Germany
.55	Other European regions or countries, A-Z
	Asia
.6	India
.65	Pakistan
.7	China
.75	Japan
.76	Other Asian regions or countries, A-Z
.8	Africa. By region or country, A-Z
.9	Australia
.95	Oceania, A-Z
9765	Congresses
	Dictionaries. Encyclopedias, see TL509

<pre>
               Air transportation - Continued
9768   Directories. Guides. Time-tables
                     Cf. HD9711, Directories of the aircraft industry
                         TL512, Directories of aircraft manufactures
                         TL512.7, Registers of air pilots
                         TL725+, Air pilot guides
                         TL723.5.T5, Time schedules, etc., for
                             making time-tables
                     For special countries, see HE9801+, subdivisions,
                     .A2 and .A9-Z6

               Registers of aircraft
9769.A3   General works
    .A5-Z   By region or country
                     Under each country:
                     .x   General works
                     .x2 Local, A-Z
9770   Special types of aircraft, A-Z
                   Cf. TL685.4+, Passenger planes
                       TL685.7, Transport planes
                 .A4   Airships
                 .A8   Atomic powered

                       Helicopters, see HE9792+
                 .J4   Jets
                           Cf. TL709+, Aeronautical engineering

                 .R6   Rocket propelled
                           Cf. TL780+, Aeronautical engineering
                 .S9   Supersonic transport planes
                 .V47 Vertically rising

               Collected works (nonserial)
9771   Several authors
9772   Individual authors
               Museums. Exhibitions, see TL506

               History
                   Cf. TL515+, History of aeronautics
                   For special countries, see HE9801+, subdivisions
                       .A3 and .A35
9774   General works
9775   General special
               Biography, see HD9711, TL539, etc.
9776   General works
    .5   Addresses, essays, lectures
9777   General special
    .7   Public policy (General)
               Air traffic surveys
                   For special countries, see HE9801+, subdivision
                       .A6
9778   General works
    .5   By region, A-Z
                   .A74 Arctic regions
                   .A8   Atlantic regions
</pre>

Air transportation - Continued
    Administration and operation of airlines
        Including international airlines
           For special countries, see HE9801+, subdivision
             .A4

9780	General works. Policy
9781	Management. Public relations
9782	Finance. Taxation. Cost of operation

          Cf. HF5686.A38, Accounting
          For special countries, see HE9801+, subdivision
            .A5

    Rates

9783	General works
.3	By region or country, A-Z

        Under each country:
          .x   General works
          .x2 Local, A-Z
     Passenger tariff
        Including schedules

.5	General works
.55	By region or country, A-Z

     Freight tariff
        Including schedules

.7	General works
.74	Rates on particular articles, A-Z
.75	By region or country, A-Z

    Accidents
        Cf. TL553.5, Accidents and their prevention.
           Air safety
          TL697.S3, Safety devices (General)

9784	General works
.5	By region or country, A-Z

        Under each country:
          .x   General works
          .x2 Local, A-Z

9785	Local service
9786	Transoceanic service

    Passenger service
        Including baggage service

9787	General works
.5	By region or country, A-Z

    Freight and express service

9788	General works
.4	Special commodities, A-Z

        .C37 Cattle
        .F58 Flowers
        .R3   Radioactive substances

.5	By region or country, A-Z
9789	Airlines in relation to other carriers

    Air-mail service, see HE6238
    Helicopter service
        Cf. TL716, Technical aspects

9792	General works
9793	By region or country, A-Z

        Under each country:
          .x   General works
          .x2 Local, A-Z
          .x3 By company, A-Z

Air transportation – Continued
Private aircraft. Business aircraft
    Cf. TL685.1, Private planes
       TL721.1+, Special uses of aircraft
       TL721.4, Private flying
    For business or special use, see particular
      classification, e. g. BV2082.A9, Aviation in
      missionary work; HF6146.A4, Use of aircraft
      in advertising; S494.5.A3, Aeronautics in
      agriculture; SD387.A3, Aeronautics in forestry

9795	General works
9796	By region or country, A–Z
	.x General works
	.x2 Local, A–Z

Airports, heliports, seaplane bases
    Cf. TL725+, Airways (Routes), airports and
        landing fields. Aerodomes

9797.A1	Periodicals. Societies. Serials
.A2–Z	General works
.4	By subject, A–Z

    .A2 Access to airports
        Cf. HE355.6, Access roads to airports
    .E3 Economic aspects
    .F4 Fees
    .F5 Finance

    .N6 Noise
    .P6 Police
    .S4 Security measures

.5	By region or country, A–Z
	Under each country:
	.x General works
	.x2 Local, A–Z

Air transportation - Continued

9801-9900   By region or country. Table I 1/
                                 Under each country (except the United States):

    1 no.

    .A1A-Z   Periodicals. Serials
    .A2A-Z   Directories. Guides. Time-tables
                       History
    .A3A-Z   General works
    .A35A-Z   1945-
    .A4A-Z   General works
    .A5A-Z   Finance. Government subsidies
    .A6   Statistics. Air traffic surveys. By date
    .A7A-Z   By state, province, or region, A-Z
    .A8A-Z   By city, A-Z
    .A9-Z6   Special airlines, A-Z
                           Including time-tables of individual airlines
    .Z7A-Z   Special topics, A-Z

        .C53 Chartering

        .H5   Hijacking
               Cf. JX5775.C7, International law

Note: For United States use above subarrangement except for .A7A-Z and
  .Z8A-Z. Apply proper number from Table I, p. 331, for United States local

---

1/
  For Table I, see pp. 331-340. Add country number in table to 9800

Periodicals. Serials
>Class here, by imprint of country or larger
>geographic region as indicated, all periodicals
>and serials of a general character
>For works relating to the commerce of a specific
>region or country, see HF3000+
>For societies, see HF294+

1	United States and Canada
6	Latin America
	Europe
11	Great Britain
13	Austria
15	France
17	Germany
19	Italy
21	Belgium
23	Netherlands
25	Soviet Union
	Scandinavia
27	Denmark
28	Iceland
29	Norway
31	Sweden
33	Spain
34	Portugal
35	Switzerland
37	Other European countries, A-Z
41	Asian countries
	Cf. HF52, Pacific islands
46	African countries
51	Australia
.5	New Zealand
52	Pacific islands

53   Yearbooks
>Cf. HF5003, Business yearbooks
>HF5028, Business calendars
>For annual reviews of local commerce, finance,
>trade, etc., see HF3151+ and HF3221+, subdivision
>(10) under each country
Collected works (nonserial), see HF345

54   Directories (General). By country of issue, A-Z
>Class here directories covering the world or
>several countries; for directories of particular
>countries, see HF3010+, HF3221+, subdivision
>(3) under each country; for local business
>directories, see HF5031+

55   International Trade Organization (Proposed)
.5   Organization for Trade Cooperation

Congresses
56   General. By date
Local, see HF3008, HF3212, HF3221+
61   Museums. Exhibitions

	Ministries, departments, bureaus of commerce, etc.
	Class here works on their organization, function, etc.; for serial publications issued by them, see HF3000+
	For boards of trade, chambers of commerce, etc., see HF294+
71	General works
73	By region or country, A-Z
81	Theory. Method. Relation to other subjects
(101-293.7)	Serials. Documents. By region or country, see HF3000+

	Boards of trade, chambers of commerce, merchants' associations, etc.
	Cf. HF71+, Ministries, departments, etc.
294	General works
	Including organization and works about boards of trade, etc., in general, in individual countries
295-343	Individual boards of trade, etc.
	For international boards of trade, etc., see HF294
	United States
295	State boards
296.A1-28	National boards of trade
.A29A-Z	Foreign-American boards of trade. By region or country, A-Z
	e. g. .A29B43 Chambre de commerce Belge aux Etats-Unis
.A3-Z	Cities, A-Z
298	Canada
299	West Indies, A-Z
300	Latin America. By region or country, A-Z
302	Great Britain
304	Austria
306	France
308	Germany
	Including West Germany
310	Greece
312	Italy
314	Belgium
316	Netherlands
318	Soviet Union
320	Scandinavian countries, A-Z
322	Spain
323	Portugal
324	Switzerland
326	Balkan countries, A-Z
328	Other European regions or countries, A-Z
331	Asia. By region or country, A-Z
336	Africa. By region or country, A-Z
340	Australia
341	New Zealand
343	Pacific islands, A-Z
	Collected works (nonserial)
345	Several authors
346	Individual authors

	History
	For works on the history of the commerce in a particular commodity, see the commodity in HD9000+
	General commercial history
	For works on the commercial history of a particular country, see HF3000+
351	Early works
352	Modern works
	For works on the history of the commerce of two countries, see HF3065+ or HF3211
353	Elementary textbooks
355	General special
	By period
	Ancient
357	General works
359	General special
(361)	Primitive, see GN450+
	Orient
363	General works
	Egypt
365	General works
366	General special
367	Africa
368	Assyria. Babylonia. Persia
369	Hebrews
370	Pheonicia
	Cf. HF381+, Mediterranean Sea
371	Carthage
372	Other Oriental areas (not A-Z)
	e. g. India, China
	Classic Occident
373	General works
	Greece
	Cf. HF405, Byzantine commerce
	HF3571+, Modern Greece
375	General works
376	Local, A-Z
	Rome
377	General works
378	Local, A-Z
	Special regions, seas, etc.
	Class here general works only; for special countries, see HF365+
381	Mediterranean Sea
383	Black Sea
385	Red Sea
386	Persian Gulf. Indian Ocean
387	Atlantic Ocean
388	Baltic Sea
389	Other, A-Z
391	Medieval and modern
	Middle Ages (476-1400/1492)
393	Sources and documents. Account books, etc.
	General works, treatises
394	Early works
395	Modern works

```
                    History
                      By period
                        Middle Ages (476-1400/1492) - Continued
                          By period
397                         Early to 1100.  Before Crusades
398                         12th and 13th centuries.  Period of Crusades
399                         14th century
400                         15th century
                          Special topics, regions, etc.
401                         Institutions, etc., A-Z
                              .S8  Staple system
403                         Trade routes
                                Cf. HE323+, Transportation and communication
                                    HF1021+, Commercial geography
404                         Levant
    .5                      Black Sea
405                         Byzantine commerce
406                         Arabs.  Moors
                          By region or country
408                         Orient
                            Italy
411                           General works
413                           Venice
414                           Genoa
415                           Pisa
416                           Florence
417                           Other local, A-Z
                            France
421                           General works
423                           General special
                            Portugal
425                           General works
    .5                        General special
                            Spain
426                           General works
427                           General special
                            Netherlands (Low Countries)
431                           General works
433                           Flanders.  Brabant
434                           Ghent
435                           Bruges
437                           Antwerp
439                           Other special
                            Germany
441                           General works
442                           General special
                                  e. g. The mercantile houses: Fugger, Welser
                              By place
444                             South Germany.  Danube River region
450                             Rhine River region
453                             Other local, A-Z
                            Hansa
455                           General works
456                           General special
                              By period
458                             Through 1500
459                             16th century
461                             17th and 18th centuries
463                             By place, A-Z
```

```
                         History
                            By period
                               Middle Ages (476-1400/1492)
                                  By region or country - Continued
         467                         Russia
                                     Scandinavia
         471                            General works
         473                            By city, A-Z
         475                         Other regions or countries
                               Modern (1400/1492-1789)
                                  Cf. HF455+, Hansa
         479                      General works
                                  The great commercial companies
         481                         General works
                                     By country
                                        Netherlands
         482                               General works
         483                               By company, A-Z 1/
                                              e. g.  .E5-6   East India Company
                                                     .W59-6  West India Company
                                        England
         485                               General works
         486                               By company, A-Z 1/
                                              e. g.  .E5-6  East India Company
                                                            For historical works
                                                            on the East India
                                                            Company, as well as
                                                            its records, see
                                                            DS465
                                                     .S6-7  South Sea Company
                                                            For the South Sea
                                                            scheme, see HC6008
                                        France
         488                               General works
         489                               By company, A-Z 1/
         491                            Other companies, A-Z 1/
         493                         16th century
         495                         17th and 18th centuries
                                     1789-
         497                            19th century
         499                            20th century


                         Dictionaries.  Encyclopedias
        1001                General
        1002                Bilingual and polyglot
           .5            Terminology.  Abbreviations.  Notation
                         General works, treatises, and advanced textbooks
        1003                Early through 1600
        1005                1601-1800
        1007                1801-1978
        1008                1979-
        1009.5           Export sales.  Export and international marketing
```

1/
Under each company:
  (1) Periodicals. Serials
  (2) General works. History

1010	Handbooks, manuals, etc.
	For United States, see HF3035; for other regions or
	countries, see HF3221+, nos. (2.5) or (7)
1014	Balance of trade
	Cf. HG3882, Balance of payments
	Statistics
1016	Collections of statistics
1017	Theory
	Commercial geography
1021	Periodicals. Societies. Serials
.5	Congresses
1022	Expeditions
	Atlases, see G1046.G1
1025	General works, treatises, and advanced textbooks
1027	Elementary textbooks
	By region or country, see HC92+
	Commodities. Commercial products
1040	Periodicals. Societies. Serials
.4	Collected works (nonserial)
.5	Dictionaries. Encyclopedias
.7	General works
	By region or country
.8	United States
.9	Other regions or countries, A-Z
	Commodity and commercial products classification
1041	General works
	By region or country
1042	United States
1044	Other regions or countries, A-Z
	Raw materials
1051	General works
	By region or country
1052	United States
1054	Other regions or countries, A-Z
	Weights and measures, see HF5711+
	Shipping, see HF5761+
	Commercial education
	Cf. HD30.4+, Management
	HF5415.4, Distributive education
	LC2780.4, Vocational education of Blacks
1101	Periodicals. Societies. Serials
1102	Congresses
	Collected works (nonserial)
1103	Several authors
1104	Individual authors
1106	General works, treatises, and textbooks
1108	History
1111	Higher commercial education
1116	Correspondence schools, home-study courses, etc.
1118	Problems, exercises, examinations
1121	General special
	By region or country
	United States and Canada
1131	General works
1132	Schools. Business colleges. By place, A-Z
1133	Correspondence schools and courses. By place, A-Z
1134	Higher commercial education. College and university
	courses. By place, A-Z

```
                         Commercial education
                            By region or country - Continued
                               Latin America
        1135.A2A-Z               General works
            .A6-Z                By region or country, A-Z
        1136                     By city, A-Z
                               Europe
        1140                     General works
                                 Great Britain
        1141                       General works
        1142                       Local, A-Z
        1143-1144                Austria 1/
        1145-1146                France 1/
        1147-1148                Germany 1/
        1149-1150                Greece 1/
        1151-1152                Italy 1/
        1153-1154                Belgium 1/
        1155-1156                Netherlands 1/
        1157-1158                Soviet Union 1/
        1159-1160                Scandinavia 1/
        1161-1162                Spain and Portugal 1/
        1163-1164                Switzerland 1/
        1165                     Other European regions or countries, A-Z
                               Asia
        1171.A2A-Z               General works
            .A6-Z                By region or country, A-Z
        1172                     By city, A-Z
                               Africa
        1176.A2A-Z               General works
            .A6-Z                By region or country, A-Z
                                    Under each country:
                                       .x    General works
                                       .x2  Local, A-Z
        1181-1182                Australia 1/
        1185-1186                New Zealand 1/

                         Commercial policy
                            Cf. HD82+, Economic policy
        1401                   General works
                               Foreign commercial policy
                                  Including works on foreign economic policy
                                  By region or country, see HF1451+
        1410                     Periodicals.  Societies.  Serials
           .5                    Congresses
        1411                     General works
        1412                     General special
        1413                     Underdeveloped areas
           .5                    Boycotts
        1414                     Competition
           .5                    Export controls
        1417                     Export processing zones
           .5                    Foreign trade promotion
        1418                     Free ports
                                    Cf. HF5484+, Warehousing and storage
           .5                    International economic integration
```

1/
   Subarranged like HF1141-1142

Commercial policy
　　　Foreign commercial policy – Continued
1420　　　　　　Import substitution
1421　　　　　　Trade adjustment assistance
　　　　　　　　Dumping
　　　　　　　　　　i. e. selling in foreign markets at lower prices
　　　　　　　　　　than in the home market
1425　　　　　　　General works
　　　　　　　　　Special articles, see HD9000+
1428　　　　　　International commodity control
1429　　　　　　Foreign licensing agreements
　　　　　　　　　Cf. JX6271+, International law
1430　　　　　　Nontariff trade barriers (General)
　.5　　　　　　Subsidies
　　　　　　Domestic commercial policy
1431　　　　　　General works
1436　　　　　　Competition
1437　　　　　　Licenses
1451-1647　　　By region or country. Table II, modified 1/
　　　　　　　　Under each country:

2 nos.	1 no.	
(1)	.A–Z3	General works (Historical and descriptive)
(2)		Special (Controversial pamphlets, etc.). By date
(2.5)	.Z4A–Z	Relations with other regions and countries, A–Z If (2.5) is not available, use (2.15)
(2.9)	.Z5A–Z	Local, A–Z If (2.9) is not available, use (2.19)

　　　　　　For Latin America (Collectively) use: HF1480.5, General
　　　　　　　works; HF1480.52, Special ... By date; HF1480.55,
　　　　　　　Relations with other countries, A–Z. For individual
　　　　　　　countries within Latin America, see the countries
　　　　　　For European Economic Community countries (Collectively)
　　　　　　　use: HF1532.92, General works; HF1532.93, Special ...
　　　　　　　By date; HF1532.935, Relations with other countries,
　　　　　　　A–Z. For individual countries within the European
　　　　　　　Economic Community, see the countries

Tariff policy (Protection and free trade)
　　　　　Class here theoretical and controversial works; for
　　　　　　tariff schedules and customs administration, see HJ
　　　　　Including import licensing, etc.
1701　　　Periodicals. Societies. Serials
1703　　　Congresses
　　　　　Collected works (nonserial)
1704　　　　Several authors
　.5　　　　Individual authors
1705　　　Dictionaries. Encyclopedias
1711　　　History

1/
　For Table II, see pp. 331-340. Add number in table to 1450

	Tariff policy (Protection and free trade) - Cont.
1713	General works
	Drawbacks
	Cf. HF2661+, Tariffs upon exports
	HF5492+, Transportation of merchandise
	in bond
1715	General works
1716	United States
1717	Other regions and countries, A-Z
1718	By particular commodity, A-Z
	Tariff. Reciprocity. Favored nation clause, etc.
	For tariff acts and laws in general, see K.
	For discussion of particular treaties, see
	HF1750+
1721	General works
1723	Colonial tariffs
	Including policy
	By region or country
	United States
1731.A1-5	Periodicals. Societies. Serials
.A6-Z	General works
1732	Treaties with other countries, A-Z. By date
	.A4 Colonies, dependencies
	.A5 American republics
1733	Other regions or countries, A-Z
	Under each country:
	.x General works
	.x2 Treaties with other countries, A-Z
	By region or country
	United States
1750	Periodicals. Serials
1751	Societies
	Collected works (nonserial)
1752	Several authors
.5	Individual authors
	History and conditions
1753	General works
.3	Biography
	By period
1754	Through 1865
1755	1865-1897/1900
	1897/1900-
1756	General works
1757	General special

Tariff policy (Protection and free trade)
By region or country - Continued
1761-2580.7   Other regions or countries, A-Z.
Table VII, modified 1/
Under each country:

10 nos.	5 nos.	1 no.	
(1)	(1)	.A1-19	Periodicals. Societies. Serials
(2)			Collected works (nonserial)
(3)	(2)	.A5-Z6	History and conditions
(3.3)			Biography
			By period
(4)	(3)		Early
(5)	(4)		Later
(6)		.Z7A-Z	Recent
(7)		.Z8A-Z	Special
(9)	(5) 2/	.Z9A-Z	Local, A-Z

For Great Britain use:
2044   Through 1846
2045   1846-1900
2046   1901-
For France use:
2099.A1 Colonies (General)

2580.9   Underdeveloped areas

Tariff and other interests
2581   Relation to navigation interests
2591   Relation to trusts
2601   Relation to farmer interests
2611   Relation to labor interests
2619   Relation to cultural interests
Cf. HF2651.B7, Tariff on books
N8770, Tariff on works of art
2651   Tariffs on commodities. By commodity, A-Z
For tariff schedules, see HJ6041+
For tariff on advertising matter, see HF5835
Under each:
.xA2   General works
.xA3-Z By region or country, A-Z
e. g.   Copper
.C78A2   General works
.C78A3-Z   By region or country, A-Z
Cf. HD9000+, Subdivision (.8) under each country
Tariffs on exports
2661   General works
By region or country
2664   United States
2665   Canada
2666   Latin America. By region or country, A-Z
2667   Europe. By region or country, A-Z
2669   Other regions or countries, A-Z

1/
For Table VII, see pp. 331-340. Add number in table to 1750
2/
For Poland use (4.5)

	Tariff policy (Protection and free trade)
	Tariffs on exports - Continued
2671	By commodity, A-Z
	Subarranged like HF2651
2701	Export premiums
	Cf. HF1715+, Drawbacks
	By region or country
	America, see HF3211+
	United States
3000	Periodicals. Serials
	For societies, associations, boards of trade,
	see HF294+
	Statistics
3001	General works
3002	By date
	Exports
3003	General works
3004	By date
	Imports
3005	General works
3006	By date
3007	Internal commerce
	Including interstate commerce, intrastate commerce,
	retail trade, wholesale trade, etc.
3008	Congresses
	For local conventions, see HF3151+
	Directories
	Including foreign trade; for local trade, see HF5038+
3010	General
3011	Export
3012	Import
	History
3021	General works
	Biography
3023.A2A-Z	Collective
.A3-Z	Individual, A-Z
	By period
	Early through 1810
3025	General works
3027.1	The Embargo acts, 1807-1809
	Including the non-importation act of 1806
.3	1811-1860
.6	Civil war
3028	1865-1900
3029	1901-1914
3030	1914-1920. World War I
3031	1921-
3035	Handbooks, manuals, etc.
	Foreign commerce
3041	Of the Atlantic
3043	Of the Pacific
3045	With the tropics
3065-3150	With other regions. Table I, modified 1/

1/
  For Table I, see pp. 331-340. Add number in table to 3050

By region or country
  United States – Continued
    Local commerce
      Including foreign commerce of individual areas

3151	Atlantic States
3153	Southern States
	Including Confederate States
3155	Mississippi Valley
3157	Great Lakes region
3159	Pacific States
	Including Western States
3161	By state, A–W
3163	By city, A–Z
	Including annual reviews of commerce, trade, finance, etc.

America (General)

3211	General works
3212	Inter-American commissions, conferences, etc.
	Latin America, see HF3230.5
3221–4040.7	Other regions or countries. Table VII, modified 1/
	Under each country:

10 nos.	5 nos.	1 no.	
(1)	(1)	.A1–4	Periodicals. Societies. Serials
(1.5)	(1.5)	.A45A–Z	Statistics
(2)	(1.7)	.A46A–Z	Congresses
(3)	(1.8)	.A48A–Z	Directories
			For local directories, see HF5071+
	(2)	.A5–Z4	General works. History Including works on export trade
(4)			General
(4.5)			Biography
(5)			Early
(6)			Recent
(6.5)	(2.3)	.Z5A–Z	1945–
(7)	(2.5)	.Z6A–Z	Handbooks, manuals, etc.
(8)	(3)	.Z7A–Z	Foreign commerce. By region or country, A–Z Class here descriptive works; for works on policy, see HF1451+
			Local commerce Under each: .A1–3 Periodicals. Societies. Serials Directories, see HF5071+
(9)	(4)	.Z8A–Z	By state, etc., A–Z
(10)	(5) 2/	.Z9A–Z	By city, A–Z

1/
  For Table VII, see pp. 331–340. Add number in table to 3210

2/
  For Poland use (4.5)

<pre>
                          By region or country
3221-4040.7   Other regions or countries.
                          Table VII, modified - Continued

                      For Great Britain use:
                      3505   Through 1800
                        .15   Medieval
                        .2   Modern
                        .4   17th century
                        .6   18th century
                                 Early 19th century to 1870
                        .8   General works
                        .9   Orders in council
                                 Recent, 1870-
                      3506   General works
                        .2   World War I

                      For Ireland use:
                                    Local
                      3539.A2A-Z   Counties
                        .A3-Z   Cities, etc.

                      For British Commonwealth use:
                      3540   General works

                      For Germany use:
                               Recent
                      3566   General works
                        .2   World War I

4045   North Atlantic region
4050   Communist countries
</pre>

BUSINESS

Including business methods, "How to do it," i.e.
 the practical aspects of commerce
For special lines of business, <u>see</u> HD, HE, HG

<pre>
5001   Periodicals. Societies. Serials
5003   Yearbooks
5004   Congresses
              Collected works (nonserial)
5006   Several authors
5007   Individual authors
5011   Addresses, essays, lectures
              Dictionaries. Encyclopedias, <u>see</u> HF1001
5028   Calendars
                  Cf. HF53, Commerce yearbooks (General)
                      HF5003, Business yearbooks
</pre>

```
                        Business - Continued
                        Directories
                            Cf. D, E, F, Local residence directories which
                               include business directories
                               HC, General industrial directories of a
                                  country
                               HF54, General export and import directories
                               HF3010+, HF3211+, Trade directories
                               T, Directories of technical industries and
                                  manufactures
      5030                  General
                            By region or country
                              United States
      5035                      General
                                Local
      5041                        Atlantic States region
      5044                        Southern States region
      5047                        Middle Western States region
      5050                        Pacific and Western States region
      5065                        By state, A-W
      5068                        By city, A-Z
  5071-5330                   Other regions or countries.  Table III 1/
                              Under each country:
```

	3 or 2 nos.	1 no.	
	(1)	.A3A-Z	General
	(2)	.A5-Z	By place, A-Z

```
                        By business, see HD9000+, HG1536+, etc.
                        History
      5341                  General works
                            By region or country
      5343                    United States
      5349                    Other regions or countries, A-Z
      5351              General works, treatises, and textbooks
                        Handbooks, manuals, etc.
      5356                  North American
      5358                  Latin American
      5361                  English (except North American)
      5363                  Other (not A-Z)
      5371              Forms
      5376              Syllabi.  Outlines
                        Vocational guidance
                            For works on vocational guidance for a specific
                               occupation or profession, see the occupation
                               or profession
   5381.A1A-Z           Periodicals.  Societies.  Serials
       .A2-Z            General works
       .2               Juvenile works
       .5               Vocational interests
       .7               Occupational aptitude tests
      5382              Occupation descriptions (Collective)
```

1/
  For Table III, see pp. 331-340. Add number in table to 5030

	Business
	Vocational guidance – Continued
5382.5	By region or country, A–Z
	Including manuals of vocational opportunities
	For United States use:
	.U5 General
	.U6 By state, A–W
5383	Applications for positions
5386	Success in business
	Cf. BF637.S8, Psychological aspects of success
	BF1729.B8, Business and business cycles
	(Astrology)
5387	Business ethics
5391	Popular works. Reminiscences. Personal narratives, etc.
5392	Juvenile works
	Occupations for women, see HD6058
	Marketing. Distribution of products
	For export and international marketing, see HF1009.5
	For statistics, see HF3001+
	For works on the marketing of a particular commodity,
	see the commodity in HD9000+
5410	Periodicals. Societies. Serials
5411	Congresses
5412	Dictionaries. Encyclopedias
5415	General works
	By region or country
.1	United States
.12	Other regions or countries, A–Z
.122	General special
	Communication of information
.123	General works
.124	Information services
.125	Data processing
.127	Market segmentation
.129	Marketing channels
	Marketing management
.13	General works
.135	Decision making
	Product management
.15	General works
.153	New products
.155	Product life cycle
.157	Quality of products
.16	Marketing audits
	Marketing research
.2	General works
.3	Market surveys. Consumer research, motivation
	research, etc.
	For individual places, see HC
	For maps, see G
.35	Vocational guidance
.4	Distributive education
	Cf. HF1101+, Commercial education
.5	Customer service

```
                    Business
                      Marketing.  Distribution of products - Continued
                        Physical distribution
                            Cf. HF5484+, Warehousing and storage
                                HF6761+, Shipping of merchandise, etc.
                                Delivery of goods
                                TS160+, Inventory control
                                TS195+, Packaging
5415.6                          General works
     .7                         Physical distribution management
     .9                         Product recall
5416                        Product coding
                            Price policy
     .5                         General works
5417                            Price maintenance
     .5                     Loss leaders

                      Wholesale trade.  Commission business, agencies.
                            Brokers.  Factors.  Jobbers
5419                        Periodicals.  Societies.  Serials
5420                        General works
                            By region or country
5421                            United States
     .5                         Other regions or countries, A-Z
5422                        Jobbers.  Factors.  Commission merchants.  Brokers
                      Retail trade
5428                        Periodicals.  Societies.  Serials
5429                        General works
     .15                    Data processing
                            Discount stores
     .2                         General works
     .215                       By region or country, A-Z
     .22                     Employee theft
     .225                    Equipment and supplies
                            Franchises
     .23                        General works
     .235                       By region or country, A-Z
     .25                     Inventories
     .26                     Personnel management
     .265                    Records and correspondence
     .27                     Security measures
                            Store location
     .275                       General works
     .28                        By region or country, A-Z
     .29                     Vocational guidance
                            By region or country
                                United States
     .3                             General works
     .4                             By region or state, A-Z
     .5                             By city, A-Z
     .6                         Other regions or countries, A-Z
```

```
                    Business - Continued
                      Shopping centers
                          Cf. HE336.S5, Traffic engineering
                             NA6218, Architecture
      5429.7              Periodicals.  Societies.  Serials
      5430                General works
                          By region or country
                            United States
         .3                   General works
         .4                     By region or state, A-Z
         .5                     By city, A-Z
         .6                   Other regions or countries, A-Z

                      Buying
      5437.A2A-Z           Periodicals.  Societies.  Serials
         .A3-Z             General works
                      Selling
      5438                Periodicals.  Societies.  Serials
         .2                Study and teaching.  Research
         .25               General works
                          By mail, see HF5730
         .3               By telephone
         .4               Sales management
         .5               Sales promotion
         .8               Other special topics, A-Z

                             .A9   Audiovisual aids
                             .C6   Competitions

                             .M4   Meetings
                             .P75  Psychological aspects
                             .R4   Reporting

      5439               By product, A-Z

                             .A4   Agricultural machinery
                             .A43  Air conditioning
                             .A46  Airplanes

                             .A5   Aluminum products
                             .A55  Antiques
                             .A8   Automobiles

                             .B3   Baked products
                                   Bonds, see HD4621
                                   Books, see Z278+
                             .B6   Boots and shoes
                             .B65  Bricks

                             .B7   Brushes
                             .B8   Building materials
                             .B85  Business forms

                             .C3   Calcium carbide
                             .C35  Carpets
                             .C4   Cemetery lots
                             .C42  Chemicals
```

Business
Selling – Continued
5439   By product, A–Z – Continued

      .C43   Christmas decorations
      .C435   Cigarettes

      .C6   Clothing
      .C67   Computers
      .C68   Confectionery

      .C69   Corsets
      .C7   Cosmetics

      .D3   Dairy products
      .D48   Diesel motors

      .D5   Directories
      .D7   Drapery

      .D75   Drugs. Medicines
      .D8   Dry goods

      .E4   Electric apparatus and appliances
      .E45   Electric power

      .E5   Embroidery
      .E55   Enamel and enameling
      .F64   Food
      .F7   Fountain pens
      .F75   Freight and freightage

      .F79   Fur garmets
      .F8   Furniture

      .G3   Garages. Service stations
      .G35   Gas appliances

      .G4   Gems
      .G43   Glassware

      .G68   Graphic arts
               For lithographs, see .L4
      .G75   Groceries

      .H27   Handicrafts
      .H3   Hardware

      .H4   Hats
      .H6   Hosiery

      .H78   House furnishings
      .H8   Household appliances

      .H82   Household supplies
      .I25   Ice

Business
<u>Selling</u>
5439   By product, A-Z - Continued

      .I3   Ice cream, ices, etc.
      .I4   Industrial equipment

      .I44   Industrial painting
              Insurance, <u>see</u> HG8091+

      .J4   Jewelry
      .K5   Kitchen utensils

      .K55   Knit goods
      .L3   Laundries

      .L35   Linen
      .L4   Lithographs
      .L9   Lumber

      .M18   Machine tools
      .M2   Machinery

      .M264   Magazine advertisements
      .M27   Meat

      .M35   Medical supplies
              Medicines, <u>see</u> .D75

      .M5   Millinery
      .M57   Mobile homes

      .M6   Motor trucks
      .M8   Musical instruments

      .N4   Newspapers
      .N8   Nursery stock

      .O4   Office equipment and supplies
      .O5   Oil burners

      .P28   Packinghouse products
      .P3   Paint

              Painting, Industrial, <u>see</u> .I44
      .P32   Paper

      .P36   Pens
      .P4   Phonographs

      .P43   Photographs
              Photographs, Wedding, <u>see</u> .W4

              Pipes, Tobacco, <u>see</u> .T55
      .P6   Pottery
      .P65   Poultry

```
                        Business
                          Selling
        5439                By product, A-Z - Continued

                            .P7    Printing
                            .R3    Radiators

                            .R36   Radio advertisements
                            .R37   Radio apparatus and supplies
                                   Real estate, see HD1375+

                            .R4    Refrigeration and refrigerating machinery
                            .R6    Roofing

                            .S37   Sausages
                                   Securities, see HG4621

                            .S42   Seeds
                                   Shoes, see .B6

                            .S47   Sign painting
                            .S48   Silicones

                            .S49   Silverware
                            .S55   Soft drinks
                            .S64   Sporting goods
                            .S8    Stainless steel

                            .T4    Tea
                            .T45   Telephone apparatus and supplies

                            .T48   Textiles
                            .T55   Tobacco pipes

                            .T6    Toys
                            .T9    Typewriters

                            .V3    Vaccum cleaners
                            .W3    Watches

                            .W4    Wedding photographs
                            .W5    Wine

                        Sales personnel
            .25             Periodicals.  Societies.  Serials
                            Biography
            .3                 Collective
            .32                Individual, A-Z
            .5              General works
            .55             Ability testing
            .6              Rating
            .65             Recruiting
            .7              Salaries, commissions, etc.
            .8              Training
                        Traveling sales personnel.  Commerical travelers
        5441                General works
        5444                Special.  By business, A-Z
                                For list of businesses, see HF5686
```

	Business – Continued
	Canvassing
5446	General works
5451	General agents
5456	By business, A–Z
	For list of businesses, see HF5686
	For electric power, etc., see TK445
	Peddling
5457	Periodicals. Societies. Serials
5458	General works
5459	By region or country, A–Z
	Department stores
	Including five-and ten-cent stores
5460	Periodicals. Societies. Serials
5461	General works
5463	General special
5465	By region or country, A–Z
	Under each country (using successive Cutter numbers):
	.x Periodicals. Societies. Serials
	.x2 General works
	.x3 History, policy, taxation, etc.
	.x35 Local, A–Z
	.x4 Particular firms, A–Z
	Mail order business
.5	Periodicals. Societies. Serials
5466	General works
5467	By firm, A–Z
5468	Branch stores. Chain stores
	Supermarkets
	Cf. HD9320+, Grocery industry
.5	Periodicals. Societies. Serials
5469	General works
	Convenience stores
	Cf. HD9320+, Grocery industry
.25	Periodicals. Societies. Serials
.5	General works
	Markets. Fairs
.7	Periodicals. Societies. Serials
5470	General works
5471	History
	By region or country
	Under each country:
	.x General
	.x2 Local, A–Z
5472	North America. By region or country, A–Z
5473	Latin America. By region or country, A–Z
5474	Europe. By region or country, A–Z
5475	Other areas. By region or country, A–Z
	Auctions
5476	General works
5477	By region or country, A–Z
	Charity fairs, see HV544
5481	Street fairs
	Trade fairs, see T391+

Business - Continued

Stock exchanges, see HG4551+

Secondhand trade

5482   General works

.3   Garage and yard sales

Black market

.6   General works

.65   By region or country, A-Z

5483   Vending machines

.5   College stores

Warehousing and storage

Warehousing. Customs warehouses

Including bonded warehouses in general and
warehouse warrants and receipts

For cold storage, see TP493; factory storage
facilities, see TS189+

General works

5484   Early through 1800

5485   1801-

By region or country

United States

5487.A1-3   Periodicals. Societies. Serials

.A7-Z   General works

5488   Companies. By city and company, A-Z

Assign 2 Cutters, the first for the
name of the city, and the second
for the name of the company

5489   Other regions or countries, A-Z

Under each country:

.x Periodicals. Societies. Serials

.x3 General works

.x4 By company, A-Z

Transportation of merchandise in bond

5490   General works

By region or country

United States

5491   General works

5493   Special articles, A-Z

5494   Other regions or countries, A-Z

Under each country:

.x Periodicals. Societies. Serials

.x2 General works

.x3 General special

.x4 Special articles, A-Z

5495   Storage methods and appliances

Business organization and administration, see HD28+,
HF5351+

Personnel

See HF5549+, Personnel management see

Executives. Executive ability HD38.2+

Cf. HD4965.2+, Executive salaries

5500.2   General works

.3   By region or country, A-Z

5501   Clerks

Class here organization, training, etc. For
labor conditions, see HD8039.M39

5506   Inspectors

Business — Continued
Equipment
    Cf. HD9999.B93, Business machines
        HF5688+, Accounting supplies, equipment,
           mechanical devices, etc.
        HF5735+, Filing and indexing

5520	General works
5521	Store and office fixtures
	Point-of-sale systems
5530	General works
5531	Cash registers
5541	Other appliances, A-Z

    .C3 Calculating machines
    .C8 Copying process
        Cf. Z48, Process of duplicating
    .S8 Stamps
    .T3 Tabulating machines
    .T4 Telephone
    .T9 Typewriters

Office organization and management

5546	Early works through 1900
	1901-
5547.A2A-Z	Periodicals. Societies. Serials
.A3-Z	General works
.2	Office layout
.25	Office location
.5	Office practice. Secretarial work

    .A1A-Z Periodicals. Societies. Serials
    .A2-Z   General works

Office equipment and supplies
    Cf. HD9999.04, Office equipment and supplies
        industry
        HF5688+, Accounting supplies, equipment, etc.
        HF5679, Methods of machine accounting

5548	General works

Electronic data processing
    Cf. JK468.A8, Automatic data processing
        (Government administration)
        QA76+, Electronic calculating machines

.125	Periodicals. Societies. Serials
.2	General works
.3	Real-time data processing
.4	Particular equipment or processes, A-Z

    .D17 DAFIN
    .L4 Leo computer
    .06 Optical scanners

.5	Computer program languages, A-Z

    .A17 ALGEC
    .A2   ALGOL
    .A23 APL   A8   A-STAT
    .A9   AUNTIE

    .B3   Basic
    .C2   COBOL
    .C24 COST

    .D2   DYNAMO
    .D24 DYNFOR

```
                    Business
                      Office organization and management
                        Office equipment and supplies
                          Electronic data processing
5548.5                      Computer program languages, A-Z  -  Continued
                              .F2   FORTRAN
                              .N2   NEBULA
                              .N25  NICOL

                              .P2   PL/1
                              .R2   RPG
                              .S2   SIMSCRIPT
     .6                     Computer leases
                      Industrial psychology
                        Cf. BF481, Psychology of work
                            BF482, Psychology of fatigue
                            BF905, Graphology in personnel management
     .7                 Periodicals.  Societies.  Serials
     .8                 General works
     .85                Job stress
                      Personnel management.  Employment management
                        Cf. HD5261+, Vacations
                        For works on personnel management in a
                          specific occupation or profession, see
                          the occupation or profession
5549.A2                Periodicals.  Societies.  Serials
     .A23              Dictionaries.  Encyclopedias
     .A3-Z             General works
     .15               Study and teaching.  Research
     .2                By region or country, A-Z
     .5                By topic, A-Z
                          .A34  Affirmative action program
                                   Cf. HD4903+, Freedom of labor
                          .A4   Alcoholism
                          .A43  Alien labor
                          .A83  Attitude surveys

                                Communication
                          .C6     General works
                          .C62    In-house publications, manuals, etc.
                                     Cf. PN4784.E6, Practical journalism
                          .C67  Compensation management
                          .C7   Competition
                          .C8   Counseling
                          .D55  Dismissal of employees
                                   Cf. HD5853+, Labor market
                          .D7   Drug abuse
                          .E42  Employee assistance programs
                          .E43  Employee theft
                          .E45  Employment in foreign  countries
                          .E5   Employment tests
                          .G7   Grievance procedures
                          .G73  Group relations training.  T-groups
                          .H3   Hardcore unemployed

                          .I5   Incentives
                                   Cf. HD4926+, Methods of remuneration
                          .I53  Induction
                          .I6   Interviewing
```

Business
Personnel management. Employment management

5549.5   By topic, A- Z - Continued

    .J6   Job analysis
    .J616 Job enrichment
    .J62   Job evaluation

    .J63   Job satisfaction
    .L3   Labor discipline
          Cf. HD6490.D5, Discipline by
                 employee groups
    .M3   Manpower planning
    .M5   Minorities
    .M6   Morale
    .M63   Motivation
    .O44   Older employees

    .P35   Performance standards
    .P4   Personnel records
    .P7   Promotions

    .R3   Rating
    .R44   Recruiting of employees
    .R45   References
    .R47   Relocation of employees
    .R5   Research
    .R54   Resignation of employees

    .S38   Selection of employees
    .S4   Seniority, Employee
    .S8   Suggestion systems
          T-groups, see .G73
    .T5   Time study
    .T54   Timekeeping

    .T7   Training of employees
    .T8   Turnover of employees
             Cf. HD5701+, Labor supply

Finance, see HG4001+
Credit, see HG3701+

5599   Other activities not elsewhere provided for, A-Z
              Advertising, see HF5801+
   .M3 Mailing
       Shipping, see HF5761+

Accounting. Bookkeeping
     Cf. HC79.F55, Flow of funds accounting
        HC79.I5, National income accounting
        HJ9701+, Public accounting

5601   Periodicals. Societies. Serials
5603   Congresses
         Collected works (nonserial)
  .5   Several authors
  .6   Individual authors
         Biography
5604   Collective
  .5   Individual,A-Z

Business
Accounting. Bookkeeping – Continued
History

5605	General works
	By period
5607	Ancient
5609	Medieval
	Cf. HF393, Sources and documents
5611	Modern
5616	By region or country, A–Z
.5	Underdeveloped areas
5621	Dictionaries. Encyclopedias
5625	Theory. Method. Relation to other subjects
5627	Certified public accountants. Expert accounting. Examination of accounts
	Cf. HF5667, Auditing
	HJ9701+, Public accounting
5629	Addresses, essays, lectures
5630	Study and teaching. Research
	Class here schools of accounting only; for commercial education in general, schools, etc., see HF1101+
	General works, treatises, and textbooks
	English and American
5631	Through 1800
5633	1801–1850
5635	1851–
	French
5641	Through 1800
5642	1801–
	German
5644	Through 1800
5645	1801–
	Italian
5647	Through 1800
5648	1801–
	Spanish
5650	Through 1800
5651	1801–
5653	Russian and other Slavic
5655	Other languages, A–Z
5657	General special
.5	Current value accounting
5658	Disclosure in accounting
.5	Inflation, price fluctuations and accounting
5659	Shortcuts, helps, etc., for bookkeepers
5661	Problems, exercises, examinations
	Auditing
	Cf. HF5627, Expert accounting
5667	General works
.15	Audit committees
.6	Auditor's reports
	Internal auditing
5668	Periodicals. Societies. Serials
.15	Congresses
.25	General works
5669	Installation of accounts

Business
Accounting. Bookkeeping – Continued
Special forms

5671		Card system
5673		Columnar and tabular
5677		Loose sheet
5679		Machine methods. Electronic data processing
		Accounts and books
5680		General works
5681		Special, A–Z
	.A2	Accounts current
	.A3	Accounts receivable
	.A4	Adjustment accounts
	.A5	Amortization
	.A8	Assets
	.B2	Balance sheet. Financial statements
	.B5	Bill book
	.B7	Branches
	.B9	Buying
	.C25	Capital
	.C28	Cash handbook
	.C4	Checkbook
	.C5	COD sales
	.C6	Consignment
	.C67	Contingencies
	.D38	Deferred credit
	.D39	Deferred tax
	.D5	Depreciation. Obsolescence
	.E9	Expense
		Financial statements, see .B2
	.F84	Fund accounting
	.G55	Going concern
	.G6	Good will
	.H8	Human capital
	.I48	Income
		Cf. HF5681.E9, Expense
	.I49	Industrial research
	.I5	Installment plans
	.I55	Intangibles
	.I6	Interest
		Cf. HG1621+, Bank management
		Inventories, see .S8
	.I7	Invoices
	.J6	Journal
	.L2	Labor costs
	.L3	Leases
	.L5	Ledger
	.L6	Liabilities
		Loss and profit, see .P8
	.M3	Maintenance
		Obsolescence, see .D5
	.N65	Non-wage payments
	.O8	Overhead
	.P3	Patents
	.P8	Profit and loss
		Purchasing account, see .B9
	.R25	Ratio analysis
	.R3	Realization
	.R34	Replacement costs

Business
Accounting. Bookkeeping
Accounts and books
5681   Special, A-Z - Continued
                        Research, Industrial, see .I49
     .R4   Reserve
     .R6   Reversion
     .S3   Sales records

     .S5   Sinking funds
                    Cf. HF5681.D5, Depreciation
     .S8   Stock. Stocktaking. Inventories
     .S85   Stock rights
     .S9   Summaries
     .S93   Surplus
     .T3   Taxation
     .T4   Timekeeping
     .V3   Valuation
     .V7   Vouchers
     .W3   Wages
     .W4   Wastage
5686   By business or activity, A-Z
     .A15   Abrasives
     .A2   Accountants' accounts
                Administrators, see .E9
                Advertising, see HF5824
                Aeronautics
                    Air transportation, see .A38
                    Airplane industry, see .A4
     .A26   Agency business. Commercial agents
     .A3   Agricultural cooperative credit associations
     .A35   Agricultural machinery
                Agriculture. Cooperative agriculture, see S567+
     .A38   Air transportation. Airlines
     .A4   Airplanes

     .A5   Aluminum

     .A65   Apartment houses
                Architects, see .P9A1+
     .A73   Artisans
     .A76   Associations, industries, etc.
                    Including voluntary associations, etc.
                Asylums, see .C2+
     .A8   Auctioneers
     .A9   Automobiles
                    Cf. HF5686.G25, Garage
                Automotive transportation, see HE5618

     .B2   Bakers
                Banking, see HG1706+
     .B3   Bankruptcy
                    Cf. HF5686.R4, Receivers
     .B34   Beauty shops
     .B36   Board of trade
     .B37   Books
     .B4   Boots and shoes
     .B45   Bowling centers.   Bowling alleys
     .B5   Breweries
     .B6   Brickmakers

Business
Accounting. Bookkeeping

5686   By business or activity, A–Z – Continued

.B65   Brokers
          For commission business (Produce),
            see .C5
          For cotton industry, see .C85

.B7   Builders. Contractors. Construction
.B8   Building and loan associations
.B9   Butchers
.C13   Canning
.C14   Carbonated water. Carbonated beverages
.C15   Carriage builders
.C155 Caterers and catering
.C17   Cement
.C175 Cemeteries
.C18   Chain stores
       Charitable institutions
.C2   Public
.C3   Private
.C35   Chemists. Chemicals
       Churches, see BV773; BX1947
.C42   Cigars
.C425 Clay industries
.C427 Cleaning and dyeing
.C43   Clock and watchmaking
.C44   Clothing
.C45   Clubs
.C48   Coal
       Coal mining, see .M6
.C49   Coffee
       Colleges, see LB2342
       Colliery, see .M6
.C495 Commercial finance companies
.C5   Commission business (Produce)
       Companies, see .C7
.C63   Confectionery
       Construction, see .B7
       Contractors, see .B7
.C67   Cooperative societies
          For cooperative banks, see HG2033+
.C68   Corn products
.C7   Corporations
         Cf. HF5686.N56, Nonprofit corporations.
            Conversion of business into cor-
            poration. Reconstruction
          HJ9768+, Government corporations
.C8   Cost finding
         For special businesses, see the business,
          e. g. .M3, Manufacturers' accounts
.C85   Cotton
       Cotton manufacturers, see .T4
.C87   Cottonseed oil
       Dairy, see SF261
.D4   Dentifrices
.D5   Department stores
       Doctors, see .P9P1+
       Domestics, see TX326
.D7   Drugs. Drugstores
.E27   Electric household appliances

Business
Accounting. Bookkeeping
5686   By business or activity, A–Z – Continued
             .E3   Electric industries
             .E35   Electric power distribution
                    Electric street railways, see HE4351
             .E4   Electric utilities
                    Engineering, see TA185
             .E9   Executors. Estate accounting. Fiduciary
                       accounting
                         For probate, see .P85

                    Factories, see .M3
                    Farms, see S567
             .F4   Fertilizers
                    Finance companies, Commercial, see .C495
                    Finance companies, Personal, see .L6
             .F5   Fisheries
             .F6   Flour and feed
             .F616 Food
                    Foreign exchange, see HG3851
             .F62   Forest industries
                         For lumber, see HF5686.L9
                         For wood-using industries, see .W8
                    Forest management, see SD393
             .F63   Forging
             .F64   Forwarding agents
             .F65   Foundries
             .F67   Freight
                         Cf. TF664+, Railroad engineering
             .F7   Fruit
             .F75   Fuel
             .F78   Fur
             .F8   Furniture

             .G23   Gambling
             .G25   Garage
             .G3   Gas
             .G35   Geological research
             .G38   Glass
             .G4   Glaziers
             .G45   Goldsmithing
             .G5   Grain
                         For commission business, see HF5686.C5
             .G6   Grain elevators
                    Granite dealers and workers, see .S79
             .G7   Greek letter societies
             .G8   Grocers
                         For supermarkets, see HG5686.S96
             .G9   Gums and resins

             .H3   Hardware
             .H4   Heating utensils
             .H5   Hides and skins
             .H6   Holding companies
             .H62   Home health care services
             .H65   Hosiery
             .H7   Hospitals
                         For nursing homes, see .N9
             .H75   Hotels, restaurants, etc.

Business
Accounting. Bookkeeping

5686   By business or activity, A-Z - Continued

    .H77   House furnishings
             Housekeeping, see TX326
    .H83   House management

    .I4   Ice
    .I42   Ice cream, ices
    .I46   Incineration
             India rubber, see .R8
    .I55   Instruments
             Insurance, see HG8077, HG8848, HG9678
             Interest, see HF5681.I6
    .I56   International business enterprises
    .I58   Investment trusts
    .I6   Investors
             Iron, see .S75
    .J6   Jewelers

    .K55   Kitchen utensils
    .L3   Laundry service
             Lawyers, see .P91+
    .L4   Lead
    .L42   Lease and rental services
             Libraries, see Z683
             Linen, see .T4
    .L46   Liquor
    .L5   Lithographers
    .L6   Loans. Personal finance companies
             Local transit, see HE4351
    .L65   Lotteries
    .L9   Lumber

    .M2   Machine shops
    .M3   Manufactures. Factories
    .M35   Marketing
    .M37   Matches
    .M4   Meat
    .M45   Metal workers
    .M48   Military supplies
    .M5   Milk
    .M6   Mining
               Including coal mining
    .M65   Missions
    .M67   Mortgage companies

    .M7   Motion pictures
             Motorbus lines, see HE5618
             Municipal, see HJ9771+
    .N4   Newspapers
    .N5   Nonferrous metal industries
    .N56   Nonprofit corporations
    .N6   Notaries
    .N9   Nursing homes

    .O3   Office buildings
    .O4   Oil industries
    .O5   Old age pensions
    .O9   Oxygen therapy equipment

Business
Accounting. Bookeeping
5686   By business or activity, A-Z - Continued
          .P15   Packing houses
          .P17   Paints
          .P2   Paper mills
          .P22   Paper
                 Parks, see SB481+
          .P225 Partnerships
          .P23   Pawnbrokers
          .P235 Peat
          .P24   Performing arts
          .P25   Personal accounts
          .P3   Petroleum
          .P33   Photo-engraving
          .P35   Photography

          .P4   Pipelines
          .P6   Planing mills
          .P7   Plumbers
                 Postal service, see HE6101, General;
                    HE6041, United States; etc.
          .P8   Printers
                 Produce, see .C5
          .P86   Productivity and analysis
                 Professional
          .P89   General
          .P9   By profession, A-Z
                       .P9A1-9 Architects. Alphabetically by author
                       .P9L1-9 Lawyers. Alphabetically by author
                       .P9P1-9 Physicians. Alphabetically by author
          .P923 Public contracts
          .P925 Public health
          .P93   Public utilities
                 Public works. Municipal, see HJ9771+
          .P94   Publishers

          .R15   Radio and television equipment
          .R2   Railroad equipment
                 Railways, see HE2241
          .R3   Real estate, rent, etc.
          .R4   Receivers
          .R45   Refractories
          .R46   Refrigeration
          .R48   Refuse disposal
                 Resin, see .G9
                 Restaurants, see .H75
                 Retail business, see HF5601+
          .R5   Rice
          .R6   Road construction and maintenance
          .R8   Rubber

          .S3   Sand
                 Savings banks, see HG1895
          .S37   Sawmills
                 Schools, see LB2380
          .S39   Scrap metals
          .S4   Screw machine products
          .S43   Service industries
          .S45   Sewage disposal plants

                 212

Business
Accounting. Bookkeeping
5686   By business or activity, A-Z - Continued
       .S5   Shipbuilders
            Shipping, see HE605
       .S53   Shopping centers
            Silk, see .T4

       .S55   Silversmithing
       .S6   Slaughterhouses
       .S7   Stationery
       .S75   Steel
            Stock exchanges, see .B65
            Stock raising, see SF111
       .S8   Stoves

            Street railways, see HE4351
            Student activities, see LB3607
       .S94   Sugar
       .S96   Supermarkets
       .T2   Tailors
       .T3   Tanners

            Telegraph, see HE7695
            Telephone, see HE8785
            Television equipment, see .R15
       .T36   Television industry
       .T4   Textile industries

            Timber, see .L9
       .T6   Tobacco
            Trade-unions, see HD6486
       .T7   Transportation
            Transportation, Air, see TL720.2
            Transportation, Automotive, see HE5618
            Transportation, Local, see HE4351
       .T73   Travel agents
       .T8   Trustees
              Cf. HF5686.P85, Probate
                   HG4315.5, Trust companies
       .T85   Tube industry
       .T9   Typewriters
       .U54   Undertakers and undertaking
            University, see LB2342

       .V3   Varnish
       .W2   Warehouse business
       .W3   Water resources development. Waterworks
              Cf. HF5686.S45, Sewage disposal plants
       .W6   Wholesale business

       .W65   Wine merchants. Wine-making
       .W68   Winter resorts
       .W8   Wood-using industries
              Including woodworking industries
            Wool, see .T4

     Supplies, equipment, mechanical devices, etc.
5688   General works
5689   Catalogs

Business - Continued
 Business mathematics. Commercial mathematics
  General works, treatises and textbooks

5691	American and English
5693	Other languages, A-Z
5694	Problems, exercises, etc.
5695	General special
.5	By business, A-Z

    For list of businesses, <u>see</u> HF5686
    For agriculture, <u>see</u> S566
    For printers, <u>see</u> Z245

5696	Average of accounts. Equation of payments

   Including tables
  Interest, <u>see</u> HG1626+
  Discount, <u>see</u> HG1651+

Tables, etc.
 Ready reckoners

5697	American and English before 1860
5698	Foreign before 1860
5699	American and English, 1860-
5702	Foreign, 1860-

 Wage tables
   For comparative tables of wages, <u>see</u> HD4961
   For salary tables of public officials,
    <u>see</u> HJ9971+

5705	General
5706	By business, A-Z

   For list of businesses, <u>see</u> HF5686
 Money, weights, and measures
  Cf. HG3854+, Foreign exchange

5711	Periodicals. Societies. Serials
5712	General works
5714	Weights and measures

   Cf. QC81+, Physics

5715	By region or country, A-Z

   Under each country:
    .x Foreign and domestic
    .x2 Domestic only

5716	Tables of cost, quantity, weight, etc.,

   of particular commodities, A-Z

   .A4 Agricultural products
   .A8 Awnings
   .B3 Beets
    Blinds, <u>see</u> .S2
   .B4 Books
   .B5 Bottles

   .B6 Boxes
    Butter, <u>see</u> SF240
   .C2 Cattle
   .C3 Cement
    Cheese, <u>see</u> SF240

   .C4 Coal
   .C5 Coffee
    Corn, <u>see</u> .G7
   .C6 Cotton

Business
  Business mathemathematics.   Commercial mathematics
    Tables, etc.
5716   Tables of cost, quantity, weight, etc. of
      particular commodities, A-Z - Continued

      .C7   Cotton goods
      .C8   Cottonseed
      .C85   Cottonseed oil
           Cream, see SF240
           Dairy products, see SF240
           Doors, see .S2
      .D8   Dry goods
      .E3   Eggs
      .E4   Electricity
           Cf. TK151, Electrical engineering
           Envelopes, see .S6
      .F3   Fertilizer
      .F35   Fish

      .F4   Flax
      .F5   Flax seed
           Flax yarn, see .Y3
      .F6   Flour
      .F9   Fruit
      .G4   Glass
      .G6   Gold
      .G7   Grain
           Granite, see .S8
           Gravel, see .S16
      .G8   Groceries

      .H3   Hardware
           Cf. HF5716.I8, Iron
                  HF5716.N3, Nails
      .H4   Hay
      .H5   Hoops
      .I8   Iron
           Cf. HF5716.N3, Nails
                  HF5716.R3, Rails
                  HF5716.S7, Steel
      .J4   Jewelry
           Liquids
           For distilled liquors, see TP609
      .L3   Through 1850
      .L4   1850-
      .L5   Gauging of tanks
      .L8   Lumber.   Wood
           Cf. HF5716.S2, Sash, doors, and blinds
                  HF5716.V4, Veneer
      .M4   Meat
      .M5   Metal industry
           Milk, see SF240
      .N4   Netting
      .O4   Oil
           Paper, see .S6
      .P4   Pearls
           Petroleum, see .O4
           Picture frames, see N8553

Business
Business mathematics.   Commercial mathematics
Tables, etc.

5716   Tables of cost, quantity, weight, etc. of
particular commodities, A–Z – Continued

.P5	Plywood
.P6	Pork
.P65	Poultry
.P7	Potatoes
	Printing, see Z245
.P8	Produce
.R4	Real estate business
.R5	Resin
.S16	Sand and gravel
.S2	Sashes, doors, and blinds
	Sheet iron, see .I8
.S5	Slate
	Cf. HF5716.S8, Stone
	Spirits, see .L3+
.S6	Stationery
.S7	Steel
	Cf. HF5716.H3, Hardware
	HF5716.I8, Iron
.S8	Stone
.S9	Sugar
	Tanks, see .L3+
.T25	Tea
.T3	Textiles
	Cf. HF5716.C6, Cotton
	HF5716.F4, Flax
	HF5716.W6, Wool
	Timber, see .L8
.T4	Tin and tin plate
	Cf. TS597, Metal manufactures
.T5	Tobacco
.V4	Veneer
.W3	Wallpaper
	Wheat, see .G7
	Windows, see .S2
.W5	Wire
	Wood (Firewood), see .L8
.W6	Woolen goods
	Cf. TS, Manufactures

Business communication
     Cf. HD30.3, Communication in management
         HF5549.5.C6+, Communication in
           personnel management
         T58.6+, Management information systems

5717   Periodicals.   Societies.   Serials
5718   General works
   .2   By region or country, A–Z
   .5   Proposal writing
5719   Business report writing
     Cf. PE1115, Commercial manuals
         PF3120.C7, Commercial English, German, etc.

```
                        Business
                          Business communication - Continued
                            Business correspondence
                                Including works of general application
                                  by government as well as private bodies
                                  or individuals.  For works applied to a
                                  specific subject, see the subject
                                Dictionaries, see HF1002
5721                            General works, treatises, and textbooks
                                Dictation exercises for stenographers, see Z56
                                Manuals, forms, etc.
5726                                English
5728                                Other languages, A-Z
                                Special
5730                                Sales letters
                                        Cf. HF5438, Selling
                                            HF5466, Mail order business
5733                                Other special, A-Z

                                    .A3  Adjustment letters
                                    .B3  Bank letters
                                    .C5  Circular letters
                                    .C7  Credit letters

                                    .F6  Form letters
                                    .L4  Letterheads

5734                                By business, A-Z
                                        For list of businesses, see HF5686
                            Filing and indexing
5735                            Periodicals.  Societies.  Serials
                                Methods.  Arrangement and classification of records
5736                                General works
5741                                Files and indexes
                                        Including catalogs of makers and dealers
5746                                Tables.  Charts.  Indexing forms
                                        For special lines of business, see the business

                        Shipping of merchandise, etc.  Delivery of goods
                            General works
5761                            American and English
5765                            Other
                            Packaging economics
                                Cf. TS195+, Packaging engineering
5770.A1A-Z                      Periodicals.  Societies.  Serials
     .A15A-Z                    Congresses
     .A2-Z                      General works
5773                            Other special, A-Z
                                .B7  Breakage, shrinkage, etc.

                                .C2  COD shipments
                                .C7  Consular requirements, invoices, etc.
                                .L3  Labels

                                .S3  Samples
                                .T3  Tare
                                .W4  Weight, Marking of

5780                            By region or country, A-Z
```

```
                         Business - Continued
                           Advertising
5801                         Periodicals.  Societies.  Serials
5802                         Yearbooks
     .5                      Congresses
5803                         Dictionaries.  Encyclopedias
                             Directories of advertisers and advertising agents
5804                            General
                                United States
5805                              General
5806                              By state, A-W
5807                              Local, A-Z
     .5                           By business, A-Z 1/
5808                            Other regions or countries, A-Z
                                    Under each country:
                                       .x   General
                                       .x2  By place, A-Z
                                       .x3  By business, A-Z
                             Biography
5810.A2A-Z                      Collective
     .A3-Z                       Individual, A-Z
                             History
5811                            General works
5813                            By region or country, A-Z
                             Study and teaching.  Research
5814                            General works
5815                            By region or country, A-Z
5816                         Competitions.  Prizes.  Awards
                             General works, treatises, and textbooks
                                Theoretical
5821                              General works
5822                              Psychology of advertising
                                Practical
5823                              General works
5824                              Office organization, accounting, etc.
5825                              Advertising writing
                                       Including lay-out and typography
5826                              Forms, etc.
     .5                           Media planning
5827                         General special
     .2                      Comparison advertising.  Positioning
     .4                      Cooperative advertising
     .6                      Corrective advertising
     .8                      Fraudulent advertising
5828                         Point of sale advertising
     .2                      Data processing
     .4                      Advertising as a profession.  Vocational guidance
5829                         Juvenile works
5831                         Ethics and aesthetics
                                  Cf. HF5843.5, Outdoor advertising
5832                         Consumer education and advertising
5833                         Regulation of and/or by the state
5834                         Self-regulation.  Industry regulation
5835                         Taxation
```

1/
    For list of businesses, see HF5686

```
                           Business
                             Advertising - Continued
                               Methods
        5837                       Campaigns
        5839                       Light and color
        5841                       Signs
                                       For history and antiquities of signs, see GT3910
                                   Outdoor advertising.  Billboards, etc.
                                       For art posters, see NC1800+
        5843                       General works
           .5                      Aesthetics, regulation, etc.
        5844                   Motion pictures

                                   Display of merchandise.  Show windows, etc.
        5845                       General works
        5847                       Special seasons of display, A-Z
        5849                       By business, A-Z
                                       For list of businesses, see HF5686
        5851                   Advertising cards
                                   Cf. TT360, Sign and card writing
        5856                   Transportation advertising.  Streetcar advertising
                                   Direct-mail advertising.  Catalogs, circulars
                                       handbills, etc.
        5861                       General works
        5862                       Making of catalogs
        5863                       Distributing business
                                       Including lists of names
        5866                   Jubilee shows, etc.
                                   Exhibitions, see T396

                                   Newspaper and magazine advertising
                                     Guides
        5871                         General
     5901-6097                       By region or country.  Table II 1/
                                     History
        6103                         General works
        6105                         By region or country, A-Z
        6107                     General works
        6111                     Rates
        6121                     By class of newspaper or magazine, A-Z
                                       .A4  Agricultural magazines
                                       .H6  House organs
                                       .M5  Medical journals
                                       .R4  Religious press
                                       .T7  Trade journals
        6122                     By newspaper or magazine, A-Z
                                   By form of advertisement
        6123                       General works
        6125                       Classified advertising.  Want ads, etc.
        6127                       Coupon ads
        6133                       Cuts
        6135                       Slogans
        6141                       Miscellaneous
```

1/
     For Table II, see pp. 331-340. Add country number in table to 5900

Business
   Advertising
     Methods – Continued
6146   Other methods, A–Z

         .A4   Aircraft
                 Including skywriting
         .B6   Blotters
         .B7   Booklets

         .C2   Calendars
         .N7   Novelties

         .P6   Postcards
         .P7   Premiums
         .P75   Prize contests

         .R3   Radio broadcasting
         .S3   Samples
                 Skywriting, see .A4

         .T4   Telephone directories
         .T42   Television broadcasting
         .T7   Trading stamps

6161   By business, A–Z
         For list of businesses, see HF5686
6169   Individual advertisers, A–Z
      Advertising agencies
6178   General works
6181   Individual, A–Z
         Cf. HF5810, Biography
6182   By region or country, A–Z
     Special lines of business, see HD, HE, HG

For public finance, see HJ

	Periodicals. Societies. Serials
1	United States
3	Canada
6	Latin America
	Europe
11	Great Britain
13	Austria
15	France
17	Germany
	Including West Germany
18	East Germany
19	Italy
21	Belgium
23	Netherlands
25	Soviet Union
27	Denmark
29	Norway
31	Sweden
33	Spain
34	Portugal
35	Switzerland
37	Other European countries, A-Z
41	Asia
46	Africa
51	Australia
52	New Zealand
61	Yearbooks
63	Congresses
	Directories
64	General
	By region or country
	United States
65	General works
66	By state, A-W
67	By city, A-Z
68	Canada
69	Latin America
	Europe
70	General works
71	Great Britain
73	France
75	Germany
77	Italy
79	Other European countries, A-Z
86	Asia
91	Africa
96	Australia
	Collected works (nonserial)
136	Several authors
138	Individual authors
151	Dictionaries. Encyclopedias

151.3	Terminology. Abbreviations. Notation
	Communication of information
.5	General works
.7	Information services
	Study and teaching. Research
152	General works
	By region or country
.25	United States
.5	Other regions or countries, A–Z
171	History
	Biography
— 172.A2A–Z	Collective
.A3–Z	Individual, A–Z
	General works, treatises, and textbooks
	Cf. HB142.5, Flow of funds accounting
173	English
.3	French
.5	German
.6	Other languages, A–Z
.8	Juvenile works
174	General special (Special aspects of the subject as a whole)
175	Addresses, essays, lectures
	Statistics
176	Collections of statistics
	For statistics by region or country, see HG181+
.5	Theory
177	Fund raising
	Cf. HV41, Charity organization and practice
178	Liquidity
	Cf. HG1656, Banking
	HG3893, International finance
	HG4028.C45, Corporation finance
179	Personal finance
	Cf. BV4397, Personal finance for clergymen
	HG3755+, Consumer credit
	HG7920+, Thrift and saving
	TX326, Home economics
	By region or country
	United States
181	General works
183	By region or state, A–Z
184	By city, A–Z
	Other regions or countries
	America
185.A2	General works
.A3–Z	By region or country, A–Z
	Europe
186.A2	General works
.A3–Z	By region or country, A–Z
	Asia
187.A2	General works
.A3–Z	By region or country, A–Z

```
                    By region or country
                        Other regions or countries - Continued
187.5                       Africa
                                .A2     General works
                                .A3-Z   By region or country, A-Z
                            Atlantic Ocean islands
188.A2                          General works
    .A3-Z                           By island, A-Z
    .5                          Indian Ocean islands
                                    .A2     General works
                                    .A3-Z   By island, A-Z
189                             Australia
    .5                          New Zealand
                            Pacific Ocean islands
190.A2                          General works
    .A3-Z                           By island, A-Z
195                     Underdeveloped areas
```

MONEY

```
201                 Periodicals.  Societies.  Serials
                    Congresses
203                     General works
205                     Individual congresses.  By date
                    Latin Monetary Union
207                     Reports
209                     General works
216                 Dictionaries.  Encyclopedias
    .5              Terminology.  Abbreviations.  Notations
                    Study and teaching.  Research
217.A1A-Z               General works
    .A3A-Z              By region or country, A-Z
    .5              Museums.  Exhibitions
                    Statistics
                        Cf. HG3854+, Foreign exchange tables
218                     Collections of statistics
                            For statistics by region or country, see HG546+
    .5                  Theory
219                 Handbooks, manuals, etc.
                    Theory.  Method.  Relation to other subjects
                        History
220.A2A-Z               General works
    .A3-Z                   By region or country, A-Z
221                     General works
    .3                  General special
    .5                  Juvenile works
222.3                   Psychological aspects
                        Functions of money
    .5                      General works
223                         Standard of value
225                     Gresham's law
```

```
                    Money
                      Precious metals.  Bullion - Continued
                        Silver
                            Cf. HD9536, Metal industries
                               TN430+, Metallurgy
301                         General works
                            Silver market
305                           General works
307                           By region or country, A-Z
                                Under each country:
                                    .x   General works
                                    .x2  Local, A-Z
                            Silver standard
309                           General works
                              By region or country, see HG451+
312                         Bimetallism
315                       Small coins
                          Tokens, see CJ4801+
                          Mints
321                         General works
                            Assaying
                                Cf. TN550+, Metallurgy
325                           Official reports
327                           Standard of weight
328                           Tables
329                           Wastage
                          Counterfeiting
                              Cf. HG1696+, Check forgery
335                         General works
336                         By region or country, A-Z
                            Coins, see CJ101
339                         Paper money
341                         Safety devices
                                Cf. HG641+, Counterfeit detectors
                          Paper money
                            Technical production
                                Including materials and processes involved in the
                                    making of bank notes, bonds, postage stamps, etc.
348                           General works
349                           Paper
350                           Engraving and printing
351                         Theory
353                         History
                                Including descriptions and catalogs
     .3                     Emergency currency
                                Cf. HE6184.E4, Use of stamps as emergency currency
     .5                     Military currency.  Occupation currency
                          Credit, see HG3701+
                          Social credit
355                         General works
                            By region or country
357                           United States
359                           Other regions or countries, A-Z
                          The legal-tender power
361                         Theory
                            History
363.A3A-Z                     General works
   .A5-Z                      By region or country, A-Z
```

                Money
                    By region or country
                       United States – Continued
                          Coinage

551	Gold
	Silver
555	History
556	Controversial literature
	Bimetallism
561	History
562	Controversial literature
566	Small coins
	Paper money
	Bureau of Engraving and Printing
571	Annual reports
573	Other works
591	History
	Including descriptions and catalogs
593	Controversial literature
	Treasury notes
601	History
602	Controversial literature
	Greenbacks
604	History
605	Controversial literature
	National bank notes
607	History
608	Controversial literature
610	Federal Reserve notes
	Local paper money
621	Bank note reporters
622	History
623	Controversial literature
627	By place, A-Z
	Counterfeit detectors
641	General works
645	Paper

                              Money
                    By region or country - Continued
651-1492.7   Other regions or countries. Table VIII 1/
                        Under each country:

20 nos.	10 nos.	5 nos.	1 no.	
				Periodicals, see HG201
				Mint
(1)	(1)	(1)	.A1-5	Reports
(2)				General works
(3.5)	(1.5)	(1.5)		Statistics
		(2)	.A6-Z7	History
(5)	(2)			General works
(6)	(3)			Early. Medieval
(7)				1600-1775
(8)				1776-1850
(9)	(4)			1851-1945
(9.5)	(5)			1945-
		(3)	.Z8A-Z	Special
				Under each:
				.A3A-Z History
				For works on early
				period to 1776,
				see the period
(10)	(6)			Gold coinage
(11)				Silver coinage
(12)				Bimetallism
(13)				Other coins
	(7)			Paper money
(14)				General works
(15)				National bank notes
(16)				Other special
(18)	(8)			Miscellaneous plans
(19)	(9)			Counterfeit detectors
(20)	(10)	(4)	.Z9A-Z	Local, A-Z

1
    For Table VIII, see pp. 331-340. Add country number in table to 650

	Money – Continued
1495	Communist Countries
1496	Underdeveloped areas

BANKING

	Periodicals. Serials
1501	American
1503	British
1505	Other
	Societies
1507	United States. Canada
1509	Latin America
1511	Great Britain
1513	Other European countries, A–Z
1515	Other
1521	Congresses
	Collected works (nonserial)
1526	Several authors
1527	Individual authors
	Dictionaries. Encyclopedias, see HG151
1531	Yearbooks
1536	Directories
	History
1551	General works
	Biography
	For United States, see HG2463
1552.A1A–Z	Collective
.A3–Z	Individual, A–Z
1555	Ancient
	Medieval
1561	General works
1563	By place, A–Z
	17th–18th centuries
1567	Contemporary works
1569	Modern works
1571	19th century
1572	20th century
1573	1971–
	Statistics
1576	Collections of statistics
1577	Theory
	By region or country, see HG2493, etc.
	Study and teaching. Research
1581	General works
1582	By region or country, A–Z
	Museums. Exhibitions
1584	General works
.2	By region or country, A–Z
	Under each country:
	.x General works
	.x2 Special. By city, A–Z

	Banking – Continued
	Theory
1586	General works
1588	General special
	Communication of information
1590	General works
.5	Information services
1591	Addresses, essays, lectures
	General works, treatises, and textbooks
	Early works (before 1800), see HG1551+
1601	English
1603	French
1605	German
1607	Other languages, A–Z
1609	Juvenile works
1611	Handbooks, manuals, etc.

Bank management

1615	General works
	Personnel management
	Cf. HD8039.B26, Bank employees
.5	General works
.7	Special topics, A–Z
	.E5 Employment tests
	.J6 Job descriptions
	.M5 Minorities
	.R3 Recruiting of employees
	.T4 Tellers
	.T7 Training of employees
1616	Other topics, A–Z
	.B7 Branch banks
	.C34 Capital
	.C55 Correspondent banks
	.C6 Costs
	.D5 Directors
	.E7 Equipment and supplies
	.F6 Forms, blanks, etc.
	.I5 Investments by banks
	Cf. HG1723, Bank stocks
	.L55 Location
	.L6 Lock box services
	.M3 Marketing
	.P8 Public relations. Customer relations
	.R4 Records and correspondence
	Safe-deposit services, see HG2251+
	.S37 Security measures
	.S4 Service charges
	.S6 Size of banks
	Trust services, see HG4301+
	.W6 Work measurement
	Organization, practice, see HG1601+
	Rate of interest \
	Including regulation
	For theory, see HB521+
1621	General works
1623	By region or country, A–Z

Banking – Continued
Interest tables
1626   General works
United States
1628   General works
1630.01-.02   Special. By percent, 1-20
Compound interest tables
1632   General works
1634   Tables for sinking funds, amortization, equal
                           payments, etc.
1636   Savings and loan associations tables
1638   Other tables. By language, A-Z
1639   Time tables

Loans. Bank credit
1641   General works
1642   By region or country, A-Z
1643   Bank credit cards and check credit plans
Discount
1651   General works
1652   By region or country, A-Z
                       Cf. HG2562.D5, Federal Reserve banks
1654   Tables
1655   Acceptances
Reserves. Liquidity
1656.A3A-Z   General works
    .A4-Z   By region or country, A-Z
                       Cf. HG2562.R4, Federal Reserve banks

Accounts and deposits
1660.A3A-Z   General works
    .A4-Z   By region or country, A-Z
Insurance of deposits
    Including state guaranty of deposits
    Cf. HG9974, Bank insurance
1662.A3A-Z   General works
    .A4-Z   By region or country, A-Z

Drafts
    Cf. HG1655, Acceptances
        HG3745, Letters of credit
1685   General works
1687   Bank drafts
1689   Bills of exchange

Checks
    Cf. HG1953, Postal checks
1691   General works
1692   Collection system. Clearing
                       Cf. HG2301+, Clearinghouses
1693   Travelers' checks
Forgeries
    Cf. HG335+, Counterfeiting
        HG9984, Forgery insurance
1696   General works
1697   Signature examiners
1698   Protective safeguards
1703   Currency exchanges
                       Cf. HG3810+, Foreign exchange

```
                    Banking - Continued
                    Accounting.  Bookkeeping
                        Cf. HG1895, Savings banks
     1706               Theory
     1707               General works
       .5               Auditing.  Bank examination
     1708               General special
       .5             Communication systems.  Telecommunications
     1709             Electronic data processing
     1710             Electronic funds transfers
     1712             Telephone bill paying services
     1720             Bank secrecy.  Confidential communications
     1722             Mergers
     1723             Bank stocks.  Banking as an investment
                          Cf. HG1616.I5, Investments by banks
                      Banks and the state.  State supervision of banks
     1725               General works
                        Taxation
     1766                 General works
     1768                 By region or country, A-Z
                            Under each country:
                              .x    General works
                              .x2   Local, A-Z
                        Examination, see HG1707.5
     1778                 By region or country, A-Z
                            Under each country:
                              .x    General works
                              .x2   Local, A-Z
                      Special classes of banks and financial institutions
                          Cf. HG3726+, Credit institutions
                      Central banks.  Banks and the treasury
     1811               General works
     1851               Banks of issue
                        Control of money market
     1854                 General works
     1855                 Open market operations
                          Discount rate, see HG1651+
                          Reserve requirements, see HG1656+
                        By region or country, see HG2559, etc.
                      Savings banks
     1881               Periodicals.  Societies.  Serials
     1883               History
     1886               General works
                        Practice
     1891                 English
     1892                 French
     1893                 German
     1894                 Other languages, A-Z
     1895               Accounting.  Bookkeeping
     1897               Investments
     1899               Savings stamps
                        By region or country
                          Under each country:
                            (1)  Periodicals.  Societies.  Serials
                            (2)  General works
                            (3)  Local, A-Z
                                    For individual savings banks, see
                                      HG2613, HG2701+, subdivision (20)
                                      under each country
   1921-1923             United States
                            For directories, see HG2441+
```

```
                      Banking
                        Special classes of banks and credit institutions
                          Savings banks
                            By region or country - Continued
1926-1928                     Great Britain
     1939                     Other European regions or countries, A-Z
     1946                     Other regions or countries, A-Z
     1949                     Communist countries
                          Postal savings banks
     1951                     General works
     1953                     Postal checks
     1956                     By region or country, A-Z
                          School savings banks
     1961                     General works
     1966                     By region or country, A-Z
                          Trade-union banks
     1968                     General works
                            By region or country
       .5                      United States
     1969                     Other regions or countries, A-Z
                          Private banks
     1978                     General works
                            By region or country
                              For individual banks, see HG2613; HG2701+
     2002                       United States
     2012                       Great Britain
     2021                       Other European regions or countries, A-Z
     2031                       Other regions or countries, A-Z

                        Cooperative banking and credit institutions.  Peoples
                            banks.  Credit unions
     2032                   Periodicals.  Societies.  Serials
     2033                   Congresses
     2035                   General works
                          By region or country
                            United States
     2037                     General works
     2038                     By region or state, A-Z
     2039                   Other regions or countries, A-Z
                        Mortgage credit agencies.  Mortgage loans
                            Cf. HG4655, Mortgages as investments
                                HG9992, Mortgage guaranty insurance
     2040                   General works
       .15                  Mortgage loans
       .2                   Discrimination in mortgage loans.  Redlining
       .3                   Mortgage closing costs.  Settlement costs
       .4                   Home improvement loans
       .45                  Home equity conversion
       .5                   By region or country, A-Z
                                Subdivided like HG2051

                        Agricultural credit agencies
                            Cf. HD1439, Theory of agricultural credit
     2041                   General works
     2051                   By region or country, A-Z
                                Under each country:
                                  .xA1-3  Periodicals.  Soceities.  Serials
                                  .xA6-Z  General works
                                  .x2A-Z  By state, province, etc., A-Z
```

Banking
　　Special classes of banks and credit institutions –
　　　　Continued
　　Money lending, see HG3701+
　　Pawnbroking
2070　　　Periodicals. Societies. Serials
2071　　　General works
　　　　State and other public institutions, monts-de-piété
2091　　　　General works
2093　　　　By region or country, A-Z
　　　　By region or country
　　　　　Including individual institutions
　　　　United States
2101　　　　　General works
　　　　　　Including history
2102　　　　　Policy
2103　　　　　Local, A-Z
2106　　　　Other regions or countries, A-Z
　　　　　　Under each country:
　　　　　　.x　　General works
　　　　　　　　　Including history
　　　　　　.x2　Policy
　　　　　　.x3　Local, A-Z

　　Savings and loan associations. Building and loan
　　　　associations
2121　　　Periodicals. Societies. Serials
2123　　　General works
　　　　　Including history
　　　　Practice
2126　　　　General works
　　　　Accounting, see HF5686.B8
　　　　Tables, see HG1636
　　　　By region or country
　　　　　For individual savings and loan associations,
　　　　　　see HG2624+, and HG2701+
　　　　United States
2150　　　　Periodicals. Serials
　　　　　Societies, see HG1507
2151　　　　General works
　　　　　　Including history
2152　　　　Policy
2153　　　　By region or state, A-Z
2156　　　Other regions or countries, A-Z
　　　　　　Under each country:
　　　　　　.x　　Periodicals. Societies. Serials
　　　　　　.x2　General works
　　　　　　　　　Including history
　　　　　　.x3　Policy

　　Safe-deposit companies
　　　　Including bank safe-deposit services
2251　　　General works
2256　　　By region or country, A-Z
　　Clearinghouses
　　　　Cf. HG1692, Check collection systems
2301　　　General works
2306　　　Practice

```
                         Banking
                           Special classes of banks and credit institutions
                             Clearinghouses - Continued
                               By region or country
                                 Under each country:
                                   (1)  Periodicals.  Societies.  Serials
                                   (2)  General works
                                             Including history
                                   (3)  Local, A-Z
2321-2323                          United States
                                       Cf. HG2562.C4, Federal Reserve banks
2331-2333                          Great Britain
2341                               Other European regions or countries, A-Z
2351                               Other regions or countries, A-Z
                             Investment banking, see HG4534
                             Military banks and banking, see UH60+
                             Trust companies, see HG4301+
                           By region or country
                             United States
2401                           Periodicals.  Serials
                               Societies, see HG1507
2416                           Collected works (nonserial)
2431                           Yearbooks
                               Directories
2441                             General
2444                             By state, A-W
2445                             By city, A-Z
                               History and policy
2461                             General works
                                 Biography
2463.A2A-Z                           Collective
     .A3-Z                           Individual, A-Z
                                 Colonial
2466                                 General works
2468                                 Local, A-Z
                                 19th century
2471                                 General works
                                 To 1860
2472                                   General works
2473                                   Controversial literature
                                 1860-1900
2477                                   General works
2478                                   Controversial literature
2479                                   Confederate States
                                 20th century
2481                                 General works
2491                                 1971-
2493                           Statistics
                               Banks of the United States (First and second)
                                 Cf. E384.7, Expunging resolutions
2525                             General works
2527                             Official reports
2529                             General special.  By date
                               Independent treasury
2535                             General works
                                     Including history
2539                             General special.  By date
2543                             Comptroller of the Currency
                                     Including history and organization
```

	Banking
	By region or country
	United States – Continued
	National banking system
	For individual banks, see HG2613
2545	Serial reports
	Administration
2548	Boards of directors
2549	Examinations
2551	Fiduciary powers
2553	Government deposits
	National bank notes, see HG607+
2555	General works
	Including history
2557	Policy. Controversial literature
	Federal Reserve banks
2559	Serial reports
	For report of Federal Reserve Board, see
	HG2401; for individual banks, see HG2613
	Administration
2562	Special, A–Z
	.B8 Branch banks
	.C4 Check collection. Clearance
	.C8 Cuban agencies
	.D5 Discount. Rediscount
	.E5 Employees
	.F7 Foreign accounts
	.F8 Fund market
	.L6 Loans
	.O5 Open market operations
	.P4 Pension funds
	.R4 Reserves
2563	General works
	Including history
2565	Policy. Controversial literature
2567	Bank holding companies
2569	Banking in foreign countries. Foreign branches
	State banks
2571	General works
	Including history
2573	Policy
2577	Local, A–Z
	For individual banks, see HG2613
	Local
2601	East
2604	South
2609	West
2611	By state, A–W
	Under each:
	.x General works
	Including history
	.x2 Other

```
                        Banking
                          By region or country
                            United States
                              Local - Continued
       2613                    By city, A-Z
                                  Under each:
                                    .x    General works
                                    .x4   Individual banks, A-Z
                                            Including savings banks and all
                                              others not elsewhere provided for
                                            Under each:
                                              .x    General works
                                              .x2   Serial reports
                                              .x3   Other works
       2626                    Savings and loan associations.  By city, A-Z
                                  Including publications (reports, etc.) of
                                    individual associations and Federal Home
                                    Loan Banks
                                  For history, practice, etc., see HG2150+
  2701-3542.7                  Other regions or countries.  Table VIII 1/
                                  Under each:
```

20 nos.	10 nos.	5 nos.	1 no.	
(1)	(1)	(1)	.A1-4	Periodicals. Serials
				Societies, see HG1507+
(4)	(3)			Yearbooks
(5)			.A5A-Z	Directories
	(4)	(2)	.A6A-Z	History and policy
(6)				General works
				Biography, see HG1552
(7)				Early
				e. g. Great Britain to
				1844; date may vary
				for different countries
(8)				Recent
(11)				Statistics
(12)	(5)			Banking in foreign countries.
				Foreign branches
	(6)	(3)	.A7A-Z	Central bank. National bank.
				Banks of issue
(14)				General works. History and
				description
				Including reports
(15)				Policy
(16)				Administration
(17)	(8)	(4)	.A8A-Z	State local banks
(18)				Other banks, A-Z
(19)	(9)	(4.5)		By region, A-Z
(20)	(10)	(5)	.A9-Z5	By city, A-Z5
				Under each:
				.x Yearbooks
				.x2 General works
				Including history
				.x3 Policy, etc.
				.x4 Individual banks, A-Z
.Z9A-Z	.Z6A-Z	.Z6A-Z	.Z6A-Z	Savings and loan associations,
				A-Z

```
       3550                    Underdeveloped areas
```

1/

For Table VIII, see pp. 331-340. Add country number in table to 2700

	Credit
	Cf. HG1641, Bank credit
	HJ8003+, Public credit
3691	Periodicals. Societies. Serials
3701	General works, treatises, and textbooks
	Credit control
3705	General works
3711	By region or country, A-Z
	Credit institutions
	Including works on credit institutions not
	provided for in HG1811+, HG4301+, e. g.
	Development credit corporations
3726	General works
3729	By region or country, A-Z
	Under each country:
	.x Periodicals. Societies. Serials
	.x2 General works
	Credit instruments
	Cf. HG1685+, Drafts
3741	General works
3745	Letters of credit
3746	Documentary bills and credit
	Commercial credit. Credit management
	Cf. HG9977, Credit insurance
3751	General works
.3	Finance companies
	Credit bureaus. Credit guides
.5	General works
	By region or country
	United States
.7	General works
.75	Local, A-Z
.8	Directories of agencies
.9	Other regions or countries, A-Z
3752	Rebates. Cash discounts
.3	Accounts receivable financing. Factoring
	Collections
.5	General works
.7	By region or country, A-Z
	Foreign credit. Export credit
	Cf. HG9977, Export credit insurance
3753	General works
3754	By region or country, A-Z
.5	By region or country, A-Z
	Consumer credit. Personal loans
3755	General works
.5	Installment plan
3756	By region or country, A-Z
	Bankruptcy. Insolvency
3760	Periodicals. Societies. Serials
3761	General works
	By region or country
	United States
3766	General works
3767	By region or state, A-Z
3769	Other regions or countries, A-Z
	Under each country:
	.x4 General works
	.x5 Local, A-Z

Foreign exchange.   International finance
     Foreign exchange

3810	Periodicals. Societies. Serials
	Congresses, see HG203+
.5	Dictionaries. Encyclopedias
	History
3811	General
3813	Medieval
3815	Modern
	Theory. Method. Relation to other subjects
3821	General works
3823	Mathematical models
3851	General works, treatises, and textbooks
3852	Floating exchange rates. Devaluation and revaluation
	Cf. HG229, Inflation and deflation
.5	Fixed exchange rates
3853	Forward exchange. Hedging and arbitrage
.7	Accounting
	Tables. Cambistry
	General
3854	Early works through 1800
3856	1801–1850
3858	1851–
	By region or country
	United States
3861	General early through 1783/1800
	Modern works
3863	General works
3864	with Latin America
3865	with Great Britain
3866	with France
3867	with Germany
3868	with other regions or countries, A–Z
3870	Other American. By region or country, A–Z
3871	Europe. By region or country, A–Z
3873	Other countries, A–Z
3875	By business, A–Z
3877	Underdeveloped areas
	By region or country, see HG3901+

International finance.   International monetary system.
     International banking
       Cf. HG381+, International currency

3879	Periodicals. Societies. Serials
	Congresses, see HG203+
3881	General works
	Balance of payments
	Cf. HF1014, Balance of trade
3882	General works
3883	By region or country, A–Z
3890	Underdeveloped areas

	Foreign exchange. International finance
	International finance. International monetary
	system. International banking – Continued
3891	Capital movements
	Cf. HG4538, Foreign investments
.5	Foreign loans. International lending
3892	International clearing
3893	International liquidity
	Monetary unions. Currency areas
3894	General works
3895	Asian dollar market
3896	Euro-bond market
3897	Euro-dollar market
3898	Special drawing rights
	Latin Monetary Union, see HG207+
3901–4000	By region or country. Table I 1/
	Financial management. Business finance. Corporation
	finance
4001	Periodicals. Serials
4005	Societies
4006	Congresses
	Collected works (nonserial)
.5	Several authors
.7	Individual authors
4007	Yearbooks
4008	Dictionaries. Encyclopedias
4009	Directories
	Theory. Method. Relation to other subjects
4011	General works
4012	Mathematical models
	Communication of information
4013	General works
.5	Information services
	Study and teaching. Research
4014	General works
4015	Problems, exercises, examinations
.5	Case studies
4016	By region or country, A-Z
4017	History
4026	General works, treatises, and textbooks
.5	Addresses, essays, lectures
	Statistics
4027	Collections of statistics
.15	Theory
.3	Handbooks, manuals, etc.
.5	International business enterprises
.7	Small business finance

1/
   For Table I, see pp. 331-340. Add country number in table to 3900

Financial management. Business finance. Corporation finance — Continued

4028		Other topics, A-Z
		Accounting, see HF5601+
	.A5	Amortization
	.B2	Balance sheets. Financial statements
	.B6	Bond transfer
	.B8	Budgeting
	.C4	Capital investments. Fixed capital
		Cf. HD39, Industrial management
		Cash management, see .C45
	.C45	Cash position. Cash management
	.C6	Charitable contributions
		Credit management, see HG3751+
	.D3	Debt
	.D4	Depreciation policy
	.D5	Dividends. Stock dividends
		Factoring, see HG3751.5
	.F3	Family corporations
		Financial statements, see .B2
		Fixed capital, see .C4
	.I5	Interest
		International business enterprises, see HG4027.5
	.I8	Issues of securities
		Leasing, see HD39.4
	.M4	Merger of corporations
	.P5	Payrolls
	.P7	Profits
	.R4	Refinancing
	.R5	Reserve funds
		Retained earnings, see .S84
	.S3	Savings
	.S43	Self-financing
	.S5	Sinking funds
		Small business finance, see HG4027.7
	.S7	Stock
	.S75	Stock splitting
	.S8	Stock transfer
	.S82	Stock warrants
	.S84	Surplus. Retained earnings
	.T4	Tender offers
	.V3	Valuation
	.W65	Working capital
		By business, see HD9000+

By region or country
   United States

4050	Periodicals. Societies. Serials
	Directories
4057.A1-5	General
.A6-Z	By region or state, A-Z
4058	By city, A-z

<u>Financial management. Business finance. Corporation</u>
     <u>finance</u>
    By region or country
     United States - Continued

4061	General works
	Including history
4063	Policy. Planning
4070	Local. By region or state, A-Z
	By business, <u>see</u> HD9000+
4090-4280.7	Other regions or countries. Table VI <u>1</u>/
	Under each country:

5 nos.	2 nos.	1 no.	
(1)	(1).A1-5	.A1-4	Periodicals. Societies. Serials
(2)	.A6-Z4	.A5-Z6	General works Including history
	.Z5A-Z		Directories
(3)			Policy. Planning
(4.5)	(1.5)	.Z7A-Z	Local, A-Z

<u>Trust services. Trust companies</u>
   Including trust departments of banks and other
    financial institutions
   For charitable trusts, <u>see</u> HV97 (U. S.)

4301	Periodicals. Serials
4303	Societies
4305	Yearbooks
4307	Directories
4309	General works
4311	History
4315	Practice
.3	Accounting
	Cf. HF5686.T8, Trustees
.5	Corporate trusts
4317	Fees
4318	Individual trusts
	Investment trusts, <u>see</u> HG4530
4319	Investments
	Life insurance trusts, <u>see</u> HG8936
	Public trustees
4323.A3	General works
.A5-Z	By region or country
4324	Trust funds
	By region or country
	United States
4341	Periodicals. Societies. Serials
4347	Directories
4352	General works
	Including history
4354	Policy
4355	By region or state, A-Z
4356	By city, A-Z
	Including individual trust companies

<u>1</u>/
 For Table VI, <u>see</u> pp. 331-340. Add country number in table to 4080

Trust services. Trust companies
By region or country - Continued
4357-4480.9   Other regions or countries. Table V 1/
Under each country:

4 nos.	1 no.		
(1)	.A1A-Z	Periodicals. Societies. Serials	
(2)	.A5A-Z	General works	
		Including history	
(3)	.A6A-Z	Policy	
(4)	.A7-Z	Local, A-Z	

Investment, capital formation, speculation
Cf. HB843, Aggregate saving and investment
HG4028.C4, Capital investments
Periodicals. Serials
Including stock exchange dailies
4501   American
4502   British
4503   Other
4505   Societies
4507   Yearbooks
4508   Congresses
Collected works (nonserial)
.3   Several authors
.5   Individual authors
4509   Directories
4513   Dictionaries. Encyclopedias
4514   Study and teaching. Research
Theory. Method. Relations to other subjects
4515   General works
.15   Psychological aspects
.2   Mathematical models
.3   Mathematics of investment
Communication of information
.7   General works
.9   Information services
4516   History
4521   General works, treatises, and textbooks
4522   Addresses, essays, lectures
4523   Capital market
Cf. HG226, Money market
4524   Policy. Investment control
4527   Handbooks, manuals, etc.
Cf. HG6021, Speculation
4528   General special
Accounting, see HF5686.I6
4529   Investment analysis
.5   Portfolio management
4530   Investment companies. Investment trusts. Mutual funds
4534   Investment banking
4537   Investment tables. Stock and bond tables
Cf. HG1626+, Interest tables
4538   Foreign investments
Including those of individual countries
For foreign investments in individual countries,
see HG4905+
Cf. HJ8083+, Foreign loans

1/
For Table V, see pp. 331-340.   Add country number in table to 4350

Investment, capital formation, speculation – Continued

4538.5	Investment guarantee insurance
	Stock exchanges
4551	General works
4553	Juvenile works

Major exchanges. By city
    For other exchanges, see HG5131, HG5151+,
        subdivision (15), (10), etc. under each country
    Under each:
        (1) Serial reports. Directories
        (2) General works. History and description
        (3) Constitution and internal regulations

4571–4573	New York. Stock Exchange
4575.1–4575.3	New York. American Exchange
4576–4578	London. Stock Exchange
4581–4583	Paris. Bourse
4586–4588	Berlin. Fondsbörse
4591–4593	Vienna. Börse
4596–4598	Tokyo. Tōkyō Shōken Torihikijo
4621	Stock brokerage. Security dealers. Investment advisers

    For directories, see HG4509, 4907, etc.
    For U. S. brokerage houses, see HG5129; for other
        firms, see subdivision (13), (10), or (5) under
        each country

4626	Bucket shops
	Cf. HV6763+, Financial crime
4631	Stock transfer. Stock clearing
	Cf. HG4028.S8, Corporation finance
4636	Prices. Values
	For valuation, see HG4028.V3
4637	Stock price forecasting
4638	Charts, diagrams, etc.

	Securities
	By form
4651	Bonds
4655	Mortgages
	Cf. HG2040.15, Mortgage loans
4661	Stocks
	Cf. HG4028.S7, Corporation finance
	Government securities
4701	Periodicals. Societies. Serials
4715	General works. History
4726	Municipal bonds
4751	Industrial securities

    For special industries, see the industry,
        e. g. Railroad securities, HE2231; Mining
        securities, HD9506+

	By region or country
	United States
	Periodicals, see HG4501
4905	Yearbooks
4907	Directories
4908	Dividend registers
4909	Directories of investors
	Including local directories

Investment, capital formation, speculation
By region or country
United States - Continued

4910	General works. History
4915	Prices. Values
4916	Charts, diagrams, etc.
4921	Handbooks, manuals, etc.
	For manuals issued annually, see HG4905
	Investments for banks, see HG1616.15, HG1897
	Insurance company investments, see HG8078, HG8850
4927	Obsolete securities
4928	Lost, stolen, or missing securities
4930	Investment companies. Investment trusts.
	Mutual funds
.5	Investment banking
	Government securities
4931	Periodicals. Societies. Serials
4936	General works
4941	Handbooks, manuals, etc.
	For serial manuals, see HG4931
	State bonds
4946	General works
4948	By state, A-Z
4949	Industrial development bonds
	Municipal bonds
4951	Periodicals. Societies. Serials
4952	General works
4953	By state, A-W
	Under each:
	.x General works
	.x2 Local, A-Z
4955	Local. By state, A-W
	Industrial securities
	For special industries, see the industry
4961	Periodicals. Societies. Serials
4963	General works
4965	Handbooks, manuals, etc.
	For serial manuals, see HG4961
5095	Mortgages
	By region
5125	South
5127	West
5128	By state, A-W
5129	By city, A-Z
	Including individual stockbrokerage firms
5131	Stock exchanges. By city, A-Z
	Under each:
	.x Serial reports
	.x2 General works. History and description
	.x3 Constitution. Internal regulations
	For the New York Stock Exchange and the
	American Exchange, see HG4571+

Investment, capital formation, speculation
By region or country - Continued
5151-5992.7   Other regions or countries. Table VIII 1/
Under each country:

20 nos.	10 nos.	5 nos.	1 no.	
(1)	(1)	(1)	.A2	Yearbooks. Directories
				For periodicals, see HG4501+
(2)	(2)	(2)	.A3A-Z	General works
				Including history
(4)	(3)			Prices. Values
(5)	(4)			Handbooks, manuals, etc.
(6)	(4.5)	(2.5)	.A35A-Z	Investment companies. Investment
				trusts. Mutual funds
(8)	(5)	(3)	.A4A-Z	Government securities
(11)	(8)	(4)	.A5A-Z	Industrial securities
(12)	(9)			Mortgages
(13)	(10)	(5)	.A6-Z	Local, A-Z
				Including individual
				stockbrokerage firms
				Stock exchanges, A-Z
(15)				For certain major interna-
				tional exchanges, see
				HG4576+. All other ex-
				changes are classed
				here

5993	Underdeveloped areas
	Speculation
	For speculation in foreign exchange, see HG3853
6001	Periodicals. Societies. Serials
	History
6005	General
	18th century
6006	General works
6007	Mississippi scheme
	Including works on John Law
6008	South Sea scheme
6009	19th century
6010	20th century
6015	General works. Treatises
6021	Handbooks, manuals, etc.
	Futures
	For particular kinds, e. g. "Cotton contracts,"
	see HG6047
6024.A3A-Z	General works
.A4-Z	By region or country, A-Z
.5	Interest rate futures
6036	General special
	Speculation in stocks
6041	General works
6042	Put and call transactions. Stock options
	Speculation in produce. Commodity exchanges
	Cf. HG6024, Futures
6046	General works

1/
    For Table VIII, see pp. 331-340. Add country number in table to 5150

Investment, capital formation, speculation
    Speculation
        Speculation in produce. Commodity exchanges – Cont.

6047	By article, A– Z
	.C3 Cattle
	.C6 Corn
	.C7 Cotton
	.C75 Cotton-seed oil
	.G8 Grain
	.O7 Orange juice
	.P6 Potatoes
	.R5 Rice
	.S5 Silk
	.S6 Soy beans
	.S8 Sugar
	.W5 Wheat
	.W6 Wool
	By region or country
6049	United States
6051	Other regions or countries, A–Z

Lotteries
6105	History
6109	Lottery tables, lists of drawings, premiums, etc.
	Class here general works only. For special by country, state, or company, see HG6133 and HG6147+
6111	General works. Treatises
6116	Lottery drawing, etc.
6123	Lotteries as savings institutions
	By region or country
	United States
6126	General works
	Including history
6128	Policy
6133	State lotteries, A–W
6134	Other lotteries. By place, A–Z
6147–6270.9	Other regions or countries. Table V 1/
	Under each country:

4 nos.	1 no.	
(1)	.A2A–Z	General works
(3)	.A5–6	State, (provincial, etc.) lotteries, A–Z
(4)	.A7–Z	Other lotteries. By place, A–Z

Thrift and saving
    Class here general works only. For saving by any particular method, e. g. savings banks, savings and loan associations, see the subject
    Cf. BJ1533.E2, Economy, thrift (Ethics)
        HB843, Aggregate saving and investment
        HC79.S7, Economic history
        HQ784.S4, Thrift education for children

7920	General works, treatises, and textbooks
	Popular works
7931	American
7933	Other

1/
    For Table V, see pp. 331–340. Add country number to table to 6140

INSURANCE

	Periodicals. Serials
8011	American
8013	British
8015	Other
8016	Societies
8017	Congresses
	Collected works (nonserial)
8018	Several authors
.5	Individual authors
8019	Yearbooks
8021	Directories
8025	Dictionaries. Encyclopedias
8026	Theory. Method. Relation to other subjects
	Cf. HG8781+, Actuarial science
	Communication of information
.3	General works
.5	Information services
	History
8027	General
8029	Medieval
8035	Modern
8039	Lloyd's
	Biography
8041	Collective
8042	Individual, A-Z
8045	Statistics. Collections of statistics
	For statistical theory and methodology, see HG8781+
	Study and teaching. Research
8047	General works
	By region or country
8048	United States
8049	Other regions or countries, A-Z
8051	General works, treatises, and textbooks
8052	Addresses, essays, lectures
.5	Juvenile works
8053	General special
	Insurance for professions. Malpractice insurance
.5	General works
.7	Contractors
8054	Physicians
.3	Police
.4	Psychiatrists
.5	Risk
	Cf. HB615, Economic theory
	HG8207, Government risks
8055	War risks. War damage compensation
.5	Multiple-line insurance
8057	Mutual insurance. Cooperative insurance
	Cf. HG9201+, Mutual life insurance
8059	Business insurance. Partnership insurance.
	Corporate insurance
	Cf. HG8937, Business life insurance
8060	Business interruption insurance
	Government insurance, see HG8205+

	Insurance – Continued
8061	Handbooks, manuals, etc.
	Rates and premiums
8065	General works
8067	Tables
	Insurance business. Insurance management
8075	General works
8076	Finance
.5	Insurance and inflation
8077	Accounting
.5	Electronic data processing
8078	Investments for insurance companies
8079	Insurance as an investment
8082	Self-insurance
8083	Reinsurance
8089	Policies
	Agents. Marketing. Selling
	For directories, see HG8021
8091	General works
	By region or country
	United States
8098	General works
8101	By region or state, A-Z
8102	Other regions or countries, A-Z
8104	Captive companies. Captive agents
	Losses. Claims
8106	General works
8107	Adjustment of claims
	Insurance and the state. State supervision
8111	General works
	Taxation
8119	General works
8121	United States
8123	Other regions or countries, A-Z
	By region or country, see HG8535, HG8550+, subdivision
	(4.5), (1.5), or .Z75 uder each country
	Insurance and crimes, see HV6763+
	Government insurance
	Cf. HD7090+, Social insurance
8205	General works
8207	Government risks. Government liability insurance
	By region or country
	United States
8210	General works
8215	By region or state, A-Z
8220	Other regions or countries, A-Z
	By region or country
	United States
8501	Periodicals. Serials
8522	Societies
.5	Congresses
8523	Yearbooks
	Directories
8525	General works
8526	By region or state, A-Z
8527	By city, A-Z
8531	General works
	Including history

```
                    Insurance
                      By region or country
                        United States - Continued
      8535                  Policy
      8538                  By region or state, A-Z
      8539                  By city, A-Z
      8540                  By company, A-Z
                              Including life, fire, and other insurance
                                combined; general casualty companies
  8550-8740.5              Other regions or countries.  Tables VI 1/
                              Under each country:
```

5 nos.	2 nos.	1 no.	
(1)	(1).A1-4	.A1-3	Periodicals. Societies. Serials
(2)	.A45	.A35A-Z	Congresses
(3)	.A5	.A4A-Z	Yearbooks
(4)	.A6	.A5-Z7	General works Including history
(4.5)	(1.5)	.Z75A-Z	Policy
(5)	(2)	.Z8A-Z	Local, A-Z
.A9	.Z9	.Z9A-Z	By company, A-Z

```
                    Life insurance
      8751            Periodicals.  Serials
      8754            Societies
                        Including actuaries' associations
      8755            Congresses
      8756            Yearbooks
      8758            Directories
      8759            Dictionaries
      8761            History
                      Biography
                        For United States, see HG8952
      8763              Collective
      8764              Individual, A-Z
      8766            Statistics.  Collections of statistics
                        For statistical theory and methodology, see HG8781+
                      Collected works (nonserial)
      8769              Several authors
      8770              Individual authors
      8771            General works, treatises, and textbooks
      8773            Popular works
      8774            Juvenile works
      8776            Addresses, essays, lectures
                      Actuarial science.  Statistical theory, and
                        methodology applied to insurance
      8779              Periodicals
                        Societies, see HG8016
      8781              General works, treatises, and textbooks
      8782              General special
                        Mortality tables
                          Cf. HB1322, Demography
      8783                General works
      8784                By region or country, A-Z
      8785                By insurance company, A-Z
```

1/
  For Table VI, see pp. 331-340.   Add country number in table to 8540

Insurance
   Life insurance
      Actuarial science. Statistical theory, and
         methodology applied to insurance - Continued
        Annuities

8790	General works
8791	General special
8793	Tables and problems
	By class insured
8799	Blacks
8801	Women
	Children, see HG9271+
8808	Physicians
	By risk
8810	Aviation risks
8811	War risks
	By plan
	Level premium
8816	General works
8817	Tontine
8818	Endowment
	Natural premium
8821	General works
8823	Flexible premium
	Assessment cooperation, see HG9201+
	Installment plan, see HG9251+
8830	Group life insurance
	Life insurance business. Management
8835	General works
	Finance
8844	General works
8848	Accounting
8850	Investments for life insurance companies
.5	Life insurance as an investment
	Rates and premiums
8851	General works
8853	Tables
	Policies
8861	General works
8866	Forms
	Agents. Marketing. Selling
	For directories, see HG8758, HG8945+, etc.
8876	General works
8877	General special
8881	Handbooks, manuals, etc.
	Medical examiners and examinations
8886	General works
8888	Company manuals
	Losses. Claims
8897	General works
8898	Adjustment of claims
8899	Disability claims. Disability benefits

```
                        Insurance
                          Life insurance - Continued
                            Life insurance and the state.  State supervision
8901                              General works
                                Taxation
8910                                General works
                                  United States
8912                                    General works
8913                                    By state, A-W
8914                                  Other regions or countries, A-Z
                                    By region or country, see HG8957+, 9010+, subdivision
                                      (4.Z9), (1.Z9), or (.Z7) under each country
8936                              Life insurance trusts
8937                              Business life insurance
                                Life insurance crimes, see HV6763+
                                By region or country
                                  United States
8941                                    Periodicals.  Societies.  Serials
8943                                    Yearbooks
8944                                    Congresses
                                      Directories
8945                                        General
8947                                        By region or state, A-Z
8949                                        By city, A-Z
8951                                    General works
                                          Including history
                                      Biography
8952.A2A-Z                                Collective
     .A3-Z                                Individual, A-Z
8955                                    Statistics
                                      Policy
8957                                        Through 1900
8958                                        1901-
8961                                    By region or state, A-Z
8962                                    By city, A-Z
8963                                    By company, A-Z
                                          Under each:
                                            .x    Serial reports
                                            .x2   General works
                                                      Including history
                                            .x3   Other
9010-9200.5                           Other regions or countries.  Table VI 1/
                                        Under each country:
```

5 nos.	2 nos.	1 no.	
(1)	(1).A1-4	.A1-3	Periodicals. Serials
(2)	.A4	.A4A-Z	Societies
(3)	.A6	.A5A-Z	Directories
(4)	.A7-Z7	.A6-Z5	General works. History. Statistics
.Z9	.Z9	.Z6A-Z	Policy
(5)	(2)	.Z7A-Z	Local, A-Z
.Z9	.Z9	.Z9A-Z	By company, A-Z

1/

For Table VI, see pp. 331-340. Add country number in table to 9000

Insurance
   Life insurance - Continued
      Mutual life insurance. Assessment life insurance.
         Fraternal life insurance

9201	Periodicals. Serials
9203	Societies
9207	Directories
9213	General works
	Including history
9217	Agents. Marketing. Selling
9221	Rates and premiums

         By region or country
           United States

9226	Periodicals. Societies. Serials
9228	Directories
9231	General works
	Including history
9237	Policy
9241	By region or state, A-Z
9242	By city, A-Z
9243	By company, A-Z
9245	Other regions or countries, A-Z

            Under each country:
               .x   Periodicals. Societies. Serials
               .x2 General works
                     Including history
               .x3 Local, A-Z
               .x4 By company, A-Z

      Industrial life insurance
         Class here insurance on small weekly or monthly
           payments, as furnished by, e. g. the Prudential.
           For social insurance, see HD7090+

9251	General works
	Including history
9255	Agents. Marketing. Selling
9257	Rates and premiums

         By region or country
           United States

9258	General works
	Including history
9259	By region or state, A-Z
9260	By city, A-Z
9261	By company, A-Z
9262	Other regions or countries, A-Z

            Under each country:
               .x   General works
                     Including history
               .x2 Local, A-Z

9271	Child insurance. Life insurance for children
9281	Marriage endowment insurance
	Maternity insurance
9291	General works
9295	By region or country, A-Z

               Insurance – Continued
                 Accident insurance
                     Cf. HD7101+, Social insurance

9301	Periodicals. Serials
9303	Societies
9311	General works
	Including history
9315	Rates and premiums
9321	Agents. Marketing. Selling
	Losses. Claims
9322	General works
.5	Adjustment of claims
.7	Disability evaluation
	Medical examinations, see HG8886
9323	War risks
9324	Athletic accident insurance
9325	The state and accident insurance. State supervision
	By region or country
	United States
9331	Periodicals. Societies. Serials
9334	Statistics
9335	General works
	Including history
9336	Policy
9338	By region or state, A–Z
9341	By company, A–Z
9343	Other regions or countries, A–Z
	Under each country:
	.x Periodicals. Societies. Serials
	.x2 General works. History. Policy
	.x25 Local, A–Z
	.x3 By company, A–Z

                 Health insurance
                     For public health insurance, see HD7101+

9371	Periodicals. Serials
9373	Societies
9383	General works
	Including history
9384	Rates and premiums
.5	Policies
9385	Agents. Marketing. Selling
	Losses. Claims
9386	General works
.5	Adjustment of claims
	Medical examinations, see HG8886
9387	Mental health insurance
9388	Group health insurance
9389	Hospitalization insurance
	By region or country
	United States
9395	Periodicals. Societies. Serials
9396	General works
9397.5	By region or state, A–Z
9398	By company, A–Z
9399	Other regions or countries, A–Z
	Under each country:
	.x Periodicals. Societies. Serials
	.x2 General works
	.x25 Local, A–Z
	.x3 By company, A–Z

```
                        Insurance - Continued
                          Old age pensions, see HD7105+
                          Burial insurance
9466                        General works
                            By region or country
                              United States
9476                          General works
9478                          By company, A-Z
9479                          Other regions or countries, A-Z
                          Social insurance, see HD7090+
                          Fire insurance
9651                        Periodicals.  Serials
9653                        Societies
9654                        Congresses
9655                        Yearbooks
9657                        Directories
    .5                      Dictionaries.  Encyclopedias
                            Collected works (nonserial)
9658                          Several authors
    .2                        Individual authors
9660                        History
9663                        Statistics.  Collections of statistics
                                For statistical theory and methodology,
                                  see HG8781+
9665                        General works, treatises, and textbooks
9667                        Handbooks, manuals, etc.
9669                        General special

                            Fire insurance business.  Management
9671                          General works
                              Finance
9674                            General works
9678                            Accounting
                              Rates and premiums
                                  For United States, see HG9769
9685                            General works
9687                            Classification of risks
                                    For special classes of risks, see HG9731
9689                            Tables
                              Policies
9695                            General works
9699                            Forms
                              Agents.  Marketing.  Selling
9706                            General works
9709                            Handbooks, manuals, etc.

                            Inspectors and inspecting.  Surveyors, etc.
                                Cf. HV8079.A7, Arson investigation
                                    TH9176, Fire inspection
9711                            General works
9715                            Handbooks, manuals, etc.
                                Special hazards, see HG9731
                              Losses.  Claims
9721                            General works
9722                            Adjustment of claims
9723                            Apportionment of loss
9725                            Handbooks, manuals, etc.
```

Insurance
  Fire insurance
    Fire insurance business. Management – Continued

9731   Special classes of risks, A–Z

                .A4   Agricultural products
                .D6   Distilleries
                .E3   Electrical risks
                .E8   Explosives
                .F2   Factories
                .F5   Fertilizer factories
                .F75   Forest fires

                .L8   Lumber
                .O5   Oils and fats
                .P5   Plastics
                .P8   Public buildings
                .S35   Schoolhouses
                .S7   Sprinkler leakage
                .W3   War risks
                .W6   Woodworking mills

          Fire insurance and the state. State supervision
9733   General works
            Taxation
9734.5   General works
9735   By region or country, A–Z
            By region or country, see HG9761, HG9781+, subdivision
            .Z7 under each country
          By region or country
            United States
9751   Periodicals. Serials
9753   Societies
9754   Congresses
9755   Yearbooks
              Cf. HG9765, Statistics
9757   Directories
9759   General works
              Including history
9761   Policy
9765   Statistics
9769   Rates and premiums
9771   Surveys
              For atlases and maps, see G1000+
9778   By region or state, A–Z
9779   By city, A–Z
9780   By company, A–Z
9781–9866   Other regions or countries. Table I/
             Under each country:
              .A1–7   Periodicals. Societies. Serials
              .A8–Z6 General works
                    Including history
              .Z7A–Z Policy
              .Z8A–Z Local, A–Z
              .Z9A–Z By company, A–Z

1/
  For Table I, see pp. 331–340. Add country number in table to 9766

```
                    Insurance
                      Fire insurance – Continued
                        Mutual fire insurance
9873                      General works
                          By region or country
9893                        United States
9899                        Other regions or countries, A–Z
                      Marine insurance, see HE961+
                      Transportation insurance
                        Including inland marine insurance
9903                      General works
9905                      By region or country, A–Z

                      Casualty insurance
                        For general casualty companies, see HG8540, etc.
9956                      General works
9958                      General special
                         Insurance for plant and equipment
9961                        General works
9963                        Boiler and machinery insurance
  .5                          Computers
  .7                          Plate glass
9964                        Employers' liability insurance
                            Workmen's compensation, see HD7103.6+
                          Agricultural insurance
9966                          General works
9968                          Crop insurance
  .3                          Forest insurance
                                Cf. HG9731.F75, Fire insurance
  .4                          Hail insurance
  .6                          Livestock insurance
  .8                          Tornado insurance
9969                          By region or country, A–Z
                            For other special, see HG9651+, HG9969.5, etc.
                            By region or country, see HG8501+

                      Other insurance
                        Under each:
                          .0    or  .5        General works
                                              Business.  Management
                          .15   or  .55         General works
                          .17   or  .57         Finance
                          .2    or  .6          Rates and premiums
                          .23   or  .63         Policies
                          .24   or  .64         Agents.  Marketing.  Selling
                          .25   or  .65         Losses.  Claims
                                              By region or country
                                                United States
                          .3    or  .7            General
                          .35   or  .75           By region or state, A–Z
                          .37   or  .77           By company, A–Z
                          .4    or  .8        Other regions or countries, A–Z

9969.5                  Atomic hazards insurance
9970                    Automobile insurance
9972                    Aviation insurance
9974                    Bank insurance
                            Cf. HG1662, Bank deposit insurance
9975                    Burglary insurance
```

Insurance
Other insurance – Continued

9977	Credit insurance. Export credit insurance
9979	Disaster insurance
9981	Earthquake insurance
9982	Fine arts insurance
9983	Flood insurance
9984	Forgery insurance
9986	Homeowners insurance
	Investment guaranty insurance, see HG4538.5
9990	Liability insurance

Cf. HG8053.5+, Malpractice insurance
HG9964, Employers' liability insurance
HG9995, Products liability insurance

9992	Mortgage guaranty insurance
9993	Motion picture insurance
9995	Products liability insurance
9997	Surety and fidelity insurance
9999	Title insurance

                Documents.   By country
                   Class here serial documents and separate
                    documents of general character not specifically
                    provided for under special subjects.   For local
                    finance documents, i. e. county, township,
                    municipality, etc., see HJ9000+

                United States

9	Collected documents (nonserial)
	Serial reports, and special documents
	Treasury department
10.A1-4	General serials
.A5-9	Annual report of receipts and expenditures
	For serial documents on the United States
	budget, see HJ2051+
	Appropriations
.B1	Estimates of appropriations
.B2	Joint committee on the budget
.B3	House of Representatives. Committee on
	appropriations
.B4	Senate. Committee on appropriations
.B46	Conference committee on appropriation bills
.B465	The President: Messages, vetoes, etc.
.B5	Digest of appropriations
.B6	"Appropriations, new offices, etc."
.B7	Supplemental or deficiency estimates
	Treasury department: Separate documents, reports,
	etc. By date
.E1	Documents, through 1800
.E3	Documents, 1801-
	House and Senate reports, etc.
	Except as elsewhere provided for
.F3	Collected works (nonserial)
.G	Documents of other departments
	Treasury administration
.R1-9	Reports of the heads of bureaus, special
	officers, etc.
.R1	Secretary of the treasury. Annual report
.R2	Report f the treasurer
.R3	Report of the register
.R4	Report of the comptroller of the treasury
	Report of the comptroller of the currency,
	see HG2401
.R7	Report of the commissioner of internal revenue
.R8	Report of the commissioner of customs
	Report of the supervising special agent of
	customs, see HJ6622
.R9	Auditors' reports
.V3	Register (List of persons employed)

Documents. By country
  United States
    Serial reports, and special documents – Continued
11   By state, A–W
          For District of Columbia appropriations, etc.,
            see HJ9013.W2; HJ9215+
          Under each (local terminology may vary):
           .x   Report of the treasurer or finance
                 department
           .x2 Report of the auditor, or comptroller
           .x4 Budget
           .x5 Report of the revenue/tax commissioner
           .x6 Report of the assessors
           .x7 Report of the state board of
                 equalization
           .x8 Report of the commissioner of excise
           .x9 Report of the commissioner of the
                 sinking fund
           .x95 Special documents. By date

  Other countries
    Under each:
      .A1–199 General reports of the department of
                 finance or treasurer
      .A2–299 Budget
      .A3–399 Receipts and expenditures
      .A4–499 Public debt
      .A5–599 Administrative reports
                 Including bureaus, special officers,
                    etc.
      .A7–799 Other. Miscellaneous
                 e. g. Colonies
      .A8–Z   Local (States, provinces, etc.)
                 Cf. HJ9000+, Municipal finance
    Canada
12   To 1867
      Dominion of Canada
13.A1–6   General
 .A8–Z   Provinces
    Latin America
15   Mexico
      Central America
16   General
 .5   Belize
17   Costa Rica
18   Guatemala
19   Honduras
20   Nicaragua
21   Panama
22   Salvador
      West Indies
 .5   Bahamas
23   Cuba
24   Puerto Rico
25   Haiti
26   Dominican Republic. Santo Domingo

```
                        Documents.  By country
                          Other countries
                            Asia - Continued
                              East Asia.  Far East
77                              Japan
  .5                            Korea
                                    Including South Korea
  .55                           North Korea
  .6                            China
  .65                           Macao
  .7                            Taiwan.  Formosa
  .75                           Hongkong
                            Africa
                              North Africa
80.2                            Morocco
  .3                            Algeria
  .4                            Tunisia
  .5                            Egypt.  United Arab Republic
  .6                            Sudan
                              Northeast Africa
  .7                            Ethiopia
  .8                            Somalia
                                    Including British and Italian Somaliland
81.2                            French Territory of the Afars and Issas
                              Southeast Africa
  .3                            Kenya
  .4                            Uganda
  .5                            Rwanda
  .6                            Burundi
  .7                            Tanzania.  Tanganyika
  .8                            Mozambique
82.2                            Madagascar
                              Southern Africa
  .3                            South Africa
  .4                            Rhodesia
                                    Including Southern Rhodesia
  .5                            Zambia.  Northern Rhodesia
  .6                            Lesotho.  Basutoland
  .7                            Swaziland
  .8                            Botswana.  Bechuanaland
83.2                            Malawi.  Nyasaland
  .3                            Namibia.  Southwest Africa
                              Central Africa.  Equitorial Africa
  .4                            Angola
  .5                            Zaire.  Congo (Democratic Republic)
  .6                            Equitorial Guinea
  .7                            Sao Tome e Principe
  .8                            French Equatorial Africa.  French Congo
84.2                            Gabon
  .3                            Congo (Brazzaville).  Middle Congo
  .4                            Central African Empire.  Central African Republic.
                                    Ubangi-Shari
  .5                            Chad
  .6                            Cameroon
```

	Documents. By country
	Other countries
	Africa – Continued
	West Africa. West Coast
84.7	Benin. Dahomey
.8	Togo
85.2	Niger
.3	Ivory Coast
.4	Guinea
.5	Mali
.6	Upper Volta
.7	Senegal
.8	Mauritania
86.2	Nigeria
.3	Ghana
.4	Sierra Leone
.5	Gambia
.6	Liberia
.7	Guinea-Bissau. Portuguese Guinea
.8	Spanish Sahara
	Atlantic Ocean Islands
87.2	Bermuda
.3	Cape Verde Islands
.4	St. Helena
.5	Falkland Islands
	Indian Ocean Islands
88.2	Seychelles
.3	Comoro Islands
.4	Mauritius
.5	Reunion
90	Australia
97	New Zealand
	Pacific Ocean Islands
98.2	Trust Territory of the Pacific
	Including Mariana, Caroline and Marshall
	Islands
.3	Guam
.4	Papua New Guinea
.5	Solomon Islands
.6	Gilbert Islands
	Including Gilbert and Ellice Islands
	Colony
.7	Tuvalu
.8	New Caledonia
99.2	New Hebrides
.3	Fiji Islands
.4	Tonga
	Somoan Islands
.5	American Samoa
.6	Western Samoa

GENERAL WORKS

For local finance, <u>see</u> HJ9103+

	Periodicals. Societies. Serials
101	English
103	French
105	German
107	Italian
108	Spanish
109	Other, A–Z
113	Congresses
	Collected works (nonserial)
117	Several authors
119	Individual authors
	Dictionaries. Encyclopedias
121	English
123	French
125	German
127	Italian
128	Spanish
129	Other languages, A–Z
	Theory. Method. Relation to other subjects
131	General works
132	History of theory
	General works, treatises, and advanced textbooks
139	Early works through 1700
	1701–
	English and American
140	Early works (1701–1850)
141	Treatises (1851–)
	French
150	Early works
151	Treatises
	German
160	Early works
161	Treatises
	Italian
170	Early works
171	Treatises
	Spanish and Portuguese
180	Early works
181	Treatises
191	Other, A–Z
	Under each:
	.x Early works
	.x2 Treatises
.8	Popular works
.9	Juvenile works
192	General special (Special aspects of the subject as a whole)
193	Public goods

General works – Continued
 Organization and administration. Intergovernmental
  fiscal relations
   Class here general works only; for special
    countries, see HJ213+
197   General works
199   Control, auditing, inspection
200   Grants-in-aid. Revenue sharing
 Study and teaching. Research
203   General works
205   Outlines, syllabi, etc.
209   Schools. By country, A-Z

HISTORY AND CONDITIONS

210   General
          Ancient
213   Egypt
214   Other Oriental (not A-Z)
              e. g. India
           Greece and Rome
215   General works
            Greece
217   General works
219   Athens
221   Other (Sparta, etc.)
            Rome
223   General works
225   Special
227   Provinces
          Medieval and modern
230   General works
           Medieval
232   Byzantine
233   Islamic
           Modern
235   General works
   .5   Special (not A-Z)
236   20th century
               Including world wars
240   Colonial finance
               Cf. HJ2025, Colonial budgets

          By region or country
           United States
241   General works
247   Revolutionary period (through 1800)
249   1800-1860/61
            Civil War and reconstruction (1861-1865/70)
251   General works
254   Confederate finances
                 Cf. HJ8110, Confederate debts
255   1865/70-1900
            20th century
257   General works
   .2   1945-

266

History and conditions
  By region or country
    United States - Continued
      Organization and administration (Practice)
        Treasury department
          Budget, appropriations, <u>see</u> HJ10.Bl+;
            HJ2050+
          History. Organization

261	General works
262	Early through 1860
263	1861-
265	Inspection, control, etc.
266	Appointments, new offices, salaries, etc.
268	Civil service
271	The keeping of the public money
272	Transportation of public money
273	Frauds, embezzlements, investigations, trials.
	By date
.5	Special topics, A-Z
	.F4 Fees
	.I4 Impoundment of appropriated funds
275	States collectively

          Including Federal grants-in-aid, revenue
            sharing, etc.
        By region (covering several states)
          Under each:
            .A1   General works
                    History
            .A3   Early through 1860
            .A5-Z3 1861-
            .Z4-9 Organization and administration

276	New England and Atlantic States
277	Southern States
278	Middle Western States
279	Pacific States

        By state
          Under each:
            (0) Collected works (nonserial)
            (1) General works
                History
            (2)   Early through 1800
            (3)   1801-1860
            (4)   1861-1900
            (5)   1901-
                Organization and administration
            (6)   Administration (General)
            (7)   Treasury administration
            (8)   Inspection, regulation, etc.
            (9)   Frauds, embezzlements, etc.

280-289	Alabama
290-299	Alaska
300-309	Arizona
310-319	Arkansas
320-329	California
330-339	Colorado
340-349	Connecticut
350-359	Delaware
	District of Columbia, <u>see</u> HJ9013.W2, HJ9215+

History and conditions
By region or country
United States
By state – Continued

370–379	Florida
380–389	Georgia
389.5–.59	Hawaii
390–399	Idaho
400–409	Illinois
410–419	Indiana
430–439	Iowa
440–449	Kansas
450–459	Kentucky
460–469	Louisiana
470–479	Maine
480–489	Maryland
490–499	Massachusetts
500–509	Michigan
510–519	Minnesota
520–529	Mississippi
530–539	Missouri
540–549	Montana
550–559	Nebraska
560–569	Nevada
570–579	New Hampshire
580–589	New Jersey
590–599	New Mexico
600–609	New York
610–619	North Carolina
620–629	North Dakota
630–639	Ohio
640–649	Oklahoma
650–659	Oregon
660–669	Pennsylvania
670–679	Rhode Island
680–689	South Carolina
690–699	South Dakota
700–709	Tennessee
710–719	Texas
720–729	Utah
730–739	Vermont
740–749	Virginia
750–759	Washington
760–769	West Virginia
770–779	Wisconsin
780–789	Wyoming

Canada
790	General works
	History
791	Early through 1867
792	1868–1900
793	1901–
	Provinces
795.A1	Collective
.A2–Z	Individual, A–Z
796–799	Organization and administration
	Subarranged like HJ286–289

History and conditions
By region or country - Continued

799.5-.53		Latin America
		Subarranged like HJ810-813
		Mexico
800		General works
		History
801		Early through 1820
802		1821-1900
803		1901-
805		States, A-Z
806-809		Organization and administration
		Subarranged like HJ286-289
		Central America
		Under each region or country:

5 nos.		2 nos.	1 no.	
(0) or (5)		(1)	.A1-Z5	General works
				History
(1)	(6).A3			Early through 1820
	.A6-Z			1821-1900
(2)	(7)			20th century
(3)	(8)	(2).A-Z6	.Z6A-Z	Organization and administration
(4)	(9)	.Z8A-Z	.Z8A-Z	Provinces, A-Z

810-813	General
814	Belize
815-819	Costa Rica
820-824	Guatemala
825-829	Honduras
830-834	Nicaragua
835-839	Panama
840-844	San Salvador
844.3	West Indies
	Subarranged like HJ810-844
.5	Bahamas
845-849	Cuba
850-854	Puerto Rico
855-859	Haiti
860-863.5	Dominican Republic. Santo Domingo
863.7	Jamaica
864	Virgin Islands of the United States
	Cf. HJ884, Danish West Indies
865-866	British West Indies
873-874	Leeward Islands
875	Trinidad and Tobago
876	Windward Islands
	Bermuda, see HJ1508.3
885-886	Netherlands Antilles. Dutch West Indies
887-888	French West Indies
889	Guadeloupe
.5	Martinique

History and conditions
By region or country
Latin America – Continued
South America
Under each region or country:

10 nos.	1 no.	
(0)	.A1–Z5	General works
		History
(1)		Early through 1820
(3)		1821–
(5)		20th century
		Organization and administration
(6)	.Z6	General works
(7)		Inspection, regulation
(8)		Frauds, embezzlements, etc.
(9)	.Z8	States, provinces, A–Z
		Under each:
		(1) General works. History
		(2) Organization and administration

890–898	General
900–909	Argentina
910–919	Bolivia
920–929	Brazil
930–939	Chile
940–949	Colombia
950–959	Ecuador
	Guianas
959.5	General works
.6	Guyana. British Guiana
.7	Surinam. Dutch Guiana
.8	French Guiana
960–969	Paraguay
970–979	Peru
980–989	Uruguay
990–999	Venezuela
	Europe
1000	General works
.5	European Economic Community countries
	Great Britain
1001	General works
1003	Biography
	History
1005	Medieval
1007	Special
1009	Local, A–Z
1011	Modern
1012	17th century
1013	18th century
1015	19th century
1017	1783–1815
1019	1816–1870
1021	1871–1900
1023	20th century

                    History and conditions
                       By region or country
                          Europe
                             Great Britain - Continued
                                Organization and administration
                                   The Exchequer
                                      History
1027   General works
1028   Early through 1688
1030   Modern
                                      Administration
1036   General
1037   Special
1038   Inspection, regulation
1039   Frauds, embezzlements
     .5   Northern Ireland
                                      .A1-Z5 General works
                                      .Z6   Organization and administration
     .6   Scotland
                                         Subarranged like HJ1039.5
     .7   Wales
                                         Subarranged like HJ1039.5
                                   Ireland
1040   General works
                                      History
1041   Early through 1800
1042   1801-1900
1043   1901-
1044   Organization and administration
                                   Austria
1055   General works
                                      History
1057   Medieval
1059   17th and 18th centuries
                                         19th century
1060   General works
1061   1800-1866/1867
1062   1866/1867-1900
1063   20th century
                                      Organization and administration
1064   General works
1065   Early through 1866/1867
1066   1866/1867-
1067   Provinces, A-Z
                                   Hungary
1068   General works. History
1069   Organization and administration
1070   Czechoslovakia. Bohemia
                                   France
1071   General works
1072   General special
                                         e. g. Caisse des dépôts et consignations
                                      History
1073   General through 1789 (Ancien régime)
                                         Medieval through 1500/1600
1076   General works
1077   Special
1078   Local, A-Z

```
                          History and conditions
                          By region or country
                            Europe
                              France
                                History - Continued
                                  1500-1800
1079                              General works
1080                              Henry IV to Louis XIV (17th century)
1081                              1715-1775 (18th century)
1082                              1775-1790 (Administrations of Turgot
                                    and Necker)
1083                            Revolution and First Empire
                                19th century
1085                              General works
1087                              1815-1871
1089                              1871-1900
1091                            20th century
                              Organization and administration
                                Administration
1093                              General works
1094                              Early through 1789
1095                              Special
                                      e. g.  Inspection
1098                              Frauds, embezzlements, etc.
1099                            Local (Departments, provinces), A-Z
                                .Z8  Colonies
1100                          Monaco
                            Germany
1101                          General works
                              History
                                Medieval
1104                              General works
1106                              Local, A-Z
                                Modern, 1500/1600
1108                              General works
1111                              17th and 18th centuries
                                19th century
1113                              General works
1115                              1800-1871
1117                              1871-1900
                                20th century
1119                              General works
1120                              1945-
1121                          Relations of the empire and the states
                              Organization and administration
                                Administration
1122                              General works
1123                              Inspection, regulation
1124                              Frauds, embezzlements, etc.
1150                          States, A-Z
                                Under each:
                                  (1)  General works.  History
                                  (2)  Organization and administration
    .5                        East Germany
```

```
                    History and conditions
                      By region or country
                        Europe - Continued
                          Greece
        1151                General works
                            History
        1152.A3               Early through 1832
            .A6-Z             1832-1900
        1153                  1901-
        1154                Organization and administration
        1155                Prefectures, A-Z
                          Italy
        1156                General works
                            History
        1157                  Medieval
        1158                  14th-16th centuries
        1159                  17th-18th centuries
        1160                  Early 19th century to 1861
        1183                  1861-
        1184                  1861-1900
        1185                  20th century
                            Organization and administration
        1186                  General works
        1187                  Special
                            Regions and provinces
            .8                Collective
                                  Including grants-in-aid
        1188                  Individual, A-Z
        1189              San Marino
            .5            Malta
```

SUBARRANGEMENT FOR HJ1190-1294 (Unless otherwise provided for)

10 nos.	5 nos.		1 no.	
(1)	(0) or (5)		.A1-Z5	General works
				History
(2)	(1)	(6).A3		Through 1789
(3)		.A6-Z		1790-1900
(4)	(2)	(7)		20th century
	(3)	(8)		Organization and administration
(6)			.Z6	General works
(7)				Early
(8)				Special
(9)	(4)	(9)		States, provinces
.A1A-Z	.A1A-Z	.A1A-Z	.Z7A-Z	Collective
				Including grants-in-aid
.A2-Z	.A2-Z	.A2-Z	.Z8A-Z	Individual

```
        1190-1193        Benelux countries.  Low Countries
        1195-1199          Belgium
        1200-1204          Netherlands
            1204.5         Luxemburg
```

	History and conditions
	By region or country
	Europe - Continued
	Soviet Union
1205	General works
	History
1206	1801-1900
1207	1901-1917
1208	1917-
	Organization and administration
1210	General works
1211	Special
.5	Local, A-Z
1212	Finland
1213	Poland
1215-1218	Scandinavia
1220-1224	Denmark
1225-1229	Iceland
1230-1234	Norway
1235-1239	Sweden
1240-1249	Spain
1250-1254	Portugal
1255-1264	Switzerland
	Cantons
1264.A2	Collective
.A5-Z	Individual
	Balkan States
.5	Albania
1265-1269	Bulgaria
1275-1279	Romania
1290-1294	Yugoslavia
1301-1616	Other regions or countries. Table X 1/
	Under each country:

10 nos.	5 nos.	1 no.	
(1)	(1)	.A1-Z5	General works
			History
(2)			Through 1800
(3)			1801-1900
(4)	(2)		20th century
			Organization and administration
(5)	(3)	.Z6A-Z	General works
(6)			Early
(7)			Special
			States, provinces, etc.
(8)	(4)	.Z7A-Z	Collective
			Including grants-in-aid
(9)	(5)	.Z8A-Z	Individual, A-Z

1620	Underdeveloped areas

1/
  For Table X, <u>see</u> pp. 331-340. Add number in Table to 620

INCOME AND EXPENDITURE. THE BUDGET

Serial documents, see HJ10+
    For serial documents on the United States budget,
        see HJ2050+

	Theory
2005	General works
2009	Preparation. Mechanism
	Control. Initiative
2011	General works
2013	By region or country, A–Z
2019	Increase. Retrenchment
2025	Colonial budgets
	Cf. HJ240, Colonial finance
2031	Program budgeting
2033	Zero-base budgeting
	History
2035	General works
	History. By period
2037	Early through 1800
2039	1800–1870
2041	1870–1900
2043	1900–

By region or country
    Under each country:

3 nos.	2 nos.	1 no.	
(1).A3	(1)	.A–Z6	Early works. Early history
.A5–Z			History (General)
			General works and history.
			By period
(2).A3			Early 19th century
.A5			Later 19th century
.A6–Z			20th century
(3)	(2)	.Z7A–Z	General special
(3.5)	(2.5)	.Z9A–Z	By state, province, etc., A–Z

2050–2052.5	United States
2052.A2	Periodicals, societies, etc.
	By state
2053.A1	Collective
.A2–W	By state, A–W
2054–2056.5	Canada
2056	By province, A–Z
.5	Saint Pierre and Miquelon
	Latin America
.7	General works
2057–2058.5	Mexico
	Central America
2060	General works
.5	Belize.
2061	Costa Rica
2062	Guatemala
2063	Honduras
2064	Nicaragua
2065	Panama
2066	Salvador

Income and expenditure. The budget
By region or country
Latin America – Continued
West Indies. Caribbean area

2066.5	General works
2067	Cuba
2068	Puerto Rico
2069	Haiti
2070	Dominican Republic. Santo Domingo
.5	Virgin Islands of the United States
2072	Jamaica
2073	Other, A-Z

South America

2074	General works
2075-2076.5	Argentina
2077-2078.5	Bolivia
2079-2080.5	Brazil
2081-2082.5	Chile
2083-2084.5	Colombia
2085	Ecuador

Guianas

2086	General works
.3	Guyana. British Guiana
.5	Surinam. Dutch Guiana
.7	French Guiana
2087-2088.5	Paraguay
2089-2090.5	Peru
2091-2092.5	Uruguay
2093	Venezuela

Europe

2094	General works
.5	European Economic Community countries
2095-2097.5	Great Britain
2098	Ireland
2100-2102.5	Austria
2103	Hungary
2104	Czechoslovakia
2105-2107.5	France
.7	Monaco
2108-2110.5	Germany
	Including West Germany
2112	East Germany
2117	Greece
2118-2120.5	Italy
2121	San Marino

Benelux countries. Low Countries

2122	General works
2123-2125.5	Belgium
2126-2128.5	Netherlands
.8	Luxemburg
2129-2130.5	Soviet Union
2131	Finland
2132	Poland

Scandinavia

2133-2134.5	Denmark
2135	Iceland
2136-2137.5	Norway
2138-2140.5	Sweden

Income and expenditure. The budget
  By region or country
    Europe - Continued

2141	Spain
2142	Portugal
2143-2145.5	Switzerland
	Balkan States
2146	Bulgaria
.5	Yugoslavia
2148	Romania
2151-2347	Other regions or countries. Table II 1/

Under each country:

	2 nos.	1 no.	
(1)	.A1-Z6	.A1-Z6	General works. History
	.Z7	.Z7A-Z	General special
(2)		.Z9A-Z	By state, province, etc., A-Z

REVENUE. TAXATION

Serial documents, see HJ10+

2240	Collected works (nonserial)
	Including publications of international societies conferences, etc.
	Study and teaching, see HJ203+
	History
2250	General works
	Ancient history, see HJ213+
2261	Ancient and medieval through 1600
2269	17th century
2271	18th century
	19th century
2273	General works
2275	Early through 1870
2277	1870-1900
2279	20th century
	Antiquities. Early forms
	Including regalia, tithes, etc.
	Cf. HJ210+, History of public finance
2281	General works
2287	By region or country, A-Z

    Under each country:
      .x   General works
      .x2 General special
      .x4 Local (not A-Z)
     e. g.   Great Britain
        .G7   General works
        .G72   General special
        .G74   Local

1/ For Table II, see pp. 331-340.   Add country number in Table to 2018

Revenue. Taxation – Continued
  Treatises. Theory and practice
2300   Early works through 1800
        Modern. Recent
2305   English
2307   French
2309   German
2311   Italian
2313   Spanish and Portuguese
2315   Other (not A-Z)
      History of theory
2317   General works
2318   By region or country, A-Z
      Incidence, shifting, distribution, equality
2321   General works
       By region or country
        United States
2322.A3   General works
   .A5-W   By state
2323   Other regions or countries, A-Z
      Progressive, proportional taxation
2326   General works
2327   By region or country, A-Z
      Exemption
        Cf. HJ4101+, Property tax
           HJ4621+, Income tax
           HJ5521+, Institutions
2336   General works
2337   By region or country, A-Z
2338   Taxation of government property
     Double taxation
       Cf. HJ5901+, Securities
2341   General works
       By region or country
        United States
2342.A3   General works
   .A5-W   By state
2343   Other regions or countries, A-Z
     Taxes on consumption, see HJ5703+
     Taxes on knowledge, see HJ5521+
     Taxation of aliens, nonresidents, etc.
2347   General works
2348   By region or country, A-Z
  .5   Tax evasion
     Taxation in international law, see K4456+
2350   Administrative fees
2351   Inflation and taxation
  .4   Tax revenue estimating
  .7   Taxation in underdeveloped areas
     Special theories
2352   General works
       Single tax, see HD1311+
     By region or country
       Including general works, history, etc.
       For administration, see HJ3231+
      United States
2360   Collected works (nonserial)
        For serial documents, see HJ10+
2362   General works
2368   Early through 1789
2369   1789-1815

```
                  Revenue . Taxation
                    By region or country
                      United States - Continued
2370                      1815-1860
2371                      1860-1865
2372                        Confederate States
                              Cf. HJ3257+, Tax administration and procedure
2373                      1865-1900
2375                        1898 (War revenue act)

2377                      1900-1950
                            War revenue acts, 1914-1918
2379.A1-4                     Documents
    .A5                       Official texts.  By date
    .A7A-Z                    Unofficial texts.  By author or editor
    .A8-Z                     Treatises, manuals, etc.  By author or editor
2380                        Defense and war revenue acts, 1938-1946
                                Subarranged like HJ2379
2381                      1950-
2383                      Facetiae, satire, etc.
2385                      States collectively

                      Regions
                        Under each:
                            .A1           General works
                            .A3             Early
                            .A4             1830-1900
                            .A6-Z8          1901-
                            .Z9           Special
2386                      New England and Atlantic States
2387                      Southern States
2388                      Middle West and Plains States
2389                      Pacific and Mountain States

                      States individually
                        Cf. HJ3260+, Tax administration and procedure
                        Under each:

                            .A2       General works
                                      History.  By period
                                        Early through 1800
                            .A29          Documents
                            .A3           Other
                                        1801-1860
                            .A39          Documents
                            .A4           Other
                                        1861-1865
                            .A49          Documents
                            .A5           Other
                                        1866-1900
                            .A59          Documents
                            .A6           Other
                                        1901-
                                          Documents
                                            For serial documents, see HJ11
                            .A7             Nonserial.  By date
                            .A8-Z2          Other
                            .Z3       Special
```

Revenue. Taxation
  By region or country
    United States
      States individually - Continued

2391	Alabama
2392	Alaska
2393	Arizona
2394	Arkansas
2395	California
2396	Colorado
2397	Connecticut
2398	Delaware
	District of Columbia, see HJ9216
2400	Florida
2401	Georgia
.5	Hawaii
2402	Idaho
2403	Illinois
2404	Indiana
2406	Iowa
2407	Kansas
2408	Kentucky
2409	Louisiana
2410	Maine
2412	Maryland
2413	Massachusetts
2414	Michigan
2415	Minnesota
2416	Mississippi
2417	Missouri
2418	Montana
2419	Nebraska
2420	Nevada
2421	New Hampshire
2422	New Jersey
2423	New Mexico
2424	New York
2425	North Carolina
2426	North Dakota
2427	Ohio
2428	Oklahoma
2429	Oregon
2430	Pennsylvania
2431	Rhode Island
2432	South Carolina
2433	South Dakota
2434	Tennessee
2435	Texas
2436	Utah
2437	Vermont
2438	Virginia
2439	Washington
2440	West Virginia
2441	Wisconsin
2442	Wyoming

```
                    Revenue.  Taxation
                      By region or country - Continued
                        Canada
      2445                General works
                          History.  By period
      2447                  Early through 1867
      2448                  1868-1900
      2449                  1901-
      2451                Special
      2460                Provinces, A-Z
                        Latin America
                          Subarranged like Central America
          .5            General works
                        Mexico
      2461                General works
                          History.  By period
      2463                  Early through 1810
      2464                  1810-1900
      2466                  1901-
      2467                Special
      2470                States, A-Z
                        Central America
                          Under each:
                              .A1A-Z  General works
                                        History.  By period
                              .A3A-Z     Early through 1820
                              .A5A-Z     1821-1900
                              .A7-Z3     1901-
                              .Z4-8     Special
                              .A9A-Z  Provinces
      2471                General works
      2472                Belize
      2473                Costa Rica
      2474                Guatemala
      2475                Honduras
      2476                Nicaragua
      2477                Panama
      2478                Salvador
                        West Indies.  Caribbean area
                          Subarranged like Central America
      2479                General works
          .5            Bahamas
      2480                Cuba
      2481                Puerto Rico
      2482                Haiti
      2483                Dominican Republic.  Santo Domingo
          .5            Virgin Islands of the United States
      2485                Jamaica
      2488                Other, A-Z
                        South America
                          Under each:
                              (1)  General works
                                     History.  By period
                              (2)    Early through 1820
                              (3)    1821-1900
                              (5)    1901-
                              (7)  Special
                              (9)  States, provinces, A-Z
 2491-2497              General
 2501-2509              Argentina
```

	Revenue. Taxation
	By region or country
	Latin America
	South America – Continued
2511–2519	Bolivia
2521–2529	Brazil
2531–2539	Chile
2541–2549	Colombia
	Guianas
	Subarranged like Central America
2550	General works
.3	Guyana. British Guiana
.5	Surinam. Dutch Guiana
.7	French Guiana
2551–2559	Ecuador
2561–2569	Paraguay
2571–2579	Peru
2581–2589	Uruguay
2591–2599	Venezuela
	Europe
2599.5	General works
.55	European Economic Community countries
	Great Britain
	Including England
2600	Collected works (nonserial)
2601	General works
	History. By period
2603	Early through 1700/1800
2605	Medieval through 1600
	Modern
2608	General works
2610	17th and 18th centuries
2612	17th century
2613	18th century
2614	1783–1815
	19th century
.5	General works
2615	1800–1850
2617	1851–1900
2619	1901–
2621	Special
	Northern Ireland
2623.A1A–Z	General works
	History. By period
.A3A–Z	Early through 1970
.A5A–Z	1701–1900
.A7–Z4	1901–
.Z5A–Z	Special
2624	Scotland
	Subarranged like HJ2623
2625	Wales
	Subarranged like HJ2623
2627	Ireland
	Subarranged like HJ2623

```
                   Revenue.  Taxation
                    By region or country
                      Europe - Continued
                        Austria
        2630              General works
                          History.  By period
        2631                Medieval through 1600/1700
                            Modern
        2632                  General works
        2633                  18th century
        2634                  19th century
        2636                  1901-1918
          .5                  1919-
        2638              States, A-Z
        2639            Hungary
        2640            Czechoslovakia
                        France
        2641              General works
                          History.  By period
                            Ancien régime
        2643                  General works
        2644                  General special
        2646                  Medieval through 1600
        2648                  17th century
        2650                  18th century
                            Modern
        2652                  General works
        2653                  Revolutionary period through 1815
        2655                  1815-1870
        2657                  1871-1900
        2659                  1901-
        2661              Special
        2669              Departments, provinces, A-Z
                        Germany
        2670              Periodicals.  Societies.  Serials
        2671              General works
                          History.  By period
                            Early through 1815
        2673                  General works
        2675                  Medieval through 1600
        2677                  17th century
        2679                  18th century
                            19th century
        2681                  General works
        2683                  1815-1870
        2685                  1871-1900
        2687                  1901-
        2690              Special
        2695              States, A-Z
        2698            East Germany
                        Greece (Modern)
        2731              General works
                          History.  By period
        2733                Early through 1832
        2735                1833-1900
        2737                1901-
        2738              Special
        2739              Prefectures, A-Z
```

Revenue. Taxation
By region or country
Europe – Continued
Italy

2741	General works
	History. By period
2742	Medieval
2744	17th and 18th centuries
2746	Early 19th century, through 1861
	Modern
2762	General works
2763	1861–1900
2765	1901–
2767	Special
2773	Regions, provinces, A–Z
2774	San Marino
.5	Malta

SUBARRANGEMENT UNDER HJ2775–2889 (Unless otherwise
provided for)

10 nos.	5 nos.	
(0)	(0)	General works
		History. By period
(1)	(1)	Early through 1800/1815
(2)		Medieval
(4)		17th and 18th centuries
(5)	(2)	1800/1815–1900
(6)		1901–
(7)	(3)	Special
(9)	(4)	Provinces, A–Z

2775–2778	Benelux countries. Low countries
2780–2789	Belgium
2790–2799	Netherlands
2799.5–.59	Luxemburg
	Soviet Union
2800	General works
	History. By period
2801	1801–1900
2802	1901–
2806	Special
.5	Republics, provinces, A–Z
2807	Finland
2808	Poland
	Scandivania
2809.5	General works
2810–2814	Denmark
2820–2824	Iceland
2830–2834	Norway
2835–2839	Sweden
2840–2849	Spain
2850–2859	Portugal

	Revenue. Taxation
	By region or country
	Europe – Continued
	Switzerland
2861	General works
	History. By period
	Early through 1815
2862	General works
2863	Medieval
2864	17th and 18th centuries
2865	1815–1900
2866	1901–
2867	Special
2869	Cantons, A–Z
	Balkan States
2870–2874	Bulgaria
2875–2879	Yugoslavia
2885–2889	Romania
2901–3192.7	Other regions or countries. Table VIII 1/
	Under each country:

10 nos.	5 nos.	1 no.	
(1)	(1)	.A1–Z5	General works
			History. By period
(2)	(2)		Early through 1800
(3)			Medieval
(4)			17th and 18th centuries
(5)			1801–1900
(6)	(3)		1901–
(7)	(4)	.Z7A–Z	Special
(9)	(5)	.Z9A–Z	States, provinces, A–Z

	Taxation. Administration and procedure
	For special subjects, see the subject, e. g.
	HJ6605+, Customs
	Collected works (nonserial)
3231	Official
3233	Nonofficial. By date of publication
3234	General works
	Administration: Theory, method
3241	Assessment. Valuation. Equalization
3245	Collection of taxes
	By region or country
	United States
	For serial documents, see HJ10+
	General works, treatises
3251.A7A–Z	Through 1860
.A8–Z	1861–1870
3252.A3A–Z	1871–1897
.A5–Z	1898–
	Confederate States
3257	Administration (Manuals, etc.)
	For nonofficial, see HJ2732

1/
For Table VIII, see pp. 331–340. Add number in table to 2350

Taxation.   Administration and procedure
By region or country
United States - Continued
Federal and state relations

3258.A2	Documents. By date
.A2A-Z	General works
.A3-Z	States collectively
	States individually. Table 1 1/
3260-3261.9	Alabama
3262-3263.9	Alaska
3264-3265.9	Arizona
3266-3267.9	Arkansas
3268-3269.9	California
3270-3271.9	Colorado
3272-3273.9	Connecticut
3274-3275.9	Delaware
	District of Columbia, see HJ9216
3278-3279.9	Florida
3280-3281.9	Georgia
3281.95-.969	Hawaii
3282-3283.9	Idaho
3284-3285.9	Illinois
3286-3287.9	Indiana
3288-3289.9	Indian Territory
3290-3291.9	Iowa
3292-3293.9	Kansas
3294-3295.9	Kentucky
3296-3297.9	Louisiana
3298-3299.9	Maine
3300-3301.9	Maryland
3302-3303.9	Massachusetts
3304-3305.9	Michigan
3306-3307.9	Minnesota
3308-3309.9	Mississippi
3310-3311.9	Missouri
3312-3313.9	Montana
3314-3315.9	Nevada
3316-3317.9	Nebraska
3318-3319.9	New Hampshire
3320-3321.9	New Jersey
3322-3323.9	New Mexico
3324-3325.9	New York
3326-3327.9	North Carolina
3328-3329.9	North Dakota
3330-3331.9	Ohio
3332-3333.9	Oklahoma
3334-3335.9	Oregon
3336-3337.9	Pennsylvania
3338-3339.9	Rhode Island
3340-3341.9	South Carolina
3342-3343.9	South Dakota
3344-3345.9	Tennessee
3346-3347.9	Texas

1/

For Table 1, see p. 287

Taxation. Administration and procedure
By region or country
United States
States individually. Table 1 (below) – Continued

3348–3349.9	Utah
3350–3351.9	Vermont
3352–3353.9	Virginia
3354–3355.9	Washington
3356–3357.9	West Virginia
3358–3359.9	Wisconsin
3360–3361.9	Wyoming

Table 1. Subdivisions under states of the
United States and foreign countries with
two numbers:

(1)	General works
	Official serial documents, see HJ11+
(2)	Special
.2	Administration
	.A1-2 Collected works (nonserial)
	.A5-Z General works
.3	Collection
.4	Delinquency
.6	Farming of taxes
.9	Tax lists

           Including cadastral survey, taxpayers'
             lists, etc.
           Cf. HJ9013, Local documents
           For United States class here state lists
             only: for lists of tax sales and taxable
             real estate, see HD268; for general tax
             lists of cities and towns, see HJ9191+

Table 2. Subdivisions under countries with
five numbers:
Serial documents, see HJ12+

(1)	Collected works (nonserial)
(5)	Administration
.A4	General works. Assessment, equalization, valuation
.A6	Collection of taxes
.A7	Farming of taxes
.A8-Z5	Local (States, provinces, etc.), A-Z
	Tax lists

           Including cadastral surveys, taxpayers'
             lists, etc.

.Z7	General
.Z8	By place

           Subarranged by date

Table 3. Subdivisions under countries with one number:

.A1-4	Collected works (nonserial)
.A6-Z	Other

Taxation. Administration and procedure
By region or country 1/ - Continued

3370-3374	Canada
	Latin America
3374.5	General works
3375-3379	Mexico
	West Indies. Caribbean area
3379.5	General works
3380-3384	Cuba
3385-3389	Puerto Rico
3390-3391	Virgin Islands of the United States
3393	Other, A-Z
	Central America
3395	General works
3396	Belize
3397-3398	Costa Rica
3399-3400	Guatemala
3401-3402	Honduras
3403-3404	Nicaragua
3405-3406	Panama
3407-3408	Salvador
	South America
3409	General works
3410-3414	Argentina
3415-3419	Bolivia
3420-3424	Brazil
3425-3429	Chile
3430-3434	Colombia
3435-3436	Ecuador
.5	Guiana
3437	Guyana. British Guiana
3438	Surinam. Dutch Guiana
3439	French Guiana
3440-3444	Paraguay
3445-3449	Peru
3450-3454	Uruguay
3455-3456	Venezuela
	Europe
3458	General works
3459	European Economic Community countries
3460-3464	Great Britain
3464.5	Ireland. Irish Republic
3465-3469	Austria
3470-3471	Hungary
3472-3473	Czechoslovakia
3475-3479	France
3480-3484	Germany
	Including West Germany
3484.5	East Germany
3511	Greece
3515-3519	Italy
3520	San Marino
3521-3524	Benelux countries. Low countries
3525-3529	Belgium
3530-3534	Netherlands
3534.5	Luxemburg

1/
For subarrangement, see tables, p. 287

Taxation. Administration and procedure
By region or country 1/
Europe - Continued

3535-3539	Soviet Union
3540	Finland
3541-3542	Poland
	Scandinavia
3543-3544	Denamrk
3544.5	Greenland
3545	Iceland
3547	Norway
3548-3549	Sweden
3550-3554	Spain
3555-3559	Portugal
3560-3564	Switerland
	Balkan States
3565	Bulgaria
3566	Yugoslavia
3568	Romania
3600-3696	Other regions or countries. Table III 2/

Under each country:

3 nos.	2 nos.	1 no.	
(1)	(1) .A1-4	.A1-4	Periodicals. Societies. Serials
(2)	.A5-Z	.A5-Z5	General works
(3)	(2)	.Z6A-Z	States, provinces, etc., A-Z

Income from sources other than taxation

3801	General works
	Fees, see HJ5301+
	Fisheries, waters, see SH1+
	Forests, see SD
	Industries, see HD, etc.
	Licenses, see HJ5301+
	Lotteries, see HG6105+
	Mines, see HD9506+
	Mints, see HG321; HG451+
	Monopolies, see HD3840+
	Regalia, see HJ2281+
	State domain, etc., see HD101+
	Transportaion and communication, see HE
	By region or country

Under each country:
    (1)   Periodicals. Societies. Serials
            General works
    (2.7)   Early works. Early history
    (3)   Recent works
    (4)   General special
    (5)   States, provinces, etc., A-Z

1/
For subarrangement, see tables, p. 287

2/
For Table III, see pp. 331-340. Add number in table to 3401

                    Taxation. Administration and procedure
                    Income from sources other than taxation
                      By region or country - Continued
                          United States
3833.A1-2   Periodicals. Societies. Serials
                            General works
     .A3   Early works
     .A5-Z   Recent works
3834   General special
3835   States, A-W

3836   Canada
3837   Mexico, West Indies, and Central America, A-Z
3838   South America. By region or country, A-Z
3840   Europe. By region or country, A-Z
3841   Asia. By region or country, A-Z
3842   Africa. By region or country, A-Z
3843   Australia
     .5   New Zealand
3844   Pacific islands, A-Z
                    Direct taxes (General)
3851   Theory
3853   History
                      General works
3861   Early works
3863   Recent works
3871-4064   By region or country
                        Under each country:

          2 nos.   1 no.

          (1).A2   .A2A-Z   Periodicals. Societies. Serials
             .A6   .A6A-Z   Early works
             .A7-Z   .A7-Z8   Recent works
          (2)   .Z9A-Z   States, provinces, etc., A-Z

3871-3924   United States
   3871   General works
3873-3924   States. Table of States II 1/
3926-3927   Canada
                          Latin America
   3927.5   General works
   3928   Mexico
                            Central America
   3929   General works
       .5   Belize
   3930   Costa Rica
   3931   Guatemala
   3932   Honduras
   3933   Nicaragua
   3934   Panama
   3935   Salvador
                            West Indies. Caribbean area
       .5   General works
   3936   Cuba
   3937   Puerto Rico

1/
For Table of States II, see p. 344. Add state number in Table to 3872.

Taxation. Administration and procedure
Direct taxes (General)
By region or country
Latin America
West Indies. Caribbean area – Continued

3938	Haiti
3939	Dominican Republic. Santo Domingo
3940	Virgin Islands of the United States
3942	Jamaica
3944	Other, A–Z
	South America
3945	General works
3946–3947	Argentina
3948–3949	Bolivia
3950–3951	Brazil
3952–3953	Chile
3954–3955	Colombia
3956	Ecuador
3957	Guianas
.3	Guyana. British Guiana
.5	Surinam. Dutch Guiana
.7	French Guiana
3958–3959	Paraguay
3960–3961	Peru
3962–3963	Uruguay
3964–3965	Venezuela
	Europe
3966–3967	Great Britain
3970.5	Ireland
3971–3972	Austria
3973	Hungary
.5	Czechoslovakia
3974–3975	France
3976	Germany
	Including West Germany
3982.5	East Germany
3983	Greece
3984–3985	Italy
3986	San Marino
3987	Benelux countries. Low countries
3988–3989	Belgium
3990–3991	Netherlands
.5	Luxemburg
3992–2993	Soviet Union
3993.3	Finland
.7	Poland
	Scandinavia
3994–3995	Denmark
3996	Iceland
3997	Norway
3998–3999	Sweden
4000–4001	Spain
4002	Portugal
4003–4004	Switzerland
	Balkan States
4005	Bulgaria
.5	Yugoslavia
4007	Romania

Taxation. Administration and procedure
Direct taxes (General) – Continued

4010.85-4056.7   Other regions or countries. Table VI 1/
Under each country:

5 nos.	2 nos.	1 no.	
(1)	(1).A2	.A1-4	Periodicals. Societies. Serials
(2)	.A6		Early works
(3)	.A7-Z	.A5-Z8	General works
(5)	(2)	.Z9A-Z	States, provinces, etc., A-Z

Direct taxes (Special)
For special forms not provided for here, see HJ5521+
General property tax
Class here all kinds of property, real and
personal

4101   Theory
History
4103   General works
4111   Early works
4113   Later and recent works
By region or country
United States
4120.A1-3   Periodicals. Societies. Serials
.A4-Z   General works
4121   By region or state, A-Z
Under each state:
.x   Periodicals. Societies. Serials
.x2   General works
Canada
4122.A1-3   Periodicals. Societies. Serials
.A4A-Z   General works
.A5-Z   By region or province, A-Z
Under each province:
.x   Periodicals. Societies. Serials
.x2   General works
Latin America
.5   General works
4123   Mexico 2/
.2   West Indies 3/
.5   Central America 3/
4124   South America 3/
Europe
4125.A1-3   Periodicals. Societies. Serials
.A4A-Z   General works
.A5-Z   By region or country, A-Z
Under each country:
.x   Periodicals. Societies. Serials
.x2   General works
.x3   States, provinces, etc., A-Z

1/
For Table VI, see pp. 331-340. Add number in table to 3856
2/
Subarranged like HJ4122
3/
Subarranged like HJ4125

```
                  Taxation.  Administration and procedure
                  Direct taxes (Special)
                     General property tax
                        By region or country - Continued
     4126                  Asia 1/
     4127                  Africa 1/
     4128                  Australia 2/
        .5                 New Zealand 2/
     4129                  Pacific islands 2/
                        Capital levy
     4132                  General works
     4133                  By region or country, A-Z
                        Land tax.  Real estate tax
     4151                  Theory
     4157                  History
                           General works
     4163                     Early works
     4165                     Recent works
                           Tax on special types of property
     4167                     Forest lands
     4169                     Mines and mineral lands
     4173                     Improvements, houses, buildings, etc.
     4175                     Betterments.  Special assessments
                        Unearned increment, see HD1315
                        By region or country
                           Under each country (except the United States):
                              (1).A1    Periodicals.  Societies.  Serials
                                 .A29   Collected works (nonserial)
                                        General works
                                 .A6       Early works
                                 .A7-Z     Recent works
                              (2)       Special
                                 .A25      Delinquency
                                 .A27      Exemption
                                 .A3       Forest lands, etc.
                                 .A4       Mobile homes
                                 .A5       Improvement, houses, etc.
                                 .A6       Betterments.  Special
                                              assessments
                              (3).A7-Z  States, provinces, etc., A-Z
                              For countries with two numbers combine (2)
                                 and (3); for countries with one number
                                 expand (1) by: Special, .Z7A-Z; Local,
                                 .Z9A-Z
                           United States
     4181                     General works
     4182                     Special
                                 .A25   Delinquency
                                 .A27   Exemptions
                                           Cf. HJ2338, Taxation of government
                                              property
                                 .A3    Forest lands
                                 .A4    Mobile homes
                                 .A6    Betterments
                                 .C35   Camp sites, facilities, etc.
                                 .C64   Condominium housing
```

1/
   Subarranged like HJ4125
2/
   Subarranged like HJ4122

Taxation. Administration and procedure
Direct taxes (Special)
Land tax. Real estate tax
By region or country
United States – Continued

4183–4286	States. Table of States, III 1/

Under each:
(1)
.A1–5 Periodicals. Societies. Serials
.A6–Z General works
(2)   Special
For subarrangement, see HJ4182
Local, see HJ9012+, HJ9191+

4291–4293	Canada
	Latin America
4293.5	General works
4294–4296	Mexico
	Central America
4297	General works
.5	Belize
4298	Costa Rica
4299	Guatemala
4300	Honduras
4301	Nicaragua
4302	Panama
4303	Salvador
	West Indies. Caribbean area
4304	General works
4305	Cuba
4306	Puerto Rico
4307	Haiti
4308	Dominican Republic. Santo Domingo
4309	Virgin Islands of the United States
4313	South America
4314–4316	Argentina
4317–4318	Bolivia
4319–4321	Brazil
4322–4324	Chile
4325–4326	Colombia
4327	Ecuador
4328	Guianas
.3	Guyana. British Guiana
.5	Surinam. Dutch Guiana
.7	French Guiana
4329–4330	Paraguay
4331–4332	Peru
4333–4334	Uruguay
4335–4336	Venezuela
	Europe
4336.5	General works
.55	European Economic Community countries
4337–4338	Great Britain
4339	Ireland
4342–4343	Austria
4344	Czechoslovakia
4345	Hungary

1/
For Tables of States III, see p. 344.   Add state number in table to 4182

Taxation. Administration and procedure
Direct taxes (Special)
Land tax. Real estate tax
By region or country
Europe - Continued

4346-4348	France
4349-4350	Germany
4356.6	East Germany
4357	Greece
4358-4360	Italy
4361	San Marino
4362	Benelux countries. Low countries
4363-4364	Belgium
4365-4366	Netherlands
4366.5	Luxemburg
4367-4368	Soviet Union
4368.3	Finland
.7	Poland
	Scandinavia
4369	Denmark
4371	Iceland
4372	Norway
4373	Sweden
4374-4375	Spain
4376	Portugal
4377-4378	Switzerland
	Balkan States
4379	Bulgaria
4380	Yugoslavia
4382	Romania
4385-4449	Other regions or countries. Table II 1/

Under each country:

2 nos.	1 no.	
(1).A1-4	(1).A1-4	Periodicals. Societies. Serials
.A5-Z6	.A5-Z6	General works
.Z7	.Z7A-Z	Special
(2)	.Z9A-Z	States, provinces, etc., A-Z

Personal property
Cf. HJ4101+, General property tax

4581	Theory
4582	History
	General works
4585	Early works
4586	Recent works
	Special, e. g. luxuries, securities, etc., see HJ5771+, HJ5901+, etc.
	By region or country
	United States
4590	General works
4591	States, A-W

1/
For Table II, see pp. 331-340. Add number in table to 4252

Taxation. Administration and procedure
  Direct taxes (Special)
    Personal property
      By region or country - Continued
        Other regions or countries
          Under each country:

	1 no.	Cutter no.	
	.A2A-Z	.x	General works
	.A3-Z	.x2	Local, A-Z

4592	Canada
.5	Latin America
4593	Mexico, West Indies, and Central America, A-Z
4594	South America. By region or country, A-Z
4595	Europe. By region or country, A-Z
4596	Asia. By region or country, A-Z
4597	Africa. By region or country, A-Z
4598	Australia
.5	New Zealand
4599	Pacific islands, A-Z

Income tax

4621	Theory
4623	History
	General works
4627	Early works
4629	Recent works
4631	Income from investments
	Including profits, rents, dividends, interest, and annuities
4633	Income from government bonds, etc.
4635	Foreign income
4637	Effect of inflation
4639	Other
	Including salaries, wages, etc.
	By region or country
	United States
	Through 1912
4651.A2	Periodicals. Societies. Serials
	For serials, see HJ9+
.A6-Z	General works
	1913-
4652.A1-4	Periodicals. Societies
.A8-Z	General works
4653	Special, A-Z
.A3	Capital income
	Including profits, rents, dividends, interest, annuities
.A7	Accounting
.A8	Administration
.A82	Aged
.A83	Aliens
.A9	Armed forces pay
.C3	Capital gains
.C35	Capital investment amortization
.C5	Civil service pensions

              Taxation. Administration and procedure
            Direct taxes (Special)
             Income tax
              By region or country
               United States

4653   Special, A-Z - Continued

         .C6   Collection at source
         .C67   Community property
         .C7   Corporations
         .C73   Credits
         .D4   Deductions
         .D5   Depreciation and depletion
         .E7   Estates and trusts
         .E75   Evasion
         .E8   Excess profits tax
         .E85   Executives
         .E9   Exemptions

         .F7   Fringe benefits
         .G5   Gifts
                Government bonds, see .P83
               Joint returns, see .C67
         .N47   Nonreimbursement certificates
         .N5   Nonresidents
         .P5   Pensions
         .P8   Public salaries
         .P83   Public securities
         .R4   Real property
         .R45   Refunds
         .R56   Returns

         .S3   Securities
         .S5   Shipping profits
                Soldier's pay, see .A9
         .S7   Statistics
         .S73   Stock rights
         .S8   Surtax
                Trusts, see .E7
         .U46   Undistributed profits
         .U5   Unearned income

          States
4655.A1   States collectively
  .A2-W   Individual states, A-W
            For subdivisions under the several states,
               use successive Cutter numbers; use a single
               digit for "General works" two digits for
               the preceding and following subdivisions

        e. g.   Michigan
           .M47   Periodicals. Societies.
                    Serials
           .M5   General works
                  Special
           .M52   Capital income
           .M53   Foreign income
           .M54   Other
           .M55   Administration

```
              Taxation.  Administration and procedure
                Direct taxes (Special)
                  Income tax
                    By region or country - Continued
                      Other regions or countries
                        Under each country:
                        For countries with three numbers:
                        (1).A2     Periodicals.  Societies
                                     For serials, see HJ9+
                                   General works
                           .A55-6    Early works
                           .A7-Z     Recent works
                        (2)          Special
                           .A3         Capital income
                                         Including profits, rents, dividends,
                                           interest, annuities
                           .A4         Capital gains tax
                           .A43        Collection at source
                           .A45        Deductions
                           .A5         Foreign income
                           .A6         Excess profits
                           .A7         Other
                                         Including salaries, wages, etc.
                           .A8         Administration
                        (3)          States, provinces, etc., A-Z

                        For countries with two numbers add .A9-Z
                          States, provinces, etc., A-Z to (2)
                        For countries with one number add .Z8A-Z
                          States, provinces, etc., A-Z to (1)
  4661-4663                 Canada
                            Latin America
     4663.5                   General works
  4664-4666                   Mexico
                              Central America
        4667                    General works
          .5                    Belize
        4668                    Costa Rica
        4669                    Guatemala
        4670                    Honduras
        4671                    Nicaragua
        4672                    Panama
        4673                    Salvador
                              West Indies.  Caribbean area
        4675                    Cuba
        4676                    Puerto Rico
        4677                    Haiti
        4678                    Dominican Republic.  Santo Domingo
        4679                    Virgin Islands of the United States
                              South America
        4683                    General works
  4684-4686                     Argentina
  4687-4688                     Bolivia
  4689-4691                     Brazil
  4692-4694                     Chile
        4695                     Colombia
        4696                     Ecuador
```

Taxation. Administration and procedure
Direct taxes (Special)
<u>Income tax</u>
By region or country
Other region or countries
Latin America
South America – Continued

4697	Guianas
.3	Guyana. British Guiana
.5	Surinam. Dutch Guiana
.7	French Guiana
4698–4699	Paraguay
4701–4702	Peru
4703–4704	Uruguay
4705–4706	Venezuela
	Europe
4706.5	General works
.75	European Economic Community countries
4707–4708	Great Britain
4709	Ireland
4712–4713	Austria
4714	Czechoslovakia
4715	Hungary
4716–4718	France
4719–4720	Germany
4726.5	East Germany
4727	Greece
4728–4730	Italy
4731	San Marino
4732	Benelux countries. Low countries
4733–4734	Belgium
4735–4736	Netherlands
4736.5	Luxemburg
4737–4738	Soviet Union
4738.3	Finland
.7	Poland
	Scandinavia
.8	General works
4739	Denmark
4741	Iceland
4742	Norway
4743	Sweden
4744–4745	Spain
4746	Portugal
4747–4748	Switzerland
4749	Bulgaria
4750	Yugoslavia
4752	Romania
4760–4824	Other regions or countries. Table II <u>1</u>/

Under each country:

2 nos.	1 no.	
(1).A1–4	.A1–4	Periodicals. Societies. Serials
.A5–Z6	.A5–Z6	General works
.Z7	.Z7A–Z	Special
(2)	.Z8A–Z	States, provinces, etc., A–Z

<u>1</u>/
  For Table II, <u>see</u> pp. 331–340. Add number in table to 4627.

Taxation. Administration and procedure
Direct taxes (Special) – Continued
Capitation. Poll tax

4911	Theory
4913	History
	General works
4917	Early works
4919	Recent works
	By region or country
	United States
4930	General works
4931	By region or state, A–Z
	Other regions or countries
	Under each country:

1 no.	Cutter no.	
.A2A–Z	.x	General works
.A3–Z	.x2	States, provinces, etc., A–Z

4932	Canada
.5	Latin America
4933	Mexico, West Indies, and Central America, A–Z
4934	South America. By region or country, A–Z
4935	Europe. By region or country, A–Z
4936	Asia. By region or country, A–Z
4937	Africa. By region or country, A–Z
4938	Australia
.5	New Zealand
4939	Pacific islands, A–Z
	Other special direct taxes, see HJ5521+
	Indirect taxes (General)
	Class here general works and works on internal revenue (Excise)
5001	Theory
5003	History
5009	General works
	By region or country
	United States
5018	Bureau of Internal Revenue
	For income tax, see HJ4651+
5020	General works
	Including general internal revenue
5021	Maladministration, "Whisky ring", etc.
5023–5074	States. Table of States II 1/

1/ For Table of States II, see p. 344. Add state number in table to 5022.

Taxation. Administration and procedure
Indirect taxes (General)
By region or country - Continued
Other regions or countries
Under each country:
(1).A1-3   Periodicals. Societies. Serials
General works
.A7   Early works
.A8-Z   Recent works
(2)   States, provinces, etc., A-Z
For countries with <u>one number</u>, use .Z8A-Z
for States, provinces, etc., A-Z

5075-5076	Canada
	Latin America
5076.5	General works
5077-5078	Mexico
	Central America
5079	General works
.5	Belize
5080	Costa Rica
5081	Guatemala
5082	Honduras
5083	Nicaragua
5084	Panama
5085	Salvador
	West Indies. Caribbean area
.5	General works
5086	Cuba
5087	Puerto Rico
5088	Haiti
5089	Dominican Republic. Santo Domingo
5090	Virgin Islands of the United States
	South America
5095	General works
5096-5097	Argentina
5098-5099	Bolivia
5100-5101	Brazil
5102-5103	Chile
5104-5105	Colombia
5106-5107	Ecuador
5107.2	Guianas
.3	Guyana. British Guiana
.5	Surinam. Dutch Guiana
.7	French Guiana
5108-5109	Paraguay
5110-5111	Peru
5112-5113	Uruguay
5114-5115	Venezuela
	Europe
5116	General works
5117	European Economic Community countries
5118-5119	Great Britain
5120	Ireland
5123-5124	Austria
5125	Hungary
.5	Czechoslovakia
5126-5127	France

	Taxation. Administration and procedure
	Indirect taxes (General)
	By region or country
	Other regions or countries – Continued
5128	Germany
	Including West Germany
5134.5	East Germany
5135	Greece
5136–5137	Italy
5138	San Marino
	Benelux countries. Low countries
5139	General works
5140–5141	Belgium
5142–5143	Netherlands
5143.5	Luxemburg
5144–5145	Soviet Union
5145.3	Finland
.7	Poland
	Scandinavia
5146	Denmark
5148	Icelnad
5149	Norway
5150	Sweden
5151–5152	Spain
5153	Portugal
5154–5155	Switzerland
	Balkan States
5156	Bulgaria
.5	Yugoslavia
5158	Romania
5161–5225	Asia, Africa, etc. Table II 1/
	Under each country:

2 nos.	1 no.	
(1).A1–3	.A1–3	Periodicals. Societies
		Serials
.A5–Z6	.A5–Z6	General works
(2)	.Z8A–Z	States, provinces, etc., A–Z

	Indirect taxes (Special)
	For excise, internal revenue, see HJ5001+
	For customs, see HJ6603+; K
	For octroi, see HJ9120, etc.

	Fees, licenses, stamp tax
5301	Theory
5303	History
	General works
5307	Early works
5309	Recent works
5315	Revenue stamps
	Class here general works only; for works on
	special countries, see HJ5321+

1/
   For Table II, see pp. 331–340. Add number in table to 5028

Taxation. Administration and procedure
Fees, licenses, stamp tax - Continued
By region or country
Under each country:

(1)		Periodicals. Societies. Serials
		General works
.A6		Early works
.A7–Z4		Recent works
.Z5		Pamphlets. By date
.Z7A–Z		Revenue stamps
(2)		States, provinces, etc., A–Z

                                   For countries with <u>one number</u>
                                   use .Z8A–Z for States,
                                   provinces, etc.

5321	United States
	Use (1) from table above
5323–5374	States. Table of States II 1/
	For cities, <u>see</u> HJ9191+
5375–5376	Canada
	Latin America
5376.5	General works
5377	Mexico
	Central America
5378	General works
.5	Belize
5379	Costa Rica
5380	Guatemala
5381	Honduras
5382	Nicaragua
5383	Panama
5384	Salvador
	West Indies. Caribbean area
.5	General works
5385	Cuba
5386	Puerto Rico
5387	Haiti
5388	Dominican Republic. Santo Domingo
5389	Virgin Islands of the United States
	South America
5393	General works
5394	Argentina
5395	Bolivia
5396	Brazil
5397	Chile
5398	Colombia
5399	Ecuador
.2	Guianas
.3	Guyana. British Guiana
.5	Surinam. Dutch Guiana
.7	French Guiana
5400	Paraguay
5401	Peru
5402	Uruguay
5403	Venezuela

1/   For Table of States II, <u>see</u> p. 344. Add state number in table to 4322

	Taxation. Administration and procedure
	Fees, licenses, stamp tax
	By region or country – Continued
	Europe
5403.5	General works
.55	European Economic Community countries
5404–5405	Great Britain
5406	Ireland
5409–5410	Austria
5411	Hungary
.5	Czechoslovakia
5412–5413	France
5414	Germany
	Including West Germany
5420.5	East Germany
5421	Greece
5422–5423	Italy
5424	San Marino
	Benelux countries. Low countries
5425	General works
5426	Belgium
5427	Netherlands
.5	Luxemburg
5428–5429	Soviet Union
5429.3	Finland
.7	Poland
	Scandinavia
5430	Denmark
5431	Iceland
5432	Norway
5433	Sweden
5434–5435	Spain
5436	Portugal
5437–5438	Switzerland
	Balkan States
5439	Bulgaria
.5	Yugoslavia
5441	Romania
5444–5508	Other regions or countries. Table II [1]/
	Under each country:

2 nos.	1 no.	
(1).A1–3	.A1–3	Periodicals. Societies. Serials
.A5–Z	.A5–Z6	General works
(2)	.Z8A–Z	States, provinces, etc., A–Z

---

[1]/ For Table II, see pp. 331–340. Add number in table to 5311

Taxation. Administration and procedure – Continued
  Other special forms
    Class here works on taxes and on the theory of
      taxation, institutions, transactions, articles,
      etc. For descriptive, statistical works, see
      HD, HE, etc.
    Mortmain. Foundations. Institutions
      Including churches, schools, etc.
        Cf. HD2753, Taxation of corporations

5521	General works
	By region or country
	United States
5523	General works
5527	By region or state, A–Z
5529	Other regions or countries, A–Z

      Art galleries, see N
      Charitable and benevolent institutions, see HV
      Churches, see BV777
      Corporations, see HD2753
      Libraries, see Z
      Museums, see AM
      Schools, see LC
      Societies (Literary, scientific, social), see AS; HS
      Theaters, concert halls, etc., see GV; PN
    Corporations, see HD2753
    Industries, occupations, business, professions
      Cf. HD; HE, etc.
      See note preceding HJ5521
      General works

5621.A3	Early works
.A4–Z	Recent works
	By region or country
	United States
5623.A1–6	General works
.A7–Z	Local
5625	Canada
5626	Latin America. By region or country, A–Z
	Including West Indies
5627	Europe. By region or country, A–Z
5628	Asia. By region or country, A–Z
5629	Africa. By region or country, A–Z
5630	Australia
5631	New Zealand
5632	Pacific islands, A–Z

      Industries, see HD, T, etc.
      Occupations. Trades, see HD, T, etc.
      Business, see HD, HF, etc.
      Professions, see HD, T, etc.

    Articles of consumption, raw materials, manufacutures

5703	General works on consumption taxes
5707	By region or country, A–Z
	Articles of consumption. Sales tax. Spendings
	tax. Turn over tax. Value–added tax
5711	General works
5715	By region or country, A–Z
	Special articles, see HD, HF, etc.

Taxation. Administration and procedure
  Other special forms
    Articles of comsumption, raw materials,
      manufactures - Continued
        Raw materials
5751   General works
5754   By region or country, A-Z
            Special materials, see HD, HF, etc.
        Manufactures
5761   General works
5764   By region or country, A-Z
            Special articles, see HD, HF, etc.
        Luxuries
            Cf. HJ4581+, Personal property tax
5771   General works
            By region or country
              United States
5773   General works
5774   By region or state, A-Z
5775   Other regions or countries, A-Z
            Special
              Furniture, instruments, vehicles, boats, yachts
5777   General works
5780   Special, A-Z
                  .B6   Boats
                  .V4   Vehicles
5783   Wearing apparel. Jewelry
              Animals (Pets, etc.)
5788   General works
              Dogs
5791   General and United States
5792   By region or country, A-Z
5793   Horses, etc.

5797   Other (not A-Z)
                    e. g. Amusements, books, club dues, motion
                             pictures, playing cards, servants,
                             soft drinks, theater tickets
    Acts, instruments, inheritance and transfer taxes
          Cf. HJ5301+, Fees, licenses, stamp tax
5801   General works
          By region or country
            United States
5804   Congresses
5805   General
5806   States collectively
5807   By region or state, A-Z
5809   Canada
5811   Latin America. By region or country, A-Z
                Including West Indies
5813   Europe. By region or country, A-Z
5815   Asia. By region or country, A-Z
5817   Africa. By region or country, A-Z
5819   Australia
5821   New Zealand
5823   Pacific islands, A-Z

Taxation. Administration and procedure
Other special forms - Continued
Securities, credits, bonds, mortgages, etc.
Class here notes, checks, etc., as forms of
property; for taxes on the execution of
instruments, on transfers, etc., see HJ5801+
Cf. HJ2341+, Double taxation
HJ4581+, Personal property, etc.

5901	General works
	By region or country
	United States
5905	General works
5907	By region or state, A-Z
5909	Canada
5911	Latin America. By region or country, A-Z
	Including West Indies
5913	Europe. By region or country, A-Z
5915	Asia. By region or country, A-Z
5917	Africa. By region or country, A-Z
5919	Australia
5921	New Zealand
5923	Pacific islands, A-Z

Transportation and traffic
General works, see HE197
Road taxes

5951	General works
5953-5957	By region or country
	United States
5953.A1-5	General works
.A6-Z	By region or state, A-Z
5954	Canada
5955	Other American regions or countries, A-Z
5956	Europe. By region or country, A-Z
5957	Other. By region or country, A-Z

Navigation: Shipping, see HE384+,
Inland (Rivers), see HE387+,
Exterior (Harbors, straits, etc.), see
HE386; HE951+
Railroads, see HE1071+
Telegraph, see HE7647, etc.

CUSTOMS ADMINISTRATION

For protection and free trade policy, see HF1701+
For tariff upon particular commodities, see HF2651

6603	International congresses, etc.
6605	Periodicals. Societies. Serials
6606	Dictionaries. Encyclopedias
6607	Terminology. Abbreviations. Notation

	Customs administration - Continued
6609	Treatises and advanced textbooks
6613	General special
6617	Certificate of origin
6619	Smuggling
	By region or country
	United States
6620	Congresses
6621	Colonial period
6622.A1-57	Periodicals. Societies. Serials
.A6	History. Antiquities. By date
	Including reform pamphlets, criticism, etc.
.A7-Z	Treatises. Manuals. Guidebooks
	Class here works for importers, etc.
6623	Particular ports, A-Z
	Cf. HJ6640, Customhouses
6625	Collection, cost, etc. Collectors
6630	Inspection. Surveyors of the port, etc.
6633	Solicitor of customs
6634	Special agents
	Ports of entry, delivery, etc. Lists, etc.
6635	General works
6637	By region or state, A-Z
6640	Customhouses, A-Z
	Cf. HJ6623, Ports
6645	United States Coast Guard. Revenue cutter service
	Cf. V437, Revenue cutter service schools
	VK1023, Lighthouse service
	Biography
6647.A2A-Z	Collective
.A3-Z	Individual
	Entry. Appraisement. Liquidation
6650	General works
	Vessels
	Cf. HE, Transportation and communication
	VK, Navigation. Merchant marine
6655	Registration, etc.
6660	Fees
6665	Entry
6670	Appraisement
6675	Liquidation
6680	Refunding
	Cf. HF1715+, Drawbacks
	Warehousing, see HF5484+
6685	Customhouse broker
	Smuggling. Frauds
6690	General works
6695	Maladministration
	Undervaluation, etc.
6700	General works
6705	Special classes
	e. g. Silks, woolens
6710	Seizure of books and papers
6715	Penalties
	Cases
6720.A1-6	Collections
.A7-Z	Individual, A-Z

Customs administration
  By region or country
    United States — Continued
      Special articles, see HD9000+; HF2651

6731	Personnel. Appointments. Civil service
6735	Blanks, forms, etc.
6740	Confederate States of America

  Other regions or countries
    Under each country:

10 nos.	5 nos.	4 nos.	2 nos.	1 no.	
		(1)	(1).A3-A5	.A3-A5	Periodicals. Societies. Serials
(0)	(0) or (5)				Early
(1).A1-3	(1) or (6).A1-25				Recent
.A6A-Z	.A3A-Z	(2).A2A-Z	.A55A-Z	.A55A-Z	History. Antiquities
.A7-Z	.A4-Z5	.A3-Z5	.A6A-Z	.A6A-Z	Treatises, manuals, etc.
(2)	.Z7A-Z	.Z7A-Z	.A7-Z	.A7-Z4	Individual ports, A-Z
			(2)	.Z5A-Z	Special
					Cf. HJ6622+, United States colonial period serial collections
(3)	(2) or (7)	(3)			Collection
(5)	(3) or (8)				Entry, appraisement, etc.
(7)	(4) or (9)	(4)			Smuggling
(9)	(4.5) or (9.5)	(4.5)			Other

6750-6757	Canada
	Latin America
6759.5	General works
6760-6767	Mexico
	Central America
6767.5	General works
6768-6769	Belize
6770-6774	Costa Rica
6775-6779	Guatemala
6780-6784	Honduras
6785-6789	Nicaragua
6790-6794	Panama
6795-6799	Salvador
	West Indies. Caribbean area
6799.5	General works
6800-6804	Cuba
6805-6809	Puerto Rico
6810-6811	Haiti
6813-6814	Dominican Republic. Santo Domingo
6815-6816	Virgin Islands of the United States
	Cf. HJ6829+, Danish West Indies
6821-6822	Jamaica
6823	Bahamas
6824	Barbados
6833-6836	Dutch West Indies
6837-6838	French West Indies

Customs administration
  By region or country
    Other regions or countries
      Latin America - Continued
        South America

6839	General works
6840–6844	Argentina
6845–6849	Bolivia
6850–6854	Brazil
6855–6859	Chile
6860–6864	Colombia
6865–6868	Ecuador
6869	Guianas
.3	Guyana. British Guiana
.5	Surinam. Dutch Guiana
.7	French Guiana
6870–6874	Paraguay
6875–6879	Peru
6880–6884	Uruguay
6885–6889	Venezuela

Europe

6889.5	General
.55	European Economic Community countries

Great Britain

6890–6897	General works
6898	Personnel, appointments, civil service
6899	Ireland
6900–6904	Austria
6905–6906	Hungary
6908–6909	Czechoslovakia
6910–6917	France

Germany
    Including West Germany

6920–6921	General
6923–6924	States collectively, 1816–1871
6925–6926	Zollverein, 1816–1871
6927–6928	States collectively, 1871–
6929–6932	Empire, 1871–
6933	States separately, 1871–
6934	East Germany
6935–6939	Greece
6940–6947	Italy
6949	San Marino
.5	Malta

Benelux countries. Low countries

6954–6955	Belgium
6957–6958	Netherlands
6960–6967	Soviet Union
6968	Finland
6969	Poland
.8	Scandinavia
6970–6974	Denmark
6975	Iceland
6976–6979	Norway
6980–6984	Sweden
6985–6992	Spain

                              Customs administration
                                By region or country
                                  Other regions or countries
                                    Europe – Continued
6995–6999   Portugal
7000–7007   Switzerland
                                     Balkan States
7010–7011   Bulgaria
7012–7015   Yugoslavia
7018–7019   Romania
7030–7174.7   Asia, Africa, etc. Table IX 1/
                                     Under each country:

      5 nos.   1 no.

                                            Periodicals. Societies. Serials
      (1)   .A3A–Z   Early
      (2).A1–25   .A5A–Z   Recent
         .A3A–Z   .A55A–Z   History. Antiquities
         .A4A–Z   .A6A–Z   Treatises, manuals, etc.
         .A5   Official. By date
         .A7–Z5   Nonofficial
         .A7A–Z   .A7–Z4   Individual ports, A–Z
                           .Z5A–Z   Special
      (3)   Collection
      (4)   Entry, appraisement, etc.
      (5)   Smuggling
      (5.15)   Other

      7390   Underdeveloped areas

1/
    For Table IX, see pp. 331–340. Add number in table to 6754.

EXPENDITURE

For budget, see HJ2005+

7451	Theory
7461	General works. History, statistics, etc.
7465	Increase, retrenchment
	Cf. HJ2019, The budget
7469	Comparative expenditures of different countries
7475	Administration
	e. g. Disbursements, etc.
	Special expenditures
7481	Salaries
	Cf. HD, Social insurance
	JF1661, Civil service
7491	Pensions
	Cf. HD, Social insurance
	JF1671, Civil service
7495	Public works
	Cf. HD, Social insurance
	T, Technology
	Cost of armaments, see UA17
	By region or country
	United States
7531	General works
	History. By period
7533	Through 1860
7535	1860-1900
7537	1900-
7539	General special
7541	Disbursements
7543	Special expenditures
	Cf. HJ7481+, Salaries
7550	States collectively
7551-7654	By region or state. Table of States, III 1/
	Under each state:
	.x General
	.x2 Special
	Other regions or countries
	Under each country:

10 nos.	5 nos.	2 nos.	1 no.	
(0)	(0) or (5)	(1)	.A-Z4	General works
				History. By period
(1)	(1) or (6).A3A-Z			Early through 1600
(2)	.A4A-Z			1600-1789
(3)	.A5-Z			Later, 1789-1870
(4)	(2) or (7)			Recent, 1870-
(6)	(3) or (8)	(2)	.Z7A-Z	General special
				e. g. Increase,
				comparative
				expenditures
(7)				Special expenditures
(8)	(4) or (9)			Administration

1/
For Tables of States III, see. p. 344. Add state number in table to 7550

```
                      Expenditure
                        By region or country
                          Other regions or countries - Continued
7660-7664                     Canada
                              Latin America
      7664.5                    General works
7665-7669                       Mexico
                                Central America
      7670                        General works
      7671                        Belize
7672-7673                         Costa Rica
7674-7675                         Guatemala
7676-7677                         Honduras
7678-7679                         Nicaragua
7680-7681                         Panama
7682-7683                         Salvador
                                West Indies.  Caribbean area
      7684                         General works
7685-7686                          Cuba
7687-7688                          Puerto Rico
7689-7690                          Haiti
7691-7692                          Dominican Republic.  Santo Domingo
7693-7694                          Virgin Islands of the United States
7700-7704                       South America
7705-7709                         Argentina
7710-7714                         Bolivia
7715-7719                         Brazil
7720-7724                         Chile
7725-7729                         Colombia
7730-7733.5                       Ecuador
      7734                         Guianas
         .3                           Guyana.  British Guiana
         .5                           Surinam.  Dutch Guiana
         .7                           French Guiana
7735-7739                         Paraguay
7740-7744                         Peru
7745-7749                         Uruguay
7750-7754                         Venezuela
                              Europe
      7755                      General works
      7757                      European Economic Community countries
                                Great Britain
      7760                        Periodicals.  Societies.  Serials
         .3                        General works
                                   History.  By period
      7761                           Early through 1800
      7762                           1800-1870
      7763                           1870-1900
      7764                           1901-
      7766                         General special
      7767                         Special expenditures
      7768                         Administration
      7769                      Ireland
7770-7774                       Austria
      7775                      Hungary
7777-7778                       Czechoslovakia
7780-7788                       France
```

	Expenditure
	By region or country
	Other regions or countries
	Europe - Continued
7790-7794	Germany
	Including West Germany
7805.5	East Germany
7806-7810	Greece
7811-7815	Italy
7816	San Marino
7817-7818	Benelux countries. Low countries
7820-7824	Belgium
7825-7829	Netherlands
7830-7834	Soviet Union
7834.3	Finland
.7	Poland
	Scandinavia
7835-7839	Denmark
7840	Iceland
7841-7844	Norway
7845-7849	Sweden
7850-7854	Spain
7855-7859	Portugal
7860-7864	Switzerland
	Balkan States
7865-7866	Bulgaria
7867-7868	Yugoslavia
7871-7872	Romania
7881-7977	Other regions or countries. Table III 1/
	Under each country:

3 nos.	1 no.	
(1)	.A-Z4	General works. History, statistics, etc.
(3)	.Z7A-Z	Special

PUBLIC CREDIT. DEBTS. LOANS

For documents, <u>see</u> HJ9+

	History. Statistics
8003	General
8005	Through 1800
8007	Early 19th century through 1870
8009	1870-1900
8011	1901-
	Including general works on European war loans
	General works, treatises
8013	Early works through 1800
	Modern
8015	English
8017	French
8019	German
8021	Italian
8023	Spanish
8025	Other, A-Z

1/
   For Table III, <u>see</u> pp. 331-340. Add number in table to 7682

Public credit. Debts. Loans - Continued
    Special
        For topics having a predominate local interest,
            e. g. Funding, Foreign loans, see classification
            by country and period, HJ8101+
        Public debts in relation to state policy, welfare, etc.

8030	General works
	By region or country
	United States
8032.A2	Federal
.A3	States collectively
.A4-Z	States individually, A-Z
8033	Other regions or countries, A-Z
8034	Public debts and the rights of creditors

        Public debts in relation to particular interests
            e. g. The money market

8036	General works
	By region or country
8038	United States
8039	Other regions or countries, A-Z
8041	Increase
	Colonial debts
	Cf. HJ240, Colonial finance
8043	General works
8045	By region or country, A-Z
	For debts of special colonies, see the colony

Creation of debt. Borrowing. Forms of loans
        Including forced loans, subscriptions, bonds
            (short-term, long-term, etc.) paper money,
            annuities, etc.

8046	General works
8047	Forced loans
8049	Premium bonds
8052	Funding system. Sinking funds. Amortization
8055	Reduction. Conversion. Liquidation
	Taxation of income from bonds, see HHJ4633
8061	Insolvency. Bankruptcy
8064	Repudiation
8071	Partition. Allotment
8079	Floating debts

        Foreign loans
            Class here works relating to the investment of
            capital in the public securities of a foreign
            state. For works relating to loans contracted
            in a foreign country, see the debtor country,
            e. g. HJ8101+, under the period

8083	General works
	By creditor region or country
8085	United States
8086	Other regions or countries, A-Z

        Domestic claims, see HJ8903+
    By region or country
        United States

8101	General works
8102.4	Funding system

```
                  Public credit.  Debts.  Loans
                    By region or country
                      United States - Continued
                        History.  By period
    8105                    Early through 1789.  By date
    8106                    1789-1812
    8107                    1812-1836/1840
    8108                    1836/1840-1860
    8109                    1860-1865/1870
    8110                      Confederate debts
                                Cf. HJ254, Confederate finances
    8112                    1865/1870-1898
    8114                    1898
                                Including war tariff, bond issue, etc.
                          1899-1939
    8115                      General works
    8117                      World War I, 1917-1919.  "Liberty loans," etc.
    8118                      War-savings stamps
    8119                      1939-
                        States collectively
    8223                      General works
    8224                      Special
                                e. g. Constitutional limitations, repudiation
    8225                      Early through 1860
    8227                      1861-
                        Regions
    8230                      New England and Atlantic states
    8235                      South
    8240                      Middle West
    8245                      Pacific States
                        States individually
                          Under each:
                            (0) or (5)  General works
                            (1)    (6)  Special
                                        History.  By period
                            (2)    (7)    Early through 1860
                            (3)    (8)    1860-1900
                            (4)    (9)    1901-
    8250-8254           Alabama
    8255-8259           Alaska
    8260-8264           Arizona
    8265-8269           Arkansas
    8270-8274           California
    8275-8279           Colorado
    8280-8284           Connecticut
    8285-8289           Delaware
    8290-8294           District of Columbia
                          Cf. HJ9215+, Local finance
    8295-8299           Florida
    8300-8304           Georgia
       8304.2-.6        Hawaii
    8305-8309           Idaho
    8310-8314           Illinois
    8320-8324           Indiana
    8325-8329           Iowa
    8330-8334           Kansas
    8335-8339           Kentucky
```

	Public credit. Debts. Loans
	By region or country
	United States
	States individually – Continued
8340–8344	Louisiana
8345–8349	Maine
8350–8354	Maryland
8355–8359	Massachusetts
8360–8364	Michigan
8365–8369	Minnesota
8370–8374	Mississippi
8375–8379	Missouri
8380–8384	Montana
8385–8389	Nebraska
8390–8394	Nevada
8395–8399	New Hampshire
8400–8404	New Jersey
8405–8409	New Mexico
8410–8414	New York
8415–8419	North Carolina
8420–8424	North Dakota
8425–8429	Ohio
8430–8434	Oklahoma
8435–8439	Oregon
8440–8444	Pennsylvania
8445–8449	Rhode Island
8450–8454	South Carolina
8455–8459	South Dakota
8460–8464	Tennessee
8465–8469	Texas
8470–8474	Utah
8475–8479	Vermont
8480–8484	Virginia
8485–8489	Washington
8490–8494	West Virginia
8495–8499	Wisconsin
8500–8504	Wyoming
	Canada
8510	General works
	History. By period
8512	Early through 1867
8513	1867–
8514	Provinces, A–Z
	Latin America
.5	General works
	Mexico
8515	General works
.3	London loan
	History. By period
	Through 1869/1865
8517.A1A–Z	Early through 1822/1823
.A2–Z	1822/1823–1860/1865
8518	1860/1865–1900
8519	1901–

```
                     Public credit.  Debts.  Loans
                        By region or country
                          Latin America - Continued
                            Central America
                              Under each country:
                                (1)  General works
                                       History.  By period
                                  (2)    Early through 1860/1870
                                  (3)     1860/1870-
        8520                        General works
     8523-8525                      Costa Rica
     8526-8528                      Guatemala
     8529-8531                      Honduras
     8532-8534                      Nicaragua
     8535-8537                      Panama
     8538-8540                      Salvador
                            West Indies.  Caribbean area
        8540.5                      General works
                                    Cuba
        8541                          Spanish rule, through 1898
        8542                          1898-
        8543                        Puerto Rico
        8546                        Haiti
        8548                        Dominican Republic.  Santo Domingo
        8549                        Virgin Islands of the United States
        8552                        Jamaica
        8555                        Other, A-Z
                            South America
        8560                      General works
                                  History.  By period
        8562                        Early through 1900
        8563                        1901-
                                By region or country
                                  Under each country:
```

5 nos.	1 no.	
(1)	.A-Z5	General works
		History. By period
(3).A2		Early through 1822/1823
.A3-Z		1822/1823-1860/1865
(4)		1865/1870-1900
(5)		1901-
(5.9)	.Z7A-Z	By state, etc.

```
     8565-8569                      Argentina
     8570-8574                      Bolivia
     8575-8579                      Brazil
     8580-8584                      Chile
     8585-8589                      Colombia
     8590-8594                      Ecuador
        8594.2                      Guiana
            .3                        Guyana.  British Guiana
            .5                        Surinam.  Dutch Guiana
            .7                        French Guiana
     8595-8599                      Paraguay
     8600-8604                      Peru
     8605-8609                      Uruguay
     8610-8614                      Venezuela
```

Public credit. Debts. Loans
By region or country - Continued
Europe
Under each country (unless otherwise provided for):

5 nos.	2 nos.	1 no.	
(1)	(1)	.A2	General works
(2)			Special
			History. By period
(3)			Through 1800
(4)			1800–1900
(5)			1901–
(5.9)	(2)	.A3–Z	By region, state, etc., A–Z

8615	General works
8616	European Economic Community countries
	Great Britain
8620	General works
	History. By period
8623	Early through 1776
8624	1776–1816
8625	1816–1860
8626	1860–1900
8627	1901–
8630	Ireland
	Austria
8631	General works
8634	Early through 1867
8635	1867–1918
8636	Republic, 1918–
.5	By state, province, A–Z
8637	Hungary
8638	Czechoslovakia
	France
8641	General works
8643	Ancien regime
8644	1789–1870/71
8645	War indemnity, 1871
8646	1870/71–
8649	Local (Departments, etc.), A–Z
	Germany
8650	General works
8652	States collectively through 1871
8654	Empire, 1871–
8655	States, A–Z
8671.5	East Germany
	Greece
8672	General and early
8673	Recent, 1898–
	Italy
8675	General works
8677	States collectively before 1861
8678	Kingdom, 1861–
8679	States, A–Z
8695	San Marino

Public credit. Debts. Loans
    By region or country
       Europe – Continued
          Benelux countries. Low countries

8696	General works
8699	Luxemburg
8700-8704.9	Belgium
8705-8709.9	Netherlands
	Soviet Union
8710	Collected works (nonserial)
8711	General works
8713	Early
8714	Recent
8715	States, provinces, etc., A-Z
8717	Poland
8718	Finland
	Scandinavia
8720-8724.9	Denmark
8725	Iceland
8728	Norway
8730-8734.9	Sweden
8735-8739.9	Spain
	Portugal
8740	General works
8742	Through 1815
8743	1815-1910
8744	1910-
8745-8749.9	Switzerland
	Balkan States

             Under each:

	(1)	General works
	.1-9	Special
	(2)	Early through 1856/78
		After 1856/78
	.A4	Serial
	.A5-Z	Nonserial

8750-8751	Bulgaria
8752-8753	Yugoslavia
8757-8758	Romania
8770-8898	Other regions or countries. Table IV 1/

           Under each country:

4 nos.	1 no.	
(1)	.A1-Z5	General works
(4)	.Z7A-Z	States, provinces, etc., A-Z

8899	Underdeveloped areas

1/
   For Table IV, see pp. 331-340. Add number in table to 8505

CLAIMS

Cf. HJ8052, Funding
HJ8064, Repudiation
JX238, Foreign claims

8903	General works
8905	Public claims
8907	Private claims
	Administration
8911	General works
8915	Claim departments
8916	Commissions
8919	Lists

By region or country
    Under each country (using successive Cutter numbers):
        .x   Periodicals. Societies. Serials
        .x2   General works. Principles
        .x3   Administration
        .x4   Special claims
    For clamis which are of primary interest in connection
    with a special subject, see the subject
    For foreign claims, e. g. claims by citizens or government
    of one country against government or citizens of
    another country, see JX238+; JX351+

	United States
8931	Periodicals. Societies. Serials
8932	Lists
8933	General works
8934	Administration
8936	Special claims, A-Z
8941	By region or state, A-Z
8943	Confederate States
8945	Canada
8949	Latin America. By region or country, A-Z
	Including West Indies
8951	Europe. By region or country, A-Z
8953	Asia. By region or country, A-Z
8955	Africa. By region or country, A-Z
8957	Australia
8959	New Zealand
8963	Pacific islands, A-Z

LOCAL FINANCE

Including county, borough, commune, municipality, etc.

	Documents
9000-9010	General collections
	By region or country
	United States
9011.A1-4	General works
.A5-Z	By region or state, A-Z
9012	Counties, townships
	Arranged by state, A-W

	Local finance
	Documents
	By region or country
	United States - Continued
9013	Cities, towns, A-Z

       Under each:
        a Early documents
        b Main financial report
        c Auditor
        d Comptroller
        e Estimates, appropriations, etc.
        g Taxes and assessments
        h Commissioners of sinking fund
        k Board of supervisors
        l Local (Boroughs, etc.), A-Z

	Canada
9014.A1-6	General works
.A7-Z	Provinces

     Under each province:
      .x General works
      .x2 Local, A-Z

9015-9099.6	Other regions or countries

     Subarranged like HJ15-99
     Under each country:
      .A1-5   National documents
      .A55A-Z By region or state, A-Z
      .A6-Z By city
         Under each city:
          .A1+ General works
          .B1+ Budgets
          .C1+ Receipts and expenditures
          .D1+ Public debt
          .R1+ Administrative reports
          .S1+ Other. Miscellaneous

9103	Periodicals. Societies. Serials
9104	Collected works (nonserial)
	General works
9105	English
9106	French
9107	German
9108	Italian
9109	Other languages, A-Z
9110	National supervision and control. Relations of general and local government
9111	Budget
	Revenue. Taxation
	General works
9115	English
9117	Other, A-Z
	Special taxes
9119	General works
9120	Octroi

      Class here general works only. For special
        local, see HJ9470.P5, etc.

9123	Other, A-Z
	.V5 Visitors' taxes

Local finance – Continued
  Expenditure

9125	General works
9126	Increase, retrenchment, etc.
9127	Administration. Disbursements, etc.

  Credit. Debts. Loans

9129	General works
9131	Increase, limits, etc.
9132	Funding. Reduction. Conversion
9133	Insolvency. Repudiation
9135	Administration

Accounting, <u>see</u> HJ9771+

By region or country
  United States

9141	General works
	History. By period
9143	Through 1860
9144	1861–1900
9145	1901–
9147	Budget
	Taxation
9150	General works
	History. By period
9151.A3	Through 1860
.A5–Z	1861–1900
9152	1901–
	Special taxes
9153	Real estate
9154	Personal property
9155	Income
9156	Other
9157	Expenditure
	Credit. Debt. Loans
9159	General works
	History. By period
9160.A3	Through 1860
.A5–Z	1861–1900
9161	1901–
	Administration
9165	General works
9167	General special
	Regions
	Under each:

(0) or (5)		General (including works on the budget and expenditure)
		History. By period
(1)	(6).A3A–Z	Through 1860
	.A5–Z	1861–
(2)	(7)	Taxation
(3)	(8)	Credit. Debt. Loans
(4)	(9)	Administration

9170–9174	New England and Atlantic States
9175–9179	Southern States
9180–9184	Middle Western States
9185–9189	Pacific States

Local finance
  By region or country
    United States - Continued
      States
        Under each (except District of Columbia):

(1)	General works	
(2)	Taxation	
.A3A-Z	Early through 1860	
.A5-Z	1861-	
.4	Credit. Debt. Loans	
.7	Administration	
(3)	Local, A-Z	

                Each arranged according to the
                    following example:

.M5-69	Montgomery	
.M5	General works	
.M52	Taxation	
.M57	Credit. Debt. Loans	
.M63	Administration	
.M67-69	Tax rolls	

              Serial documents, <u>see</u> HJ9013+

9191-9193	Alabama
9194-9196	Alaska
9197-9199	Arizona
9200-9202	Arkansas
9203-9205	California
9206-9208	Colorado
9209-9211	Connecticut
9212-9214	Delaware
9215-9217	District of Columbia

        For serial documents and appropriations,
          <u>see</u> HJ9013.W2

HJ9215	General	
.A3A-Z	Early	
.A5A-Z	1860-1900	
.A7-Z	1901-	
9216	Taxation	
.A3A-Z	Early	
.A5A-Z	1860-1900	
.A7-Z	1901-	
9217	Credit. Debt. Loans	
.A3A-Z	Early	
.A5A-Z	1860-1900	
.A7-Z	1901-	
.1	Administration	

9218-9220	Florida
9221-9223	Georgia
9223.5-.7	Hawaii
9224-9226	Idaho
9227-9229	Illinois
9230-9232	Indiana
9236-9238	Iowa
9239-9241	Kansas
9242-9244	Kentucky
9245-9247	Louisiana
9248-9250	Maine

                Local finance
                  By region or country
                    United States
                      States - Continued

9251-9253	Maryland
9254-9256	Massachusetts
9257-9259	Michigan
9260-9262	Minnesota
9263-9265	Mississippi
9266-9268	Missouri
9269-9271	Montana
9272-9274	Nebraska
9275-9277	Nevada
9278-9280	New Hampshire
9281-9283	New Jersey
9284-9286	New Mexico
9287-9289	New York
9290-9292	North Carolina
9293-9295	North Dakota
9296-9298	Ohio
9299-9301	Oklahoma
9302-9304	Oregon
9305-9307	Pennsylvania
9308-9310	Rhode Island
9311-9313	South Carolina
9314-9316	South Dakota
9317-9319	Tennessee
9320-9322	Texas
9323-9325	Utah
9326-9328	Vermont
9329-9331	Virginia
9332-9334	Washington
9335-9337	West Virginia
9338-9340	Wisconsin
9341-9343	Wyoming

              Other regions or countries
              Under each country (unless otherwise indicated):

4 nos.	3 nos.	2 nos.	1 no.	
(1)	(1)	(1)	.A1-2	General works
.A3A-Z	.A3A-Z	.A3A-Z		Early
(2)	(2)	.3	.A3A-Z	Taxation
.4	.4	.5	.A4A-Z	Credit. Debt. Loans
.7	.7	.7	.A5A-Z	Administration
(3)	(3).A2	(2).A2	.A6A-Z	Provinces, states, regions, A-Z 1/
(4)	.A5-Z	.A5-Z	.A7-Z	Cities, towns, etc. 1/

9350-9353	Canada
	Latin America
9353.5	General works
9354-9357	Mexico
	Central America
9357.5	General works
.55	Belize
9358-9359	Costa Rica

1/
  Subarranged like HJ9193

	Local finance
	By region or country
	Other regions or countries
	Latin America
	Central America - Continued
9360-9361	Guatemala
9362-9363	Honduras
9364-9365	Nicaragua
9366-9367	Panama
9368-9369	Salvador
	West Indies. Caribbean area
9369.5	General works
9370-9371	Cuba
9372-9373	Puerto Rico
9374	Haiti
9375	Dominican Republic. Santo Domingo
9376	Virgin Islands of the United States
9379	Other, A-Z
	South America
9380-9382	Argentina
9383-9385	Bolivia
9386-9388	Brazil
9389-9391	Chile
9392-9394	Colombia
9395-9397	Ecuador
9397.2	Guianas
.3	Guyana. British Guiana
.5	Surinam. Dutch Guiana
.7	French Guiana
9398-9400	Paraguay
9401-9403	Peru
9404-9406	Uruguay
9407-9409	Venezuela
	Europe
9415	General works
9420	European Economic Community countries
	Great Britain
9421	General works
	History. By period
9422.A3	Through 1700
.A4	18th century
.A5	1800-1860
.A6-Z	1861-1900
9423	1901-
9424	National supervision and control. "Grants in aid," etc.
	Other special
	Under each:
	(1) General works
	History. By period
	.A3A-Z Early works through 1800
	.A5A-Z 1801-1860
	(2) 1861-1900
	(3) 1901-
	(4) Special, A-Z
9425-9428	Taxation. Revenue
9429-9432	Credit. Debt. Loans
9433-9436	Administration
9438	Cities, towns, A-Z
	Subarranged like HJ9193

	Local finance
	By region or country
	Other regions or countries
	Europe
	Great Britain
	Other special – Continued
9439	Colonies
	Class here general works only; for special topics, <u>see</u> the colony
9440–9441	Northern Ireland
9442–9443	Scotland
9444–9445	Wales
9445.5	Ireland
9446–9448	Austria
9449–9450	Hungary
9451–9452	Czechoslovakia
	France
9453	General works
	History. By period
9454.A3A–Z	Through 1700
.A4A–Z	1701–1789
.A5A–Z	1789–1870
.A6–Z	1870–
9456	National supervision and control. "Subvention de l'etat," etc.
	Other special
	Subarranged like (1) – (4) above HJ9425–9428
9457–9460	Taxation
9461–9464	Credit. Debt. Loans
9465–9468	Administration
	Departments
9469.A1–5	General works
.A6–Y	By department, A–Y
9470	Cities, towns, A–Z
	Germany
	Including West Germany
9473	General works
.A3	Early
9474	Credit. Debt. Loans
9475	Administration
9493.5	States
	.A2A–Z Collective
	.A5–Z6 Individual, A–Z
	Under each:
	.A5–Z5 General works
	.Z6A–Z Special
9494	Cities, towns, A–Z
	Subarranged like HJ9193
.5	East Germany
9495–9496	Greece
9497–9500	Italy
	For San Marino, <u>see</u> HJ9499
	Benelux countries. Low countries
9501	General works
9503–9506	Belgium
9507–9510	Netherlands
9510.5	Luxemburg
9511–9514	Soviet Union
9514.3	Finland

Local finance
 By region or country
  Other regions or countries
   Europe – Continued

9514.7	Poland
	Scandinavia
9515	General works
9516–9518	Denmark
9519	Iceland
9520–9522	Norway
9523–9524	Sweden
9525–9528	Spain
9529–9531	Portugal
9532–9535	Switzerland
	Balkan States
9536–9537	Bulgaria
9538	Yugoslavia
9540–9541	Romania

9550–9694.7   Other regions or countries. Table IX 1/
        Under each country:

5 nos.	1 no.	
(1)	.A–Z5	General works
	.Z6A–Z	Special
(2)		Taxation
(2.5)		Credit. Debt. Loans
(3)		Administration
(4)	.Z7A–Z	Provinces, states, regions, A–Z
(5)	.Z9A–Z	Cities, towns, etc., A–Z

PUBLIC ACCOUNTING

Cf. HF5601+, Commercial accounting

	Periodicals. Societies. Serials
9701	English
9703	Other
9705	Congresses
	General works
9731	Early
	Modern
9733	English
9735	French
9737	German
9739	Italian
9741	Other languages, A–Z
9745	Special methods
	e. g. Machine methods
9750	Cost accounting

1/
 For Table IX, see pp. 331–340. Add number in table to 9274

```
                  Public accounting - Continued
                  Government corporations
9768                  General works
9769                  By region or country, A-Z
                  Municipal accounting
                     Including local accounting
9771              Periodicals.  Societies.  Serials
9773              General works
                  United States
9777.A1               Periodicals.  Societies.  Serials
    .A3               General works
    .A5-Z             By region or state, A-Z
                         Under each state:
                            .x   General works
                            .x2  Local, A-Z
9779              Other regions or countries, A-Z

              By region or country
                 United States
                    General works
9801.A3              Official.  By date
    .A5-Z            Nonofficial
9802              General Accounting Office
                  Treasury Department
9803                 General works
9805.A               Auditor
    .C               Comptroller
    .P               Paymaster
    .T               Treasurer
9807                 Internal revenue
                         Including collection, rating, etc.
9809                 Customs
                  Post Office Department, see HE6311+
9813              Special accounts, A-Z
9816              States collectively
9817-9920         States separately.  Table of States III 1/
                     Under each:
                     (1)          General works
                                     Official series, see HJ11+
                          .A3        Official monographs.  By date
                     (2)          Special
                                     Departments
                                        Treasury
                          .A2            General works
                          .A23           Auditor
                          .A25           Comptroller
                          .A27           Paymaster
                          .A29           Treasurer
                          .A3            Internal revenue.  Taxation
                          .A4            Other
                          .A5-Z       Special accounts
```

1/
  For Table of States III, see p. 344. Add state number in table to 9816

```
                    Public accounting
                      By region or country - Continued
                        Canada
                          General works
9921.A2                       Official
     .A4-Z2                    Nonofficial
                            Departments
     .Z3                       Treasury
     .Z31                        Auditor
     .Z33                        Comptroller
     .Z35                        Paymaster
     .Z37                        Treasurer
     .Z4                         Internal revenue
     .Z5                         Customs
     .Z6                       Other
     .Z8                     Special accounts
     .Z9                     Provinces, A-Z
                        Other American regions or countries, A-Z
                          Under each country:
                                      General works
                 .xA3-49               Official
                 .xA5-Z                Nonofficial
                 .x2                 Treasury
                 .x3                 Auditor
                 .x5                 Paymaster
                 .x6                 Treasurer
                 .x7                 Internal revenue
                 .x8                 Customs
                 .x85                Special accounts
                 .x9                 Local, A-Z
                        Europe
9924                      General works
9925                      By region or country, A-Z
                        Asia
9926                      General works
9927                      By region or country, A-Z
                        Africa
9928                      General works
9929                      By region or country, A-Z
9931                    Australia
9932                    New Zealand
9933                    Pacific islands, A-Z
                      Tables, calculators, etc.
                      Salaries
                        United States
9971.A3A-Z                General works
     .A5-Z                 By department
                            e. g.              Treasury
                                   .T7         Official.  By date
                                   .T7A-Z      Nonofficial.  By author
9975                    Other regions or countries, A-Z
                          Under each country:
                            .x   General works
                            .x2  Government departments
                      Taxes
9991                    General works
9993                    United States
                          Subarranged like HJ9971
9995                    Other regions or countries, A-Z
                          Subarranged like HJ9975
```

TABLES OF GEOGRAPHICAL DIVISIONS

Division	I	II	III	IV	V	VI	VII	VIII	IX	X
America. Western Hemisphere	1	1-2	1-2	1-2	1	1				
North America	2	3-4	3-4	3-4	2	2				
United States	3	5-6	5-6	5-8	3-6					121-130
Northeastern States. New England	4	7-8	8-10	9-12						
Middle Atlantic States.	5	9-10	11-13	13-16						
Middle States	6	11-12	14-16	17-20						
Southern States	7	13-14	17-19	21-24						
Central States. Plains States	8	15-16	21-22	25-28						
Great Lakes region	9	17-18	23-25	29-32						
Mississippi Valley	10	19-20	26-28	33-36						
Southwestern States	11	21-22	29-31	37-40						
Northwestern States.	12	23-24	32-34	41-44						
Rocky Mountain region	13	25	35	45						
Pacific States	14	27	38	49						
States, A-W	15	29-30	41-43	53-56						
Including regions and counties	15.25	30.25	43.25	56.25						
Cities, A-Z	15.5	30.5	43.5	56.5						
Canada	16	31-32	44-46	57-60	7-10	10	11-20	1-10	1-10	151-160
Saint Pierre and Miquelon Islands	17	33-34	47	61-64	10.25	10.25	20.25	10.25	10.25	160.25
Greenland, see 99.5 ...	17.5	35-36	48	65-68						
Latin America	18	37-38	49-51	69-72	10.5	11.5	20.5	10.5	10.5	160.5
Mexico	19	39	52-54	73-74	11	12	21-30	11-20	11-15	161-170
Central America	20	40	55-56	75-76	13	13	31-35	21-25	16-20	171-175
Belize. British Honduras	21	41	57-58	77-78	13.5	13.25	36-40	26-30	20.5	181-185
Costa Rica	22	42-43	59-60	79	14	13.5	41-50	31-40	21-25	191-195
Guatemala	22.5	43.5	61	80	15	13.75	51-60	41-50	26-30	201-205
Honduras	23	44	62-64	81-84	16	14	61-70	51-60	31-35	206-210
Nicaragua					17	14.25	71-80	61-70	36-40	216-220
Panama					18	14.5	81-85	71-75	41-45	221-225
Panama Canal Zone					18.5	14.75	86-90	76-80	45.5	226-230
Salvador					19	15	91-100	81-90	46-50	231-235

TABLES OF GEOGRAPHICAL DIVISIONS

Latin America – Continued
West Indies. Caribbean

	I	II	III	IV	V	VI	VII	VIII	IX	X
area	24	45–46	65–67	85–88	20	16	101–105	91–95	51	241–245
Bahamas	24.5	47–48	68–70	89–92	20.5	16.2	106–110	96–100	53	246–250
Cuba	25	49–50	71–73	93–96	21	16.3	111–120	101–110	56–60	251–260
Haiti	26	51	74–75	97–98	22	16.4	121–125	111–115	61	261–265
Dominican Republic. Santo Domingo	26.5	52	76	99–100	22.5	16.5	126–130	116–120	64	266–270
Jamaica	27	53–54	77–79	101–104	23	16.6	131–140	121–130	66–70	271–280
Puerto Rico	28	55–56	80–82	105–108	24	16.7	141–150	131–140	71–75	281–285
Virgin Islands of the United States	28.3	56.3	83	109	24.3	16.8	150.3	141	75.3	286–290
British West Indies	28.5	56.5	83.5	110	24.5	16.9	151	142	75.4	291
Leeward Islands	28.7	56.7	83.7	110.7	24.7	17	153	144	75.5	293
Windward Islands	28.9	56.9	83.9	110.9	24.9	17.3	154	145	75.6	294
Trinidad and Tobago	29	57	84	111	25	17.4	155	146	75.7	295
Netherlands Antilles. Dutch West Indies	29.3	57.3	84.3	111.3	25.3	17.5	156	147	75.8	296
French West Indies	29.5	57.5	84.5	111.5	25.5	17.6	157	148	75.85	297
Guadeloupe	29.7	57.7	84.7	111.7	25.7	17.7	158	149	75.9	298
Martinique	29.9	57.9	85	112	25.9	17.9	159	150	75.95	299
South America	30	58	86–88	113–116	26	18–19	161–170	151–160	76–80	301–310
Argentina	31	59–60	89–91	117–120	27–30	20–24	171–180	161–170	81–85	311–320
Bolivia	32	61–62	92–94	121–124	31	25–26	181–190	171–180	86–90	321–330
Brazil	33	63–64	95–97	125–128	32–35	28–32	191–200	181–190	91–95	331–340
Chile	34	65–66	98–100	129–132	36	33–37	201–210	191–200	96–100	341–350
Colombia	35	67–68	101–103	133–136	37	38–39	211–220	201–210	101–105	351–360
Ecuador	36	69–70	104–106	137–140	38	40–41	221–230	211–220	106–110	361–370
Guianas	37	71–72	107–109	141–144	39	42–43	231–240	221–230	111–115	371–380
Guyana, British Guiana	37.3	72.3	109.3	144.3	39.3	43.3	240.3	230.3	115.3	380.3
Surinam. Dutch Guiana	37.5	72.5	109.5	144.5	39.5	43.5	240.5	230.5	115.5	380.5
French Guiana	37.7	72.7	109.7	144.7	39.7	43.7	240.7	230.7	115.7	380.7

TABLES OF GEOGRAPHICAL DIVISIONS

	I	II	III	IV	V	VI	VII	VIII	IX	X
Latin America										
South America – Continued										
Paraguay	38	73–74	110–112	145–148	40	44–45	241–250	231–240	116–120	381–390
Peru	39	75–76	113–115	149–152	41	46–47	251–260	241–250	121–125	391–400
Uruguay	40	77–78	116–118	153–156	42	48–49	261–270	251–260	126–130	401–410
Venezuela	41	79–80	119–121	157–160	43	50–51	271–280	261–270	131–135	411–420
Europe	42	81–82	122–124	161–164	44	52–53	281–290	271–280	136–140	421–430
European Economic Community countries	42.8	82.5	124.5	164.5	44.5	53.5	289.5	280.5	140.5	430.5
Great Britain	43	83–84	125–127	165–168	45	54–58	291–300	281–300[1]	141–150[1]	431–440
England and Wales	44	85–86	128–130	169–172	46	60–61	301–310			441–450
Scotland	45	87–88	131–132	173–176	47	62–63	311–320			451–460
Northern Ireland	45.5	88.5	132.5	176.5	47.5	63.5	320.5			460.5
Ireland. Irish Republic	46	89–90	133–135	177–180	48	64–65	321–330	301–320	151–160	461–470
Austria	47	91–92	136–138	181–184	49–52	66–67	331–340			471–480
Czechoslovakia	47.3	92.3	138.3	184.3	52.3	69.3	340.3	320.3	160.3	480.3
Hungary	47.5	92.5	138.5	184.5	52.5	69.5	340.5	320.5	160.5	480.5
Liechtenstein	47.9	92.9	138.9	184.9	52.9	69.9	340.9	320.9	160.9	480.9
France	48	93–94	139–141	185–188	53–56	70–74	341–350	321–340	161–170	481–490
Monaco	48.5	94.5	141.5	188.5	56.5	74.5	350.5	340.5	170.5	490.5
Germany	49	95–96	142–144	189–192	57–60	75–79	351–360	341–360	171–180	491–500
Including West Germany	49.5	96.5	144.5	192.5	60.5	79.5	360.5	360.5	180.5	500.5
East Germany	51	99–100	148–150	197–200	62–65	85–89	371–380	371–390	186–195	511–520
Italy	51.3	100.3	150.3	200.3	65.3	89.3	380.3	390.3	195.3	520.3
San Marino	51.5	100.5	150.5	200.5	65.4	89.5	380.5	390.5	195.5	520.5
Malta	52	101–102	151–153	201–204	65.5	90–94	381–390	391–400	196–200	521–530
Benelux countries. Low countries										
Belgium	53	103–104	154–156	205–208	66–69	95–99	391–400	401–410	201–205	531–540
Netherlands	54	105–106	157–159	209–212	70–73	100–104	401–410	411–420	206–210	541–550
Luxemburg	54.5	106.5	159.5	212.5	73.5	104.5	410.5	420.5	210.5	550.5

---

1 Class the constituent countries of Great Britain as particular localities of Great Britain in the Local, A–Z number provided

TABLES OF GEOGRAPHICAL DIVISIONS

I	II	III	IV	V		VI	VII	VIII	IX	X
					Europe – Continued					
55	107–108	160–162	213–216	74–77	Russia	105–109	411–420	421–430	211–215	551–560
55.3	108.3	162.3	217	77.3	Finland	110	421–425	431–435	215.5	561–565
55.7	108.7	162.7	218	77.7	Poland	111	426–429.5	436–439.5	215.7	566–569.5
56	109–110	163–165	219–220	78	Scandinavia	113–114	430	440	216–220	570
57	111–112	166–168	221–224	79	Denmark	115–119	431–440	441–450	221–225	571–580
58	113–114	169–171	225–228	79.5	Iceland	120–124	441–450	451–460	226–230	581–590
59	115–116	172–174	229–232	80	Norway	125–129	451–460	461–470	231–235	591–600
60	117–118	175–177	233–236	81–84	Sweden	130–134	461–470	471–480	236–240	601–610
61	119–120	178–180	237–240	85–88	Spain	135–139	471–480	481–490	241–245	611–620
61.3	120.3	180.3	240.3	88.3	Andorra	139.3	480.3	490.3	245.3	620.3
61.5	120.5	180.5	240.5	88.5	Gibraltar	139.5	480.5	490.5	245.5	620.5
62	121–122	181–183	241–244	89	Portugal	140–144	481–490	491–500	246–250	621–630
63	123–124	184–186	245–248	90	Switzerland	145–149	491–500	501–510	251–255	631–640
64	125–126	187–189	249–252	91	Balkan States	150–154	501–510	511–520	256–260	641–650
64.5	126.5	189.5	252.5	91.4	Albania	154.4	510.5	520.5	260.5	650.5
65	127–128	190–191	253–254	91.5	Bulgaria	154.5	511–520	521–530	261–265	651–660
65.5	128.5	192–193	255–256	91.6	Yugoslavia	154.6	521–525	531–535	265.5	661–665
67	131–132	196–198	261–264	91.8	Romania	154.8	531–540	541–550	271–275	671–680
67.5	132.5	198.5	264.5	91.83	Greece	154.83	540.5	550.5	275.5	680.5
68	133	199	265	91.85	Asia	154.85	541–545	551–555	276	681
68.2	133.3	200	265.5	91.9	Middle East, Near East	154.9	546	556	276.5	682
68.25	133.4	200.5	265.7	91.93	Turkey	154.93	546.5	556.5	276.7	682.5
68.3	133.5	200.6	266	91.95	Cyprus	154.95	547	557	277	683
68.35	133.7	200.9	266.5	92	Syria	155	548	558	277.5	684
68.4	133.9	201	267	92.15	Lebanon	155.15	549	559	278	685
68.45	134	201.3	267.5	92.2	Israel, Palestine	155.2	550	560	278.5	686
68.5	134.3	201.6	268	92.25	Jordan	155.25	551	561	279	687
68.55	134.5	201.9	268.5	92.3	Arabian Peninsula, Arabia	155.3	552	562	279.5	688
68.6	134.7	202	269	92.35	Saudi Arabia	155.35	553	563	280	689
68.65	134.9	202.3	269.5	92.4	Yemen (Yemen Arab Republic)	155.4	554	564	280.5	690

TABLES OF GEOGRAPHICAL DIVISIONS

Geographical Division	I	II	III	IV	V	VI	VII	VIII	IX	X
Asia										
Middle East. Near East										
Arabian Peninsula.										
Arabia – Continued										
Yemen (People's Democratic Republic). Southern Yemen, Aden (Colony and Protectorate)	68.7	135	202.6	270	92.43	155.43	554.5	564.5	280.7	691
Oman. Muscat and Oman	68.75	135.3	202.9	270.5	92.44	155.44	555	565	281	692
United Arab Emirates. Trucial States	68.8	135.5	203	271	92.45	155.45	556	566	281.5	693
Qatar	68.85	135.7	203.3	271.5	92.5	155.5	557	567	282	694
Bahrein	68.9	135.9	203.6	271.6	92.52	155.52	558	568	283	695
Kuwait	68.95	136	203.9	271.7	92.53	155.53	559	569	284	696
Iraq	69	136.3	204	272	92.55	155.55	560	570	285	697
Iran	69.2	136.4	204.2	272.2	92.56	155.7	560.2	570.2	285.2	698
South Asia	69.3	136.5	204.3	272.3	92.57	156	560.3	570.3	285.3	700
Afghanistan	69.6	136.6	204.6	272.6	92.6	156.6	560.6	570.6	285.6	700.6
Burma	69.7	136.7	204.7	272.7	92.7	156.7	560.7	570.7	285.7	700.7
Sri Lanka. Ceylon	69.8	136.8	204.8	272.8	92.8	156.8	560.8	570.8	285.8	700.8
Nepal	69.9	136.9	204.9	272.9	92.9	156.9	560.9	570.9	285.9	700.9
India	71	139–140	208–210	277–280	97–100	160–164	571–580	581–590	291–295	711–720
Bhutan	71.3	140.3	210.3	280.3	100.3	164.3	580.3	590.3	295.3	720.3
Pakistan	71.5	140.5	210.5	280.5	100.5	164.5	580.5	590.5	295.5	720.5
Bangladesh	71.6	140.6	210.6	280.6	100.6	164.55	580.6	590.6	295.6	720.6
Southeast Asia. Indochina. Including French Indochina	72	141–142	211–213	281–284	101	164.6	580.8	590.8	295.8	721–730
Burma, see 69.7 ...										
Cambodia	73.3	144.3	216.3	288.3	102.3	164.63	590.3	600.3	300.3	740.3
Laos	73.4	144.4	216.4	288.4	102.4	164.64	590.4	600.4	300.4	740.4

Division	I	II	III	IV	V	VI	VII	VIII	IX	X
Asia										
Southeast Asia. - Continued										
Indochina - Continued										
Vietnam	73.5	144.5	216.5	288.5	102.5	164.65	590.5	600.5	300.5	740.5
Thailand	73.55	144.55	216.55	288.55	102.55	164.655	590.55	600.55	300.55	740.55
Malaysia. Malaya	73.6	144.6	216.6	288.6	102.6	164.66	590.6	600.6	300.6	740.6
Singapore	74	145	217	289	103	164.67	590.67	600.67	300.67	741
Brunei	74.3	146.3	218.3	290	103.3	164.68	590.68	600.68	300.68	742
Indonesia	75	147-148	220-222	293-296	104	164.7	591-600	601-610	301-305	751-760
Philippine Islands	76	149-150	223-225	297-300	105	164.8	601-610	611-620	306-310	761-770
East Asia. Far East										
Japan	76.5	150.5	225.5	300.5	106	164.9	610.5	620.5	310.5	770.5
Korea	77	151-152	226-227	301-304	107	165-166	611-620	621-630	311-315	771-780
Including South Korea	77.5	152.5	228	304.5	108	167	620.5	630.5	315.5	780.5
North Korea (Democratic People's Republic)	77.6	152.6	228.6	304.6	108.6	167.6	620.6	630.6	315.6	780.6
Outer Mongolia. Mongolian People's Republic	77.8	152.8	229	305	109	168	620.8	630.8	315.8	780.8
China	78	154	230	306	110	169	621-630	631-640	316-320	781-790
Macao	79	155	231	307	111	170	631-635	641-645	321-325	791-795
Taiwan. Formosa	80	156	232	308	112	171	636-640	646-650	326-330	796-800
Hongkong	81	157	233	309	113	172	641-645	651-655	331	801-805
Arab countries (Collective)	81.5	160	239	319	116	178	656	666	334	816
Islamic countries (Collective)	81.7	160.5	240	320	116.5	179	658	668	335	818
Africa	82	161	241-243	321-324	117	180-181	661-670	671-680	336-340	821-830
North Africa	82.2	161.2	244	325	118	182	671	681	340.5	831
Morocco	82.3	161.3	244.3	325.3	118.3	182.2	672	682	341	832
Algeria	82.4	161.4	244.5	325.5	118.5	182.3	673	683	341.5	833
Tunisia	82.5	161.5	244.7	325.7	118.7	182.4	674	684	342	834
Libya	82.6	161.6	245	326	118.9	182.5	675	685	342.5	835
Egypt. United Arab Republic	82.7	161.7	245.3	326.3	119	182.6	676	686	343	836
Sudan	82.8	161.8	245.5	326.5	119.3	182.7	677	687	343.5	837

TABLES OF GEOGRAPHICAL DIVISIONS

I	II	III	IV	V		VI	VII	VIII	IX	X
					Africa – Continued					
					Northeast Africa					
82.9	161.9	245.7	326.7	119.5	Ethiopia	182.8	678	688	344	838
83	162	246	327	119.7	Somalia	182.9	679	689	344.5	839
83.2	162.2	246.3	327.3	119.9	Including British and Italian Somaliland	183	680	690	345	840
83.3	162.3	246.5	327.5	120	French Territory of the Afars and Issas	183.2	681	691	345.5	841
					Southeast Africa					
83.4	162.4	246.7	327.7	120.3	Kenya	183.3	682	692	346	842
83.5	162.5	247	328	120.5	Uganda	183.4	683	693	346.5	843
83.6	162.6	247.3	328.3	120.7	Rwanda	183.5	684	694	347	844
83.7	162.7	247.5	328.5	120.9	Burundi	183.6	685	695	347.5	845
83.8	162.8	247.7	328.7	121	Tanzania. Tanganyika. Zanzibar	183.7	686	696	348	846
83.9	162.9	248	329	121.3	Mozambique	183.8	687	697	348.5	847
84	163	248.3	329.3	121.5	Madagascar. Malagasy Republic	183.9	688	698	349	848
84.2	163.2	248.5	329.5	121.7	Southern Africa	184	689	699	349.5	849
84.3	163.3	248.7	329.7	121.9	South Africa	184.2	690	700	350	850
84.4	163.4	249	330	122	Rhodesia	184.3	691	701	350.5	851
84.5	163.5	249.3	330.3	122.3	Including Southern Rhodesia	184.4	692	702	351	852
84.6	163.6	249.5	330.5	122.5	Zambia. Northern Rhodesia	184.5	693	703	351.5	853
84.7	163.7	249.7	330.7	122.7	Lesotho. Basutoland	184.6	694	704	352	854
84.8	163.8	250	331	122.9	Swaziland	184.7	695	705	352.5	855
84.9	163.9	250.3	331.3	123	Botswana. Bechuanaland	184.8	696	706	353	856
85	164	250.5	331.5	123.3	Malawi. Nyasaland	184.9	697	707	353.5	857
85.2	164.2	250.7	331.7	123.5	Southwest Africa (Namibia)	185	698	708	354	858

TABLES OF GEOGRAPHICAL DIVISIONS

I	II	III	IV	V	Division	VI	VII	VIII	IX	X
					Africa – Continued					
85.3	164.3	251	332	123.7	Central Africa. Equatorial Africa	185.2	699	709	354.5	859
85.4	164.4	251.3	332.3	123.9	Angola	185.3	700	710	355	860
85.5	164.5	251.5	332.5	124	Zaire. Congo (Democratic Republic)	185.4	701	711	355.5	861
85.6	164.6	251.7	332.7	124.3	Equatorial Guinea	185.5	702	712	356	862
85.7	164.7	252	333	124.5	São Tomé e Príncipe	185.6	703	713	356.5	863
85.8	164.8	252.3	333.3	124.7	French Equatorial Africa. French Congo	185.7	704	714	357	864
85.9	164.9	252.5	333.5	124.9	Gabon	185.8	705	715	357.5	865
86	165	252.7	333.7	125	Congo (Brazzaville). Middle Congo	185.9	706	716	358	866
86.2	165.2	253	334	125.3	Central African Republic. Ubangi-Shari	186	707	717	358.5	867
86.3	165.3	253.3	334.3	125.5	Chad	186.2	708	718	359	868
86.4	165.4	253.5	334.5	125.7	Cameroon	186.3	709	719	359.5	869
86.5	165.5	253.7	334.7	125.9	West Africa. West Coast	186.4	710	720	360	870
86.6	165.6	254	335	126	French-speaking West Africa	186.5	711	721	360.5	871
86.7	165.7	254.3	335.3	126.3	Benin. Dahomey	186.6	712	722	361	872
86.8	165.8	254.5	335.5	126.5	Togo	186.7	713	723	361.5	873
86.9	165.9	254.7	335.7	126.7	Niger	186.8	714	724	362	874
87	166	255	336	126.9	Ivory Coast	186.9	715	725	362.5	875
87.2	166.2	255.3	336.3	127	Guinea	187	716	726	363	876
87.3	166.3	255.5	336.5	127.3	Mali	187.2	717	727	363.5	877
87.4	166.4	255.7	336.7	127.5	Upper Volta	187.3	718	728	364	878
87.5	166.5	256	337	127.7	Senegal	187.4	719	729	364.5	879
87.6	166.6	256.3	337.3	127.9	Mauritania	187.5	720	730	365	880
87.7	166.7	256.5	337.5	128	Nigeria	187.6	721	731	365.5	881
87.8	166.8	256.7	337.7	128.3	Ghana	187.7	722	732	366	882
87.9	166.9	257	338	128.5	Sierra Leone	187.8	723	733	366.5	883

TABLES OF GEOGRAPHICAL DIVISIONS

I	II	III	IV	V		VI	VII	VIII	IX	X
					Africa					
					West Coast – Continued					
88	167	257.3	338.3	128.7	Gambia	187.9	724	734	367	884
88.2	167.2	257.5	338.5	128.8	Liberia	188	725	735	367.5	885
88.3	167.3	257.7	338.7	129	Guinea-Bissau. Portuguese Guinea	188.2	726	736	368	886
88.4	167.4	258	339	129.3	Spanish Sahara	188.3	727	737	368.5	887
					Atlantic Ocean Islands					
					Iceland, see 58 ...					
88.5	167.5	258.3	339.3	129.5	Azores	188.35	728	738	369	888
88.53	168	258.5	340	129.53	Bermuda	188.4	728.3	738.3	369.3	888.3
88.55	168.5	258.7	340.5	129.55	Madeira Islands	188.5	728.5	738.5	369.4	888.5
88.6	169	259	341	129.6	Canary Islands	188.6	728.7	738.7	369.5	888.7
88.63	169.5	259.3	341.5	129.63	Cape Verde Islands	188.7	728.9	738.9	369.6	888.9
88.65	170	259.5	342	129.65	St. Helena	188.8	729	739	369.7	889
88.7	170.5	259.7	342.5	129.7	Tristan da Cunha	188.9	729.3	739.3	369.8	889.3
88.73	171	260	343	129.73	Falkland Islands	189	729.5	739.5	369.9	889.5
					Indian Ocean Islands					
88.75	171.5	260.3	343.5	129.75	Maldive Islands	189.2	729.7	739.7	370	889.7
88.8	172	260.5	344	129.8	Seychelles	189.3	729.9	739.9	370.3	889.9
88.83	172.5	260.7	344.5	129.83	Comoro Islands	189.4	730	740	370.4	890
88.85	173	261	345	129.85	Mauritius	189.5	730.3	740.3	370.5	890.3
88.9	173.5	261.3	345.5	129.9	Reunión	189.6	730.5	740.5	370.6	890.5
88.93	174	261.5	346	129.93	Kerguelen Islands	189.7	730.7	740.7	370.7	890.7
89	175-176	262-264	349-352	130	Australia	190-194	731-740	741-750	371-375	891-900
97.5	192.5	288.5	384.5	130.4	New Zealand	194.6	820.5	830.5	415.5	980.5
97.55	192.55	288.55	384.55	130.43	Pacific Ocean Islands	194.7	820.7	830.7	415.6	980.7
97.6	192.6	288.6	384.6	130.45	Trust Territory of the Pacific Including Mariana, Caroline and Marshall Islands	195	821	831	415.7	981

TABLES OF GEOGRAPHICAL DIVISIONS

I	II	III	IV	V		VI	VII	VIII	IX	X
					Pacific Ocean					
					Islands – Continued					
					Hawaii, see 13 ...					
97.7	192.7	288.7	384.7	130.47	Guam	195.5	821.5	831.5	416	982
97.8	192.8	288.8	384.8	130.5	Papua New Guinea	196	822	832	416.5	983
97.9	192.9	288.9	384.9	130.52	Gilbert Islands	196.3	822.3	832.3	416.6	983.3
98	193	289	385	130.53	Solomon Islands	196.5	823	833	416.7	984
98.3	193.3	289.3	385.3	130.55	New Caledonia	197	824	834	417	985
98.4	193.4	289.4	385.4	130.57	New Hebrides	197.5	825	835	417.5	986
98.5	193.5	289.5	385.5	130.6	Fiji Islands	198	826	836	417.7	987
98.6	193.6	289.6	385.6	130.63	Tonga	198.5	827	837	418	987.5
					Samoan Islands					
98.7	193.7	289.7	385.7	130.65	American Samoa	199	828	838	418.5	988
98.8	193.8	289.8	385.8	130.67	Western Samoa	199.5	829	839	418.7	989
99	195	292-293	389-390	130.69	Arctic regions	200	830	840	420	991-995
99.5	196	294	391	130.7	Greenland	200.5	830.5	842.5	420.5	995.5
100	197	295	393	130.9	Antarctic regions	200.7	830.7	842.7	420.7	996

TABLE OF REGIONS AND COUNTRIES IN ONE ALPHABET

The following table is usable in cases where the scheme calls for an alphabetical arrangement of regions and countries. It is provided as a guide for the best distribution of numbers. The numbers themselves sould not be regarded as fixed since it may be necessary to adjust them to conform with particular shelflist situations

Afghanistan	.A3	Italy	.I8
Albania	.A38	Ivory Coast	.I9
Algeria	.A4	Japan	.J3
Antarctic regions	.A6	Jordan	.J6
Argentina	.A7 .A75	Kenya	.K4
Australia	.A8 Asia	Korea	.K8
Austria	.A9	Latin America	.L29
Bangladesh	.B3	Lebanon	.L4
Belgium	.B4	Liberia	.L7
Benin	.B45	Libya	.L75
Bolivia	.B5	Luxemburg	.L9
Brazil	.B6	Madagascar	.M28
Bulgaria	.B9	Malawi	.M3
Burma	.B93	Malaysia	.M4
Canada	.C2	Mexico	.M6
Caribbean area	.C27	Morocco	.M8
Central America	.C35	Mozambique	.M85
Chile	.C5	Namibia	.N3
China	.C6	Netherlands	.N4
Colombia	.C7	New Zealand	.N45
Costa Rica	.C8	Nicaragua	.N5
Cuba	.C9	Nigeria	.N6
Czechoslovakia	.C95	Norway	.N8
Denmark	.D4	Oman	.O5
Dominican Republic	.D65	Pakistan	.P18
Ecuador	.E2	Panama	.P2
Egypt	.E3	Papua New Guinea	.P25
Ethiopia	.E8	Paraguay	.P3
Europe	.E85	Peru	.P4
Europe, Eastern	.E852	Philippines	.P6
Europe, Western	.E855	Poland	.P7
Finland	.F5	Portugal	.P8
France	.F8	Puerto Rico	.P9
French Guiana	.F9	Romania	.R6
Germany	.G3	Russia	.R9
Including West Germany		Salvador	.S2
Germany, East	.G35	Santo Domingo	.S3
Ghana	.G4	Saudi Arabia	.S33
Great Britain	.G7	Scandinavia	.S34
Greece	.G8	Senegal	.S38
Greenland	.G83	Sierra Leone	.S5
Guam	.G85	Somalia	.S58
Guatemala	.G9	South Africa	.S6
Guyana	.G95	Soviet Union, see .R9	
Haiti	.H2	Spain	.S7
Honduras	.H8	Sri Lanka	.S72
Hungary	.H9	Sudan	.S73
Iceland	.I2	Surinam	.S75
India	.I4	Sweden	.S8
Indonesia	.I5	Switzerland	.S9
Iran	.I7	Syria	.S95
Iraq	.I72	Taiwan	.T28
Ireland	.I73	Tanzania	.T34
Israel	.I75	Thailand	.T5

Tunisia	.T8	Uruguay	.U8
Turkey	.T9	Venezuela	.V4
Uganda	.U33	Yugoslavia	.Y8
United States	.U6	Zaire	.Z28

A unique feature of Class H is the use of A-Cutters for individual regions of the United States. Unless otherwise provided for, the following Cutters should be assigned in all cases where the scheme indicates Cuttering for the regions of the United States. Two standard captions, both occurring with great frequency throughout the schedule, provide for this treatment:

Case 1:　United States
　　　　　　General works
　　　　　　By region or state, A-Z ◄──── Assign A-Cutters here

Case 2:　By region or country, A-Z
　　　　　　Under each country:
　　　　　　　.x　General works
　　　　　　　.x2　Local, A-Z ◄──────── Assign A-Cutters here
　　　　　　　　　　　　　　　　　　　　　　under the United States

As an illustration of the practice, Cuttering subarrangements of one class number have been provided in full in the schedule at HC107.

```
.A1-195 ......... Regions
.A11 ............. New England
.A115 ............ Northeastern States
.A118 ............ Atlantic States
.A12 ............. Middle Atlantic States
.A124 ............ Potomac Valley
.A127 ............ Appalachian region
.A13 ............. South
.A135 ............ Tennessee Valley
.A137 ............ Ozark Mountain region
.A14 ............. North Central States
                      Including Great Lakes region and
                          Old Northwest
.A145 ............ Northwestern States
.A15 ............. Mississippi Valley
.A16 ............. Ohio Valley
.A165 ............ Southwestern States
.A17 ............. Western States
.A172 ............ Missouri Valley
.A175 ............ Pacific Southwestern States
.A18 ............. Pacific coast
.A19 ............. Pacific Northwestern States
.A195 ............ Columbia Valley
```

I (Cutter number)		II (1 number)	III 1/ (2 numbers)
A2	Alabama	1	1
A4	Alaska	2	3
A6	Arizona	3	5
A8	Arkansas	4	7
C2	California	5	9
C6	Colorado	6	11
C8	Connecticut	7	13
D3	Delaware	9	17
D6	District of Columbia .	10	19
F6	Florida	11	21
G4	Georgia	12	23
H3	Hawaii	12.5	24.5
I2	Idaho	13	25
I3	Illinois	14	27
I6	Indiana	16	31
I8	Iowa	17	33
K2	Kansas	18	35
K4	Kentucky	19	37
L8	Louisiana	20	39
M2	Maine	21	41
M3	Maryland	22	43
M4	Massachusetts	23	45
M5	Michigan	24	47
M6	Minnesota	25	49
M7	Mississippi	26	51
M8	Missouri	27	53
M9	Montana	28	55
N2	Nebraska	29	57
N3	Nevada	30	59
N4	New Hampshire	31	61
N5	New Jersey	32	63
N6	New Mexico	33	65
N7	New York	34	67
N8	North Carolina	35	69
N9	North Dakota	36	71
O3	Ohio	37	73
O5	Oklahoma	38	75
O7	Oregon	39	77
P4	Pennsylvania	40	79
R4	Rhode Island	41	81
S6	South Carolina	42	83
S8	South Dakota	43	85
T2	Tennessee	44	87
T4	Texas	45	89
U8	Utah	46	91
V5	Vermont	47	93
V8	Virginia	48	95
W2	Washington	49	97
W4	West Virginia	50	99
W6	Wisconsin	51	101
W8	Wyoming	52	103

1/
    For example: Alabama, 1-2; Hawaii, 24.5-6; Wyoming, 103-104

TABLE OF CITIES IN THE UNITED STATES

Akron	A2	Kansas City	K2
Albany	A3		
Allegheny	A35	Lawrence	L4
Annapolis	A4	Lincoln	L65
Atlanta	A7	Little Rock	L67
Augusta	A9	Los Angeles	L7
Austin	A95	Louisville	L8
		Lowell	L9
Baltimore	B2	Lynn	L97
Baton Rouge	B3		
Bismarck	B63	Madison	M18
Boise	B66	Manchester	M2
Boston	B7	Memphis	M4
Bridgeport	B78	Milwaukee	M5
Buffalo	B9	Minneapolis	M6
		Mobile	M7
Cambridge	C2	Montgomery	M75
Camden	C22		
Charleston, S.C.	C3	Nashville	N2
Charleston, W.Va.	C32	New Bedford	N3
Cheyenne	C38	New Britain	N33
Chicago	C4	New Haven	N37
Cincinnati	C5	New Orleans	N4
Cleveland	C6	New York	N5
Columbia, S.C.	C68	Newark	N6
Columbus	C7	Newcastle	N63
		Newport	N67
Dallas	D2	Newton	N7
Dayton	D3	Norfolk	N8
Denver	D4		
Des Moines	D5	Oakland	O2
Detroit	D6	Olympia	O4
Dover	D7	Omaha	O5
Dubuque	D8		
Duluth	D88	Paterson	P2
		Peoria	P3
Elizabeth	E4	Petersburg	P4
Erie	E6	Philadelphia	P5
Evansville	E9	Pierre	P57
		Pittsburgh	P6
Fall River	F2	Portland, Me.	P7
Fort Wayne	F7	Portland, Oreg.	P8
Frankfort	F8	Providence	P9
Galveston	G2	Raleigh	R2
Grand Rapids	G7	Reading	R3
Guthrie	G8	Richmond	R5
		Rochester	R6
Harrisburg	H2		
Hartford	H3	Sacramento	S12
Helena	H4	Saginaw	S13
Hoboken	H6	St. Joseph	S14
Holyoke	H7	St. Louis	S2
Houston	H8	St. Paul	S3
		Salem, Mass.	S33
Indianapolis	I4	Salem, Oreg.	S34
		Salt Lake City	S35
Jackson, Miss.	J2	San Antonio	S37
Jacksonville	J3	San Francisco	S4
Jefferson City	J4	Santa Fe	S43
Jersey City	J5	Savannah	S45

Schenectady	S48		Topeka	T65
Scranton	S5		Trenton	T7
Seattle	S6		Troy	T8
Sioux City	S62			
Somerville	S69		Utica	U8
South Bend	S72			
South Omaha	S73		Washington	W3
Spokane	S76		Waterbury	W4
Springfield, Ill.	S8		Wheeling	W5
Springfield, Mass.	S82		Wilkes-Barre	W6
Springfield, Ohio	S83		Wilmington, Del.	W7
Syracuse	S97		Wilmington, N.C.	W8
			Worcester	W9
Tacoma	T2			
Tallahassee	T3		Yonkers	Y5
Terre Haute	T4		Youngstown	Y8
Toledo	T6			

Compound interest tables: HG1632+
Comptroller (United States
  Treasury Department): HJ9805.C
Comptroller of the Currency
  (United States): HG2543
Compulsory labor: HD4871+
  Wartime: HD4905.5
Compulsory loans, see Forced loans
Computer industry: HD9696.C6+
  Selling: HF5439.C67
Computer insurance: HG9963.5
Computer leases: HF5548.6
Concentration, Industrial: HD2757+
Concessions (Transportation): HE196
Conciliation and abitration, see
  Abitration and conciliation
Concrete industry: HD9622
Condominiums
  Housing for labor: HD7287.65+
  Real estate tax: HJ4182.C64
Conductors, Railroad: HD8039.R3;
  HE1811
Confectionery
  Accounting: HF5686.C63
  Grocery industries: HD9330.C65+
  Selling: HF5439.C68
Confederate states
  Debts: HJ8110
  Finances: HJ254
  Money: HG526
  Postal service: HE6500
  Telecommunication industry:
    HE7798
Confidential communications
  (Banking): HG1720
Conglomerate corporations: HD2756
Conservation of postage stamps:
  HE6184.C63
Consignment (Accounting): HF5681.C6
Consolidation
  Corporations: HD2746.5
  Labor unions: HD6490.C62
  Land holdings: HD1334+
Construction camps: HD7290
Construction industry: HD9715+
  Accounting: HF5686.B7
Construction workers (Railroads):
  HD8039.R315
Consular requirements (Shipping
  of merchandise): HF5773.C7
Consultants, Business: HD69.C6
Consumer credit: HG3755+
Consumer demand
  Economic history: HC79.C6
  Economic theory: HB820+
Consumer education and advertising:
  HF5832
Consumer protection: HC79.C63
Consumption (Economic theory):
  HB801+

Consumption, Articles of, see
  Articles of consumption
Consumption and cycles: HB3721
Consumption taxes: HJ5703
Container industry: HD9999.C74
  Employees: HD8039.C6523
Container ships: HE566.C6
Continental money: HG516
Contingencies (Accounting):
  HF5681.C67
Contraceptives industry: HD9995.C6
Contract labor: HD4871+
  State labor: HD8026+
Contract proposal, see Proposal
  writing
Contracting (Industry): HD2365+
Contractors
  Accounting: HF5686.B7
  Malpractice insurance: HG8053.7
Contracts
  Government, see Public contracts
  Public, see Public contracts
  Real estate: HD1384+
Control
  Budget: HJ2011+
  Industry: HD45+
  Public finance: HJ199
    United States: HJ265
  Water transportation: HE384+
Convenience stores: HF5469.25+
Conversion
  Credit: HJ9132
  Public debt: HJ8055
Cookware industry: HD9999.C746+
Cooperage (Telegraph codes):
  HE7677.C7
Cooperation, Industrial, see
  Industrial cooperation
Cooperation, International, see
  International cooperation
Cooperation and competition
  (Management), see Competition
  and cooperation (Management)
Cooperative advertising: HF5827.4
Cooperative agriculture: HD1491+
Cooperative banking: HG2032+
Cooperative distribution: HD3271+
Cooperative housing (Housing
  for labor): HD7287.7
Cooperative insurance: HG8057
Cooperative production: HD3120+
Cooperative societies (Accounting):
  HF5686.C67
Coopers: HD8039.C653
Copper industry: HD9539.C5+
  Copper miners: HD8039.M7
Copy writers: HD8039.C654
Copying process (Business equipment):
  HF5541.C8

Interoceanic canals (Transportation): HE528

Interurban railways: HE3601+

Interviewing (Personnel management): HF5549.5.I6

Intrusion alarm systems industry, see Electronic alarm systems industry

Invalidity: HD7105+

Inventories
  Accounting: HF5681.S8
  Economic history: HC79.I6
  Retail trade: HF5429.25

Inventories and cycles: HB3720.5

Inventory policy: HD40

Investigations
  Industrial accidents: HD7262.25
  Public finance (United States): HJ273

Investment: HG4501+
  Real estate: HD1382.5

Investment and cycles: HB3720

Investment, Banking as an: HG1723

Investment advisers: HG4621

Investment analysis: HG4529

Investment banking: HG4534

Investment control: HG4524

Investment guarantee insurance: HG4538.5

Investment trusts (Accounting): HF5686.I58

Investments
  by
    banks: HG1616.I5
  Capital (Management): HD39+
  for
    insurance companies: HG8078
      Life insurance: HG8850
  Postage stamps: HE6184.I5
  Savings banks: HG1897
  Trusts: HG4319

Investments, Income from, see Income from investments

Investors (Accounting): HF5686.I6

Invoices (Accounting): HF5681.I7

Iodine industry: HD9675.I52+

Iron
  Cost tables, etc.: HF5716.I8
  Railway freight traffic: HE2321.I7
  Telegraph codes: HE7677.I7

Iron and steel industries: HD9510+
  Employees: HD8039.I5

Iron miners: HD8039.M7

Iron molders: HD8039.I7

Iron ores (Shipping): HE595.I7

Iron shipbuilders: HD8039.B6

Irrigation: HD1711+

Islam
  and
    finance: HJ233
    labor: HD6338.4

Issues of securities (Financial management): HG4028.I8

Ivory (Animal industry): HD9429.I86+

J

Jets: HE9770.J4

Jewelers: HD8039.J5
  Accounting: HF5686.J6

Jewelry
  Cost tables, etc.: HF5716.J4
  Selling: HF5439.J4
  Taxes: HJ5783
  Telegraph codes: HE7677.J6

Jewelry, Metal, industry: HD9747

Jews
  Labor force: HD6305.J3
  Topic on postage stamps: HE6183.J4

Job analysis (Personnel management) HF5549.5.J6

Job descriptions (Banks): HG1615.7.J6

Job enrichment (Personnel management): HF5549.5.J616

Job evaluation (Personnel management): HF5549.5.J62

Job satisfaction (Personnel management): HF5549.5.J63

Job stress: HF5548.85

Job vacancies: HD5710.5

Jobbers (Business): HF5419+

Joint returns, see Community property

Journal (Accounting): HF5681.J6

Jubilee shows (Advertising): HF5866

Judaism and labor: HD6338.3

Junk industries: HD9975

Jute industry: HD9156.J7+
  Employees: HD8039.J8

Juvenile drivers: HE5620.J8

K

Kaolin industry: HD9600.K3+

Kapok industry: HD9156.K6+

Kauri gum industry: HD9769.K3+

Keeping of the public money (United States): HJ271

Kelp industry: HD9469.K4+

Kennedy, John F. (Topic on postage stamps): HE6183.K4

Keys (Postal service)
  United States: HE6497.K4

Kitchen utensils
  Accounting: HF5686.K55
  Selling: HF5439.K5
Knights of Malta (Topic on
  postage stamps): HE6183.K6
Knit goods (Dry goods industry):
  HD9969.K5+
  Selling: HF5439.K55

L

LPG, see Liquified petroleum
  gas
Labels (Shipping of merchandise):
  HF5773.L3
Labor: HD4801+
  and
    occupational mobility: HD5717+
    politics: HD8031
    the state: HD7795+
Labor, Division of, see Division
  of labor
Labor bureaus: HD4831
Labor camps: HD7290
Labor costs (Accounting): HF5681.L2
Labor day: HD7791
Labor departments, see Departments
  of labor
Labor discipline (Personnel
  management): HF5549.5.L3
Labor disputes: HD5306+
Labor exchanges: HD5860+
Labor interests and tariff: HF2611
Labor-management committees:
  HD6490.L33
  Industrial relations: HD6972
Labor market: HD5701+
Labor productivity: HD57
  Economic history: HC79.L3
Labor service: HD4869
Labor unions: HD6350+
Laborers: HD8039.L2
Lac industry: HD9769.L3+
Lace industry: HD9933
  Lace makers: HD8039.L22
Lacquer industry: HD9660.L33+
Ladies' garment workers: HD8039.C6
Laissez faire: HB95
Lamb industry: HD9436
Lamp industry: HD9697.L33+
Land Committee (United States):
  HD183.N3
Land grants (Railways): HE1063+
Land holdings, Consolidation of,
  see Consolidation - Land
  holdings
Land holding, Large, see Large
  land holdings

Land holdings, Small, see Small
  land holdings
Land reform: HD1332+
Land subdivision: HD259
  Real estate business: HD1390
Land tax: HJ4151+
Land tenure: HD1241+
Land titles (United States):
  HE537.9.L3
Land use: HD101+
Landlord and peasant: HD1330+
Large farms: HD1471
Large industry: HD2350.8+
Large land holdings: HD1326+
Laser industry: HD9999.L32+
Lathers: HD8039.L25
Latin Monetary Union: HG207+
Laundries: HD9999.L38
  Accounting: HF5686.L3
  Employees: HD8039.L3
  Selling: HF5439.L3
  Telegraph codes: HE7677.L3
Laundry machinery industry:
  HD9999.L418
Law (Telegraph codes): HE7677.L35
Law clerks: K
Lawyers (Accounting): HF5686.P9L1+
Layoffs: HD5708.5+
Lead industry: HD9539.L38+
  Accounting: HF5686.L4
  Telegraph codes: HE7677.L38
Lead miners: HD8039.M7
Leaflets dropped from aircraft,
  see Aircraft, Leaflets dropped
  from
Lease and rental services:
  HD9999.L436
  Accounting: HF5686.L42
Leases
  Accounting: HF5681.L3
  Real estate: HD1384+
Leather, Artificial, see
  Artificial leather
Leather and leather goods industry:
  HD9780+
  Employees: HD8039.L4
  Railway freight traffic HE2321.L4
  Telegraph codes: HE7677.L4
Leave of absence (Labor):
  HD5255+
Ledger: HJ5681.L5
The legal-tender power: HG361+
Leisure classes: HB831
Lemon industry: HD9259.L4+
Lenin, V.I. (Topic on postage
  stamps): HE6183.L4
Leo computer: HF5548.4.L4
Letter post: HE6141
  United States: HE6441
Letterheads: HF5733.L4

Letters of credit: HG3745
Lettuce industry: HD9235.L4+
Level premium life insurance:
  HG8816+
Liabilities (Accounting):
  HF5681.L6
Liability insurance: HG9990
Liberalism (Economic theory):
  HB95
Liberty loans: HJ8117
Liberty of speech (Radio
  broadcasting): HE8697.L5
Librarians (Topic on postage
  stamps): HE6183.L5
License plates: HE5620.L5
License taxes: HJ5301+
Licenses (Domestic commercial
  policy): HF1437
Licensing of occupations and
  professions: HD3629+
Life expectancy: HB1322.3
Life insurance: HG8751+
  as
    an investment: HG8850.5
  Trusts: HG8936
Life tables: HB1322
Light in advertising: HF5839
Light railways: HE3601+
Lighter-than-air craft industry:
  HD9711.3
Lighting industries: HD9684
  Municipal public works:
    HD4486+
Lignite industry: HD9559.L4+
Lime (Minerals) industry:
  HD9585.L49+
  Railway freight traffic:
    HE2321.L5
  Telegraph codes: HE7677.L7
Limes industry: HD9259.L5+
Limits
  of
    credit: HJ9131
  to
    growth (Production): HD88
Lincoln, Abraham (Topic on postage
  stamps): HE6183.L57
Lindbergh, Charles (Topic on
  postage stamps): HE6183.L57
Linen industry: HD9930
  Selling: HF5439.L35
Linens, Household, see Household
  linens
Linoleum industry: HD9999.L46
Linseed oil industry: HD9999.L5
Liquefied petroleum gas industry:
  HD9579.P4+

Liguidation
  Corporations: HD2747
  Customs: HJ6675
  Public debt: HJ8055
Liquidity: HG178
  Banks: HG1656
Liquids
  Cost tables, etc.: HF5716.L3+
  Freight: HE199.5.L45
Liquor industry: HD9350+
  Accounting: HF5686.L46
  Employees: HD8039.L5+
  Telegraph codes: HE7677.L75
Lists, etc. (Customs): HJ6635+
Lists of vessels: HE565
Literature (Topic on postage
  stamps): HE6183.L59
Lithium hydroxide industry:
  HD9660.L5+
Lithium industry: HD9539.L58+
Lithographers (Accounting):
  HF5686.L5
Lithographs (Selling): HF5439.L4
Lithopane industry: HD9660.L57+
Livestock
  Freight: HE199.5.L5
    Railway freight traffic:
      HE2321.L7
    Shipping: HE595.L5
  Insurance: HG9968.6
  Telegraph codes: HE7677.L78
Lloyd's register: HE565
Loans
  Accounting: HF5686.L6
  Banks: HG1641+
    Federal Reserve banks: HG2562.L6
  Compulsory, see Forced loans
  Forced, see Forced foans
  Foreign, see Foreign loans
  Forms, see Forms of loans
  International, see Foreign loans
  Local finance: HJ9129+
    France: HJ9461+
    Germany: HJ9474
    Great Britain: HJ9429+
    United States: HJ9159+
  Public: HJ8003+
Lobster industry: HD9472.L6+
Local accounting: HJ9771+
Local finance: HJ9000+
Local post stamp catalogs:
  HE6230.L6
Location
  of
    banks: HG1616.L55
    industry: HD58
    railways: HE1613+
    stores, see Store location

Lock box services (Banks):
  HG1616.L6
Lockouts: HD5306+; HD5471
  State labor: HD8004+
Locomotives
  Telegraph codes: HE7677.L8
  Topic on postage stamps:
    HE6183.L63
Lodging houses (Housing for
  labor): HD7288+
Loggers: HD8039.L9
London loan: HJ8515.3
London Stock Exchange: HG4576+
Long distance telephone rates:
  HE8779
Long-term bonds, see Bonds,
  Long-term
Longshore workers: HD8039.L8
Lontar palm, see Borassus
  sundaica
Loose sheet (Accounting): HF5677
Loss and profit, see Profit
  and loss
Loss leaders (Marketing): HF5417.5
Losses (Insurance): HG8106+
  Accident insurance: HG9322+
  Fire insurance: HG9721+
  Health insurance: HG9386+
  Life insurance: HG8897+
Lotteries: HG6105+
  Accounting: HF5686.L65
Lubricants industry: HD9579.L8+
Luggage industry: HD9970.5.L85+
Lumber industry: HD9750+
  Accounting: HF5686.L9
  Cost tables, etc.: HF5716.L8
  Employees: HD8039.L9
  Fire insurance: HG9731.L8
  Railway freight traffic:
    HE2321.L8
  Selling: HF5439.L9
  Shipping: HE595.L8
  Telegraph codes: HE7677.L9
Luminescence (Postage stamps):
  HE6184.L8
Lunchrooms (Industrial hygiene):
  HD7393
Luther, Martin (Topic on postage
  stamps): HE6183.L8
Luxuries: HB841
  Taxes: HJ5771+

M

Macaroni (Grocery industries):
  HD9330.M32+
Machine methods (Public accounting):
  HJ9745

Machine shops: HD9700
  Accounting: HF5686.M2
Machine tools: HD9703
  Selling: HF5439.M18
Machinery: HD9705+
  and
    labor: HD6331+
  Selling: HF5439.M2
  Telegraph codes: HE7677.M2
Machinery, Agricultural, see
  Implements and machinery,
  Agricultural
Machinists: HD8039.M2
Macroeconomics: HB172.5
Magazine advertisements:
  HF5439.M264
Magazine advertising: HF5871+
Magnesite industry: HD9539.M23+
Magnesium industry: HD9539.M25+
Magnet steel industry: HD9529.M3+
Mahogany industry: HD9769.M3+
Mail carriers: HE6161
Mail handling equipment, supplies:
  HE6237
Mail order business: HF5465.5+
Mail steamers: HE566.M3
Mail traffic (Railways): HE2556
Mailboxes (United States):
  HE6497.M3
Mailing (Business): HF5599.M3
Maintenance and repair
  Accounting: HF5681.M3
  Management: HD40.6
  Production: HD69.M3
Maintenance, Employee: HD4928.M3
Maize, see Corn
Maladministration
  Smuggling: HJ6695
  Taxation: HJ5021
Malpractice insurance: HG8053.5+
Malted liquors industry: HD9397
Malthus: HB861+
Mammals, see Animals
Management: HD28+
  Banks, see Bank management
  by
    exception: HD30.6
    objectives: HD30.65
  Railway companies: HE1621
Management audit: HD58.95
Management committees: HD58.4
Management games: HD30.26
Management rights: HD6971.7
Managerial economics: HD30.22
Manganese industry: HD9539.M3+
Mango industry: HD9259.M28+
Manila hemp industry: HD9156.M35+
Manpower planning (Personnel
  management): HE5549.5.M3
Manpower policy: HD5713+

Manufactures
  Accounting: HF5686.M3
  Taxes: HJ5761+
Manufacturing industries: HD9720+
Maple sugar industry: HD9119.M3+
Maps (Topic on postage stamps):
  HE6183.M3
Marble building stones industry:
  HD9621
Marble cutters: HD8039.S75
Margarine (Grocery industries):
  HD9330.M37+
Marginalists (Economics): HB98
Marine engineers: VM
Marine insurance: HE961+
Maritime economics: HE582
Market segmentation: HF5415.127
Marketing: HF5410+
  Accounting: HF5686.M35
  Banks: HG1616.M3
Marketing audits: HF5415.16
Marketing channels: HF5415.129
Marketing research: HF5415.2+
Markets: HF5469.7+
Marking devices (Artists' supplies):
  HD9793
Marriage endowment insurance:
  HG9281
Marriages (Demography): HB1111+
Married women (Labor): HD6055+
Marshallians: HB98.2
Marxian economics: HB97.5
Mary, Virgin (Topic on postage
  stamps): HE6183.M33
Masons: HD8039.M25
Mastership (Labor): HD4895
Matches industry: HD9660.M47+
  Accounting: HF5686.M37
  Employees: HD8039.M28
Maternal mortality HB1322.5
Maternity insurance: HG9291+
Maternity leave: HD6065.5
Mathematical economics: HB135+
Mathematical models
  Demography: HB849.51
  Financial management: HG4012
  Foreign exchange: HG3823
  Industrial economic growth: HD75.5
  Investment: HG4515.2
  Labor market: HD5701.6
  Land use: HD108.4
  Management: HD30.25
  Transportation: HE147.7
Mathematical programming: HB143
Mathematics of investment: HG4515.3
Mats industry: HD9999.M2613
Mattresses industry: HD9971.5.M38+
May day: HD7791
Measurement of vessels: HE538.M5

Measuring instruments industry:
  HD9706.2
Meat
  Accounting: HF5686.M4
  Cost tables, etc.: HF5716.M4
  Railway freight traffic: HE2321.M4
  Selling: HF5439.M27
Meat cutters; HD8039.B96
Meat packing industry: HD9410+
Meat products industry:
  HD9440
Mechanical industries: HD9680+
Mechanics: HD8039.M3+
Mechanism (Budget): HJ2009
Mechanization, Farm, see Farm
  mechanization
Medical botany (Topic on postage
  stamps): HE6183.M4
Medical examiners and examinations:
  HG8886+
Medical instrument industry: HD9994+
Medical journals (Advertising):
  HF6121.M5
Medical supplies (Selling):
  HF5439.M35
Medicine
  Selling: HF5439.D75
  Telegraph codes: HE7677.M4
  Topic on postage stamps: HE6183.M42
Medieval guilds, see Guilds, Medieval
Meetings
  Labor unions: HD6490.M4
  Sales: HF5438.8.M4
Melioration of agricultural land:
  HD1580
Melons (Telegraph codes): HE7677.M5
Mental health insurance: HG9387
  Public health insurance: HD7102.5+
Mercantile clerks: HD8039.M39
Mercantile system (Economic theory):
  HB91
Merchant marine: HE730+
Merchant seamen: HD8039.S4
Merchants' associations: HF294+
Mercury industry: HD9539.M4+
Mergers
  Banks: HG1722
  Corporations: HD2746.5
    Financial management: HG4028.M4
  Labor unions: HD6490.C62
Messenger service: HE9751+
Metal industries: HD9506+
  Accounting: HF5686.M45
  Cost tables, etc.: HF5716.M5
  Employees: HD8039.M5
  Manufacturing industries: HD9743+
Metals and metal products
  Freight: HE199.5.M4
    Railway freight traffic: HE2321.M45

Wedding supplies and services:
   HD9999.W37+
Weight, Marking of (Shipping
   of merchandise): HF5773.W4
Weight, Standard of, see
   Standard of weight
Weights and measures (Tables)
   HF5711+
Welders: HD8039.W4
Welding equipment industry:
   HD9697.W43+
Welfare
   and
      public debts, see Public debts
         and welfare
Welfare economics: HB99.3
Welfare funds (Labor unions):
   HD6490.W38
Welfare theory: HB846+
Welfare work: HD7260+
   Labor unions: HD6490.W4
The West (Topic on postage stamps):
   HE6183.W47
West India Company: HE483.W59+
Wharves (Waterways): HE550+
Wheat: HD9049.W3+
   Cost tables, etc.: HF5716.G7
   Freight: HE199.5.W5
      Railway freight traffic: HE2321.W5
      Shipping: HE595.W54
      Speculation: HG6047.W5
Whip makers: HD8039.W48
Whisky industry: HD9395
"Whisky ring": HJ5021
White-collar employees: HD8039.M39
White goods (Dry goods industry):
   HD9969.H83+
Wholesale trade: HF5419+
   Accounting: HF5686.W6
Wildcat strikes: HD5311
Window shade industry: HD9971.5.W56+
Windows (Cost tables, etc.):
   HF5716.S2
Wine industry: HD9370+
   Accounting: HF5686.W65
   Employees: HD8039.L7
   Selling: HF5439.W5
   Telegraph codes: HE7677.W6
Wine merchants (Accounting):
   HF5686.W65
Winter resorts (Accounting):
   HF5686.W68
Wire (Iron and steel industries):
   HD9529.W5+
   Cost tables, etc.: HF5716.W5
Wire melting (Iron and steel
   industries): HD9529.W58+
Wireless telegraph: HE8660+
Wireless telephone: HE9713+

Women
   Labor: HD6050+
   Life insurance: HG8801
   Topic on postage stamps: HE6183.W6
Women, Lodging houses for (Housing
   for labor): HD7288.5+
Women's cooperative guilds: HD3423
Women's exchanges: HD6076
Wood floor (Forest products
   industry): HD9769.W4+
Wood products
   Cost tables, etc.: HF5716.L8
   Railway freight traffic
      HE2321.W6
Wood-using industries (Accounting):
   HF5686.W8
Woodcarving industry: HD9773
   Employees: HD8039.W5
Woodpulp industry: HD9769.W5+
Woodworkers: HD8039.W6
Woodworking mills (Fire insurance):
   HG9731.W6
Wool (Textile industries): HD9890+
   Cost tables, etc.: HF5716.W6
   Employees: HD8039.T4
   Railway freight traffic: HE2321.W65
   Speculation: HG6047.W6
   Telegraph codes: HE7677.W9
Work boats: HE566.W6
Work groups (Production): HD66
Work measurement (Banks): HG1616.W6
Working capital (Financial
   management): HG4028.W65
Workingmen (Fares)
   Railways: HE1960.W7
   Rapid transit systems: HE4345.W7
Workingmen's associations: HD6350+
Workingmen's gardens: HD1519
Workmen's compensation: HD7103.6+
Wreckers: HD8039.W8
Writing, Proposal, see Proposal
   writing

Y

Yachts (Taxes): HJ5777+
Yard sales: HF5482.3
Yarns (Wool textile industries):
   HD9909.Y28+
   Telegraph codes: HE7677.Y2
Yeast (Grocery industries):
   HD9330.Y4+
Youth labor: HD6270+
   Labor unions: HD6490.Y65
Yucca industry: HD9769.Y8+

INDEX

~~Reclass project~~

Shirley Daniels